THE CAMBR
THOM

This *Companion* forms an acces⟨ ⟩ork of
Thomas Jefferson, third Presiden ⟨ ⟩⟨…⟩⟩ and author of the
Declaration of Independence. Essays explore Jefferson's political thought, his
policies towards Native Americans, his attitude to race and slavery, as well as
his interests in science, architecture, religion, and education. Contributors include
leading literary scholars and historians; the essays offer up-to-date overviews
of his many interests, his friendships, and his legacy. Together, they reveal his
importance in the cultural and political life of early America. At the same time
these original essays speak to abiding modern concerns about American culture
and Jefferson's place in it. This *Companion* will be essential reading for students
and scholars of Jefferson, and is designed for use by students of American
literature and American history.

CAMBRIDGE UNIVERSITY PRESS
Cambridge, New York, Melbourne, Madrid, Cape Town, Singapore, São Paulo, Delhi

Cambridge University Press
The Edinburgh Building, Cambridge CB2 8RU, UK

Published in the United States of America by Cambridge University Press, New York

www.cambridge.org
Information on this title: www.cambridge.org/9780521686976

First published 2009

Printed in the United Kingdom at the University Press, Cambridge

A catalogue record for this publication is available from the British Library

Library of Congress Cataloging in Publication data
The Cambridge companion to Thomas Jefferson / edited by Frank Shuffelton.
p.   cm.
Includes bibliographical references.
ISBN 978-0-521-86731-3 (hardback) – ISBN 978-0-521-68697-6 (paperback)
1. Jefferson, Thomas, 1743–1826 – Philosophy.   2. Jefferson, Thomas, 1743–1826 – Political
and social views.   3. Jefferson, Thomas, 1743–1826 – Knowledge and learning.   4. Jefferson,
Thomas, 1743–1826 – Relations with slaves.   5. Presidents – United States – Biography.
6. Statesmen – United States – Biography.   7. United States – Politics and government –
Philosophy.   I. Shuffelton, Frank, 1940–   II. Title: Companion to Thomas Jefferson.
E332.C26   2008
973.4'6092–dc22
[B]
2008041634

ISBN 978-0-521-86731-3 hardback
ISBN 978-0-521-68697-6 paperback

CONTENTS

NOTES ON CONTRIBUTORS

DOUGLAS ANDERSON is Sterling-Goodman Professor of English at the University of Georgia. He is the author of *A House Undivided: Domesticity and Community in American Literature*, *The Radical Enlightenments of Benjamin Franklin*, and *William Bradford's Books: Of Plimmoth Plantation and the Printed Word*, and he has published a wide range of articles on American literature in the *New England Quarterly*, the *William and Mary Quarterly*, and elsewhere.

ANDREW BURSTEIN is the Charles Phelps Manship Professor of History at Louisiana State University, Baton Rouge. He has published on Jefferson in the *Nation*, the *William and Mary Quarterly*, and *Journal of the Early Republic*. He is the author of *The Inner Jefferson*, *America's Jubilee*, and *Jefferson's Secrets: Death and Desire at Monticello*. He has been a consultant to Ken Burns and appeared in the PBS documentary *Thomas Jefferson*.

DOUGLAS R. EGERTON is a professor of history at Le Moyne College. His *Charles Fenton Mercer and the Trial of National Conservatism* examined the career of the founder of the American Colonization Society, a group of conservative white antislavery politicians who wished to send freed slaves to Liberia. More recent books, *Gabriel's Rebellion*, *He Shall Go Out Free: The Lives of Denmark Vesey*, and *Rebels, Reformers and Revolutionaries* explore slave rebelliousness.

JOANNE B. FREEMAN, Professor of History at Yale University, is the author of *Affairs of Honor: National Politics in the New Republic*, and the editor of *Alexander Hamilton: Writings*. She also has published articles on politics, political culture, and honor culture in the *William and Mary Quarterly*, the *Journal of the Early Republic*, and the *Yale Law Journal*, among other publications, and contributed chapters to *Novel History: History According to the Novelists*, *Neither Separate Nor Equal: Congress and the Executive Branch in the 1790s*, *The Revolution of 1800: Democracy, Race, and the New Republic*, and *The Democratic Experiment: New Directions in American Political History*. She is currently working on a study of the culture of Congress in antebellum America.

ANNETTE GORDON-REED, a professor of law at New York Law School since 1992, earned a place in history with her first book, *Thomas Jefferson and Sally Hemings: An American Controversy*, in which, prior to the DNA findings about Jefferson's probable paternity of Sally Hemings's children, she successfully managed to persuade a generation of historians to re-examine their assumptions about the Jefferson–Hemings relationship. She also holds an appointment in the Department of History at Rutgers University, Newark.

THOMAS HALLOCK is an assistant professor of English at the University of South Florida, St. Petersburg. He is the author of *From the Fallen Tree: Frontier Narratives, Environmental Politics, and the Roots of a National Pastoral*, and he is currently editing William Bartram's Manuscripts, in a forthcoming two-volume edition.

ARI HELO (Ph.D.) is a research fellow at the University of Helsinki, Renvall Institute for Area and Cultural Studies. His doctoral dissertation from 1999 handled Jefferson's republicanism and the problem of slavery. His more recent publications include "Jefferson, Morality, and the Problem of Slavery," co-authored with Peter Onuf in *William and Mary Quarterly*, and "How the Revolution Lost Its Political Meaning," in *America in the Course of Human Events*, ed. Josef Jarab, Marcel Arbeit, and Jenel Virden.

RICHARD SAMUELSON is Assistant Professor of History at California State University, San Bernardino. He completed work on his chapter while serving as the Henry Salvatori Visiting Fellow at Claremont McKenna College. He has taught at the University of Paris, 8; the National University of Ireland, Galway; the University of Glasgow; and the University of Virginia, from which he received his Ph.D. in American History in 2000. He is currently completing a book about John Adams's political thought.

GORDON M. SAYRE is a professor of English at the University of Oregon where he teaches seventeenth- and eighteenth-century American literature with a special interest in travel and captivity narratives and relations with native peoples. He has edited an anthology, *American Captivity Narratives*, and is the author of *"Les Sauvages Americains": Representations of Native Americans in French and English Colonial Literature* and *The Indian Chief as Tragic Hero*.

FRANK SHUFFELTON teaches American literature at the University of Rochester. He has written two volumes of critical annotated bibliography covering writings about Thomas Jefferson since 1826. Updates to these volumes can be found online at the Portal of the Monticello Library and elsewhere. He has also written widely about American literature from the seventeenth to the nineteenth centuries and in 2006 was honored as the MLA Distinguished Scholar of Early American Literature.

ERIC SLAUTER is an associate professor of English at the University of Chicago, specializing in American cultural, intellectual, and literary history, with additional research and teaching interests in law and political thought, art and material culture, and the history of the book. He is currently completing a book entitled *The State as a Work of Art: The Cultural Origins of the Constitution*. He has held research fellowships from the National Endowment for the Humanities, the Andrew W. Mellon Foundation, and the McNeil Center for Early American Studies at the University of Pennsylvania.

DARREN STALOFF teaches history at the City College of New York and the Graduate Center of the City University of New York. He is the author of *The Making of an American Thinking Class: Intellectuals and Intelligentsia in Puritan Massachusetts* and *Hamilton, Adams, Jefferson: The Politics of Enlightenment and the American Founding*.

LUCIA STANTON directs research at Monticello, where she is the Shannon Senior Research Historian at the Robert Smith International Center for Jefferson Studies. She has co-edited, with James A. Bear, Jr., *Thomas Jefferson's Memorandum Books 1767–1826*, and is the author of *Slavery at Monticello* and *Free Some Day: The African American Families of Monticello*. She continues to work on an oral history project to collect information about Jefferson's slaves and their descendants.

TIMOTHY SWEET teaches American literature at West Virginia University, with a particular interest in literature and the environment in the seventeenth, eighteenth, and nineteenth centuries. He is the author of several essays in this area and of *American Georgics: Economy and Environment in Early American Literature*. His earlier *Traces of War: Poetry, Photography, and the Crisis of the Union* attests to an additional interest in photography and literature.

RICHARD GUY WILSON holds the Commonwealth Professor's Chair in Architectural History at the University of Virginia. A frequent lecturer and a television commentator, he has also published widely, with many articles and books on different aspects of American and modern architecture, including *The American Renaissance*; *McKim, Mead & White, Architects*; *Machine Age in America*; *Thomas Jefferson's Academical Village*; *Campus Guide: University of Virginia*; and *The Colonial Revival House*.

1743   Born April 2 (OS) at Shadwell, Goochland (now Albemarle) County, the plantation of his father, Peter Jefferson, and his mother, Jane Randolph Jefferson.

1752–7   Attends the Latin school conducted near Tuckahoe by the Revd. William Douglas, "a superficial Latinist."

1757   Peter Jefferson dies.

1758–60   Enters the school of Revd. James Maury, whom he remembers as "a correct classical scholar."

1760–2   Attends College of William and Mary, at Williamsburg, and studies with William Small, the Professor of Natural Philosophy: "[F]rom his conversation I got my first views of the expansion of science & of the system of things in which we are placed."

1762–7   Studies law under the direction of George Wythe, one of the most learned members of the Virginia bar, a signer of the Declaration of Independence, and the first Professor of Law at William and Mary.

1764   Comes of age and inherits 2,650 acres from his father and at least twenty slaves.

1767   Is admitted to the bar and begins his own law practice.

1769   Begins building the first Monticello, following his own design, on a mountain across the Rivanna River from Shadwell. He will later tear this down and build the second Monticello on the same site.

1769–76   Member of the Virginia House of Burgesses for Albemarle County.

1772 Marries Martha Wayles Skelton, a 23-year-old widow, on January 1. Their first child, Martha (called Patsy), is born on September 27.

1773 His father-in-law, John Wayles, dies and leaves 11,000 acres of land and 135 slaves as well as debts that force Jefferson to sell over half the land. Purchasers pay in depreciated Revolutionary currency, and Jefferson struggles for the rest of his life under the burden of this debt.

   With four others proposes a committee of correspondence in each colony to "consider the British claims as a common cause." Governor Dunmore dissolves the House of Burgesses.

1774 Writes instructions for Virginia delegates to the first Continental Congress, which are subsequently published as *A Summary View of the Rights of British America.*

1775–6 Elected a delegate from Virginia to second Continental Congress. Drafts a version of the Declaration on the Necessity of Taking Up Arms. In June, 1776, drafts the Declaration of Independence.

1776–9 Member of Virginia House of Delegates. Serves on Committee of Revisors charged with drawing up a body of law for Virginia. These proposed laws, not all of which were passed, include his Bill for Establishing Religious Freedom, a Bill for the More General Diffusion of Knowledge, and bills reforming laws of inheritance.

1779 Elected governor of Virginia.

1780 Elected a member of the American Philosophical Society, the nation's premier society for the advancement of science. Re-elected governor of Virginia. On December 29, British forces under Benedict Arnold invade Virginia.

1781 A second invasion of Virginia forces Jefferson and several members of the House of Delegates to flee Monticello two days after his term of office as governor expires. A subsequent inquiry on his conduct as governor unanimously absolves him of any censure. Receives a list of questions from François Marbois, secretary to the French legation, and begins to write what would become *Notes on the State of Virginia.*

1782 Martha Wayles Jefferson dies. Jefferson emotionally devastated.

1783–4 Virginia delegate to Congress. Writes "Report of a Plan of Government for the Western Territory," which becomes basis for organizing the Northwest Territory.

1784 Appointed minister plenipotentiary to join Benjamin Franklin and John Adams in Paris.

1785 Succeeds Franklin as minister. Arranges for a private edition in Paris of *Notes on the State of Virginia*. Publishes a revised edition in 1787 in London, after a badly translated French edition appears.

1789 French Revolution begins. Jefferson meets with Lafayette and other Patriot party leaders and supports their discussions about a constitution. Returns to the United States in November.

1790–3 Serves as George Washington's first secretary of state. Objects to Alexander Hamilton's plans to increase the power of the federal government, beginning with his financial system.

1791 Jefferson and James Madison persuade Philip Freneau to edit a newspaper to counter the Federalist-dominated press. Edition of Paine's *Rights of Man* with Jefferson's comments criticizing John Adams's "political heresies" creates controversy.

1792 Hamilton attacks Jefferson in anonymous letter to the press. Jefferson begins to be seen as the leader of the opposition to Federalist interests.

1793 President Washington issues a Proclamation of Neutrality, in response to war between France and Britain. Edmond Charles Genet, the new French minister, challenges the executive's position and creates controversy, leading to Jefferson's drafting of papers demanding his recall. Jefferson retires as secretary of state at the end of December.

1794 Returns to Monticello, resumes active interest in farming. Whiskey Rebellion in Western Pennsylvania.

1796 Publication of letter written to Philip Mazzei claims "an Anglican monarchical, & aristocratical party has sprung up," leading to Federalist attacks. Elected vice president in December, with Federalist John Adams as president, because the Constitution at the time called for the candidate getting the most notes to become president, the one with the second most votes to become vice president. Assumes leadership of the opposition Republican party.

1797   Installed as president of the American Philosophical Society the day before his inauguration as vice president.

1798   Revelation of XYZ affair, in which French agents of the Directory sought bribes from an American diplomatic mission in Paris, inspires hysterical anti-Jacobin response that targets Jefferson and other Republicans. Congress passes Alien and Sedition Laws. Jefferson secretly drafts the Kentucky Resolutions, which call on individual states to reject the constitutionality of the laws and to regard them as void. Madison drafts Virginia Resolutions also protesting the Alien and Sedition Laws.

1800   Publishes appendix to *Notes* with testimony about Logan's speech. Republican caucus nominates Jefferson and Aaron Burr for president and vice president. Leading up to the election, vituperative attacks in the press appear from both Republicans and Federalists. Gabriel's slave rebellion in Virginia crushed. The Electoral College receives the same number of votes for Burr as for Jefferson, and the tie sends the decision to the House of Representatives.

1801   Federalists in Congress explore the possibility of electing Burr over Jefferson, but on the thirty-sixth ballot, Jefferson is elected. Inaugurated president on March 4. Walks from his boarding-house to the Capitol to be sworn in and deliver inaugural address. After Pasha of Tripoli declares war on the United States, sends a naval squadron to the Mediterranean to protect American shipping against depredations of Barbary pirates. On December 8 sends first annual message to Congress rather than delivering an address, thus beginning a tradition of written messages that continues through the nineteenth century.

1802   Sends letter to the Danbury Baptist Association on January 1, affirming the principle of separation of church and state. Writes to Robert R. Livingston, minister to France, about concerns regarding French control of New Orleans and Louisiana. James Callender publishes accusations that Jefferson keeps a black concubine named Sally.

1803 Louisiana Purchase Treaty signed in Paris on April 20, but Jefferson had already sent to Congress on January 18 a secret message proposing an exploring expedition into the Louisiana Territory, to be led by Meriwether Lewis. Sends his "Syllabus of the Doctrines of Jesus" to Benjamin Rush.

1804 Re-elected president with an overwhelming majority of the votes. Daughter Maria Jefferson Eppes dies.

1806 Lewis and Clark expedition returns to St. Louis. Issues proclamation warning against a plot by Aaron Burr to separate western states from the union and attack Mexico.

1807 Act barring importation of slaves after January 1, 1808, is passed. Trial of Aaron Burr for treason ends in his acquittal. HMS *Leopard* fires upon the USS *Chesapeake* after demands to search the American ship for British deserters are refused. British Orders in Council and Napoleon's Berlin Decree threaten neutral shipping. Jefferson proposes the Embargo Act, passed by Congress in December.

1809 Non-Intercourse Act, signed on March 1, repeals the Embargo Act, which had failed to have any diplomatic impact but had damaged the American economy. Retires as president on March 4.

1810 The Virginia Literary Fund established; Jefferson writes to Governor John Tyler about education.

1812 Resumes correspondence with John Adams.

1814 Becomes trustee of Albemarle Academy. Offers to sell his library to Congress, to replace the one burned by the British. Resigns as president of the American Philosophical Society.

1816 Virginia bill to establish Central College is passed. Named to the Board of Visitors.

1817 Bill embodying Jefferson's general education plan is defeated in the legislature. Cornerstone of Central College is laid in Charlottesville.

1818 Legislature passes a bill establishing a university, chartered in the following year and located on the site of the Central College. Drafts so-called Rockfish Gap Report, resulting from a meeting of the commissioners in charge of planning the university.

1820   Denounces the Missouri Compromise, fearing it will provoke sectional hostilities and is another example of federal "consolidationism" that usurps state powers.

1821   Writes memoir later referred to as his *Autobiography*.

1823   Writes to President James Monroe about foreign relations in advance of proclamation of the Monroe Doctrine.

1824   Lafayette visits Charlottesville on his triumphal return to America, is entertained at Monticello and at a dinner in the Rotunda of the University.

1825   First students arrive at the University of Virginia. Jefferson's health begins to decline.

1826   Dies at Monticello, July 4, 1826. John Adams dies on the same day.

FRANK SHUFFELTON

Introduction

Thomas Jefferson was born in 1743 at Shadwell, his father's plantation near present-day Charlottesville, Virginia. At the time of Jefferson's birth Shadwell was near the western limit of white settlement, but by the time he practiced as a lawyer twenty-five years later the frontier had moved over 100 miles further west. By the time of his death, fifty years to the day after the Declaration of Independence, Virginia was a part of a new nation, the United States, whose limits had moved over 2,000 miles farther west. Jefferson, as the author of the Declaration and as the president who acquired the Louisiana Purchase, played a key role in each of these transformations.

He was educated in local schools and at the College of William and Mary before reading law with George Wythe, who had been mentoring the young Jefferson since his arrival in Williamsburg. One of the most learned lawyers in the colonies, Wythe would go on to be a signer of the Declaration of Independence and the first Professor of Law at the College of William and Mary. Subsequently Jefferson practiced as a lawyer and also entered the Virginia legislature, where he aligned himself with the more radical members who were already questioning the authority of Parliament over the colonies. In 1774 he proposed instructions for the Virginia delegates to the first Continental Congress, which had called for representatives of the thirteen North American colonies to meet in Philadelphia in order to discuss responses to supposed British restrictions on the colonies. Subsequently published as *A Summary View of the Rights of British America* and reprinted in Philadelphia and London, this pamphlet informed King George III that "kings are the servants, not the proprietors of the people" and established Jefferson's reputation as an effective writer on behalf of the colonial cause. When he himself joined Congress, he was appointed to the committee to prepare a Declaration of Independence, along with fellow members John Adams, Benjamin Franklin, Robert Livingston, and Roger Sherman. The others delegated the main responsibility for writing the Declaration to him, and, with a few mostly minor changes, the final version as approved by Congress followed his draft.

One major change involved the deletion of a passage condemning the king for supporting and maintaining the slave trade, calling it "a cruel war against human nature." The second paragraph of the Declaration, however, with its assertion of human equality and the natural rights of life, liberty, and the pursuit of happiness struck a chord in later years and in countries around the world. Opponents of slavery frequently cited these phrases from the Declaration, the women at the Seneca Falls Convention relied on it, and other nations have modeled their own declarations of independence and human rights after Jefferson's text.

Back in Virginia, Jefferson participated in a revision of Virginia's laws and was most proud of his reform of property and inheritance law that worked against the amassing of large estates, and of a law for the freedom of religion. His two terms as governor of Virginia ended ignominiously when he was unable to mount an effective resistance to the British invasion of the state. He retired briefly to private life and began writing his one published book, *Notes on the State of Virginia*. Shaped as an answer to a questionnaire he had received from a French diplomat, *Notes* offered an extensive view of Virginia's geography, its natural resources, fauna and flora, laws and customs, and its history. *Notes* participated in important scientific debates of the time, but it is also largely responsible for the ambivalent nature of Jefferson's reputation: while it condemned slavery in no uncertain terms, it also put forward an argument for black inferiority in mind and body that is difficult to see in any other light than as racist. Subsequent critics have frequently noted Jefferson's failure to do anything to promote the end of slavery, in spite of his strong language in *Notes* condemning it.

Jefferson was subsequently appointed as minister to France from 1784 to 1789. There he saw to the publication of *Notes*, first in Paris in 1785 and in London in a revised form in 1787. He also pursued his interests in architecture and worked with the French architect Charles Louis Clérisseau when he designed the Virginia Capitol after the model of a Greco-Roman temple in Nîmes. Returning to America, he accepted an appointment as the United States' first secretary of state. Opposition to the policies of Alexander Hamilton, which sought to strengthen the powers of the central government at the expense of those of the states and which Jefferson thought privileged a narrow group of wealthy cronies, soon led him to be regarded as the leader of an emerging republican faction in Congress. By the time he retired at the end of 1793, the so-called first party system in American politics had begun to take shape, with Jefferson as putative leader of the Republicans in opposition to the Federalists who supported Hamilton's policies. In 1796 when the Republican caucus put him forward as a presidential candidate, he became vice president by virtue of finishing second to John Adams in the number of electoral ballots.

Jefferson wrote the Kentucky Resolutions in 1798 in opposition to the Federalists' passage of the Alien and Sedition Acts aimed at critics of the government, but had to preserve his anonymity in regard to the document.

In 1800 he was again nominated for president, with Aaron Burr as his running mate. When the election resulted in a tie between Jefferson and Burr – there was no provision at the time for designating candidates for the presidency and the vice presidency, a condition subsequently rectified by the twelfth amendment – the election was thrown into the House of Representatives, which elected Jefferson on the thirty-sixth ballot. The major achievement of his presidency was the acquisition of the Louisiana Territory, more by luck than by design as it turned out, but his planning for the Lewis and Clark expedition that explored its western limits was a result of his extensive reading and his deep interests in science. Re-elected overwhelmingly in 1804, his second term had to deal with the worsening conditions in Europe; war between Great Britain and Napoleonic France put the United States in an uncomfortable vise. Jefferson responded to this by calling for an embargo of all American trade, reminiscent of the non-importation acts of the pre-revolutionary years, but even less successful. His decision not to seek a third term, however, confirmed the similar choice made by George Washington and established a traditional limit for presidential office holders until Franklin D. Roosevelt broke with it in 1940.

In the years of his retirement Jefferson turned to an unrealized project he had first touched upon in his revisionary drafts of laws for Virginia. His Bill for the More General Diffusion of Knowledge had proposed a system of public education that had not been acted upon – and in its largest terms would not be until after the Civil War – but Jefferson took up the cause of creating a public university that would be free of the clerical hand that lay over the William and Mary that he had attended. His modern curriculum at the University of Virginia became an important model for later great American public universities, culminating in the founding of the land grant universities in the later nineteenth century. At the same time his architectural plan for the university created a site that would be recognized in 1976 by the American Institute of Architects (AIA) as one of the ten most significant architectural works in the United States. Jefferson was able to observe the building of his university from Monticello, his other building that made the AIA list, tying him with Frank Lloyd Wright for the most works to be recognized there. In the later years of his life he continued to carry on an extensive correspondence, of which he carefully kept copies and records. Jefferson's letters are among his most significant and powerful writings, revealing him as a man of widespread interests, extensive reading and scholarship, and challenging ideas, challenging even when seemingly mistaken or cranky.

In the years after his death on July 4, 1826, fifty years after the Declaration of Independence, Jefferson's reputation was contested by partisans of all sorts. Supporters of slavery cited his comments on the natural inferiority of blacks in *Notes*, and abolitionists quoted his condemnation of slavery. Abraham Lincoln could announce "All honor to Jefferson ... who ... had the coolness, forecast, and capacity to introduce into a merely revolutionary document, an abstract truth, applicable to all men and all times," even as Andrew Dixon White, president of Cornell University, could blame the Civil War on Jefferson's enunciation of states' rights doctrine in the Kentucky Resolutions.[1] The twentieth century saw a turn in a more straightforwardly positive direction, as evidenced by the subtitle of Gilbert Chinard's popular 1929 biography, "Apostle of Americanism." This reputation was enhanced by the New Dealers who took Jefferson for their patron saint, putting his face on the five-cent piece and providing a handsome memorial in Washington, DC, on the occasion of the 200th anniversary of his birth.

In the last three decades the reputation of Thomas Jefferson has undergone radical revision.[2] The Apostle of Democracy apotheosized during the New Deal era has, by some scholars, been accused of being a slave-owner whose deepest instincts had a racial bias, an architect of America's genocidal policy towards Native Americans, a merely lukewarm friend of civil liberties, and even an early advocate of terrorism and civil violence.[3] These attacks have certainly been based on obvious flaws in Jefferson's character and record, but they are, in their extreme versions, often merely reflections of the much more nuanced and sophisticated scholarship that has emerged in these years on Jefferson and the period of the early American republic. Jefferson continues to be a figure of major, widespread interest because, at some fundamental level, he does continue to speak for the values of equality, tolerance, and individual liberty, but also because his contradictions and ambivalences seem to reflect the contradictions of America itself. Since the mid-1990s each year has seen the publication of more than 100 books and essays on Jefferson, typically considerably more. These publications are both scholarly and popular, indicating a continuing interest in Jefferson as a person and as a bellwether of American self-reflection. The recent DNA report that offers fairly convincing evidence that Jefferson fathered a child by Sally Hemings (and quite probably fathered all those whom Hemings family tradition claims) provoked widespread discussion about the complex racial relations that are still embedded in American society. Jefferson's writings about freedom of religion and the separation of church and state are more vigorously examined and debated than ever, at a moment when religious voices clamor for a more central role in public life.

The scholarship supporting this work has been grounded in new strategies of interpretation in some cases, and new recognitions of the larger intellectual and ideological contexts in which Jefferson wrote. Scholarship in the last thirty years has by turns addressed the significance of the republican synthesis, the role of classical liberalism, the importance of moral sentiment and sentimentality, the prevailing code of honor among gentlemen, and the discourse of sociability and the public sphere. Jefferson's texts have been deconstructed, psychoanalyzed, and examined for participation in various hegemonic strategies; they have been read closely in order to unpack metaphors and tropes that might give insight into the mind of Jefferson and the mind of his time. Interpretation has also been supported by increasingly sophisticated scholarship in material culture. Archaeological investigations at Monticello, for instance, have underwritten more subtle and complex understandings of the intertwined lives of the white and black residents there and moved beyond simplistic representations of slavery, either apologetic or condemning. More exacting scholarship about the objects with which Jefferson filled Monticello has considered him as a consumer, a pioneer in a consumer revolution that would energize America in later years. Jefferson's architectural work is increasingly being understood as a human-centered creation of spaces that is intended to make possible republican forms of civic and public life as well as the rational comforts of an ideal private life. Jefferson the letter writer, the author of the Declaration of Independence, and of *Notes on the State of Virginia* increasingly draws the attention of scholars of American literature, who feel the need to fit him into any satisfactory account of their subject. In the supposed death bed words of John Adams, who died on the same day as Jefferson, "Thomas Jefferson still survives," if not as the icon he once was then as a touchstone able to generate continuing interest, debate, and inquiry. This volume addresses major topics of Jeffersonian concern that may well reflect the concerns of Americans in the twenty-first century.

The Declaration of Independence was a defining text for an American nationality, although it was not necessarily recognized as such at the time. It was simultaneously an assertion of independence, a legal document signifying that assertion, an appeal to the international community for recognition, and an attempt to appeal to the citizens of the individual states to support the cause of the whig/patriot side of an insurrection. In later years the Declaration became increasingly significant as a ceremonial text to be celebrated on its anniversary and also as an inscription of basic individual rights. Eric Slauter's chapter on the Declaration explores the implications of that document's claims and promises for a wider segment of Americans than Jefferson may have had in mind. Slauter places the Declaration in its historic context as he describes its evolution from Jefferson's draft through the debates in Congress that led to its final form, but he also presents the Declaration as a living document whose meanings were not confined to those of its mere historical moment. If not intended by Jefferson or his colleagues in Congress as a charter of rights, African American readers from the beginning read the Declaration in ways that made it a modern document by asserting that it should be so.

At the heart of Jefferson's political ideology was faith in republicanism, an idea with a long history going back to the Greeks, but one which he understood at its heart as the right of the people to choose their own government. Many of his contemporaries would have agreed with this basic notion, but they would have different notions of what was meant by "the people" and what constituted "choice," and they would have had very different notions of what the consequences of this belief in republicanism might be. Ari Helo's chapter discusses Jefferson's understanding of republicanism and how it affected his notions of government. Helo connects Jefferson's belief in popular sovereignty both with its radical dimension of empowering ordinary citizens and with its more parochial aspects, which sought to preserve individual rights by grounding them in local government and in a doctrine of states' rights. Jefferson's naturalistic theory of rights, based on human behavior and human intelligence, saw constitutions as historically contingent and in need of change and evolution as the human mind developed. For Jefferson each generation should write its own constitution, but the writing should be left to the "talented and virtuous," perhaps limiting the extent of his belief in popular sovereignty.

Notes on the State of Virginia was Jefferson's one published book and was a significant nationalistic document. Among its other intentions it meant to dispute the negative picture of climate and nature disseminated by Buffon and other European thinkers, but the *Notes* also located Virginia in the context of the confederated states and explained, or fantasized about, American culture and American prospects. Thomas Hallock explores Jefferson's thinking, or perhaps fantasizing, by thinking about *Notes* in the context of Jefferson's longstanding interest in the West and in the American Indian. For Hallock, *Notes* "may be read as the product of and blueprint for an expanding republic," but one in which the Indians will disappear, at least as Indians. Jefferson's fantasy of the future of European-American and Indian relations saw two possibilities: a nearly seamless Indian assimilation into white culture, which would erase differences, or their eventual disappearance from the American scene. Hallock shows how Jefferson's fantasy was implicitly endorsed by the blindness towards Indian knowledge and culture of Lewis and Clark, who failed to understand the skills of their Nez Perce guides. Gordon M. Sayre also addresses the problematic issues that permeate Jefferson's thinking about Indians in "Jefferson and Native Americans: policy and archive." As secretary of state, Jefferson laid the foundations for

American Indian policy for years to come. His interest in Indians, however, seems to have come from his youth; he vividly expresses his memories of Indian oratory he heard sometime before his father died in 1757. His passages in *Notes on the State of Virginia* on American Indians, including the transmission of Logan's speech, are an important part of his argument with Buffon, but he was interested in acquiring information about Indian languages and customs throughout his life. Sayre examines Jefferson's Indian archive and pays special attention to his use of Logan's speech in *Notes*, but also to how it was used by his political opponents. His examination of the speech's origins finally opens insights into the complex interplay of racial and cultural difference on the frontier that resonate with other discussions of race found here.

Jefferson's position vis-à-vis slavery was ambiguous to say the least; he professed opposition to slavery but failed to take any significant steps to deal with it. Douglas R. Egerton's "Race and slavery in the era of Jefferson" explores Jefferson's racial thinking as expressed in *Notes on the State of Virginia* and other writings. Egerton portrays Jefferson as at heart a racist, whose actions are ultimately motivated by his attitudes about race. He contends that Jefferson's supposedly scientific analysis of racial difference in the *Notes* was fundamentally a charade, bad science "out of step with the prevailing scientific trends of the late eighteenth century." Egerton explodes the coherence of Jefferson's theorizing about slavery and race as a way to explain his failure to do anything to end the "peculiar institution." Lucia Stanton's chapter, "Jefferson's people: slavery at Monticello," on the other hand offers in fascinating detail Jefferson's interaction with his slaves at Monticello and his other plantations. For Stanton, the system of slavery, and by implication perhaps the racial attitudes that justified it, was something Jefferson was born into. It was seemingly a system so entwined with every aspect of his life that he was never able to extricate himself from it. Stanton examines the actual relations of blacks and whites on Jefferson's plantations, with special attention to the members of the Hemings family but also to the teenage workers in his nailery and trusted figures like George Granger ("Great George" is George Granger). Jefferson's relationship with Sally Hemings, now accepted by serious historians since the DNA tests of 1998, is contextualized within a rich network of family and community ties at Monticello, offering a more nuanced view of Jefferson's thinking about race and slavery.

Science is the subject of Timothy Sweet's "Jefferson, science, and the Enlightenment," and he concentrates on Jefferson's argument with Buffon in *Notes*. If this was ultimately a nationalistic argument, it was carried on in scientific terms. Jefferson's scientific interests figured in his writings on paleontology, his presidency of the American Philosophical Society, his mathematical proclivities, and his interest in gardening and agriculture.

Jefferson's engagement with the scientific world of his time, as Sweet shows, exposes a fundamental belief in the rational structure of the natural world that underwrites his faith in human rational behavior. Yet at the same time Jefferson's attempt to think about "the races of black and red men ... as subjects of natural history" failed for a number of reasons, not least that Jefferson was unable to imagine himself as a "subject of natural history." If his practice of science seems curiously constricted, it might be that, as Sweet concludes, the disciplines of the sciences were changing – "biology moving inward, from structure to function; geology moving outward, to the conceptualization of deep time" – and amateur scientists like Jefferson found it increasingly difficult to engage the disciplines. Jefferson, suggests Sweet, was perhaps less interested in science itself than in its shared discursive conventions with the communicability of reason they exemplified.

The arts were an important interest of Jefferson's. He was an ardent musician until he broke his wrist and could no longer easily play his violin; he collected paintings and statuary for Monticello, and, as a lover of poetry from the classics to Ossian, he even wrote an essay on prosody for a French friend. Of all the arts, however, he may have been most interested in architecture; his life-long effort to create the perfect residence for himself led him to tear down the first Monticello and tinker endlessly to complete and improve the second. Yet for Jefferson architecture was another exploration, like his interest in science, of the communicability of reason. Richard Guy Wilson's "Thomas Jefferson and the creation of the American architectural image" thematically considers Jefferson's architectural career as a designer of public spaces. Wilson demonstrates how Jefferson intended his design for the pavilions on the Lawn at the University of Virginia as, in effect, a set of architectural lessons for aspiring students "of natural taste." As Wilson shows, Jefferson combined an intention to locate his buildings in the context of classical and Palladian precedents while also paying attention to the limits or opportunities of the site and the presence of a Virginian vernacular that offered specific materials. Jefferson's neoclassicism was not, argues Wilson, a matter of offering symbols of Roman republicanism but of their perfecting of form and proportion. His design for the Capitol of Virginia was less important for him as a symbol than as an almost mathematically perfect structural exposition of the golden mean. The communicability of Jefferson's reason seems validated by the national architecture that his building inaugurated. If we are inclined to think first about Jefferson as a political thinker, we should not neglect the buildings he designed to house political leaders of his time and beyond.

In "The politics of pedagogy: Thomas Jefferson and the education of a democratic citizenry," Darren Staloff examines Jefferson's scheme to educate the political leaders of Virginia in his university and shows that this was somewhat less than the generously democratic project it has been taken to be. One of the three items Jefferson wished to be remembered for on his grave marker was the University of Virginia, and he campaigned for improved schools in Virginia as early as 1777. The University as he conceived of it has been called the model for many subsequent state universities, particularly the land grant universities, where the whole range of (secular!) human inquiry could be pursued. He thought of the university, however, particularly as a mechanism to ensure the reproduction of republican principles in the future leaders of Virginia and the nation, or so he hoped. Staloff shows how Jefferson's plans for the university were shaped by his perceptions of a sectional threat to the slave-holding South. Staloff also provides a corrective critique of Jefferson's earlier plans for educational reform in Virginia, showing how it was not nearly so likely to rake "diamonds from the dunghill" as many have assumed it might. Jefferson's plans for educating the aristocracy of the talented and virtuous who had the misfortune to be born into poverty would not have provided for many; his plans for the university seem to turn away from his earlier proposal to educate the mass of common people. More damning in 1825 Virginia, crucial parts of the curriculum on politics and law "no longer consisted in a broad exposure to modern learning but instead took on the forms of a narrow political indoctrination."

Jefferson was proud of his authorship of Virginia's Statute for Religious Freedom, even though his comments on religious freedom in *Notes* provoked vicious attacks from Federalist clergy who considered him an atheist. Jefferson called for a "wall of separation" between church and state in a memorable letter to the Danbury Baptist Association, a phrase that in the twentieth century entered into the language of Supreme Court decisions. Yet he assured his friends in private that he was no atheist and showed a select few his personal edit of the Gospels, one that preserved the morality of Jesus and left out the "priestcraft." Richard Samuelson discusses Jefferson's evolving religious ideas and relates them to his defense of religious freedom, showing one to be a private matter of belief, the other to be more complicated because of the public dimensions of religious practice.

Jefferson's major literary output occurs in the form of the thousands of letters he wrote to friends, colleagues, constituents, and others. The letters he wrote to his friends are particularly revealing of his investment in the sentimental culture of the eighteenth-century moral sense philosophers as well as of Shaftesburean sociability. Andrew Burstein's "Jefferson and the language of friendship" examines this phenomenon with specific attention to particular friendships and exchanges. Burstein looks closely at the famous "Head and Heart" letter that Jefferson wrote to Maria Cosway, an artist he met during his stay in Paris. Here Jefferson articulates a serious moral dialogue but in language reminiscent of Laurence Sterne's discourse filled with "flirtation and sexual tease." Nowhere does Jefferson's investment in the discourse of sentiment and sentimentalism appear more clearly than in this letter and in his abiding affection for the works of Sterne. As Burstein observes, however, friendship had gendered dimensions, and Jefferson's political friendships developed in different ways and required a different language. Age differences mattered as well, and Burstein shows how Jefferson wrote differently to James Madison, his near contemporary, and to the younger James Monroe.

The next two chapters continue the theme of political and epistolary friendship as Joanne B. Freeman examines Jefferson's correspondence with John Adams, and Annette Gordon-Reed looks at Jefferson's political friendship with Madison. Jefferson and Adams exchanged their most interesting and entertaining letters in the last decade and a half of their lives, after the political differences that had divided them in the late 1790s had become less important to them than the much older friendship that had begun with their meeting in Philadelphia in 1776. These letters snap and bubble with the numerous topics that interested both men and the genuinely playful ways in which they responded to each other. Shadowed by health problems, the deaths of loved ones, their concerns about how they would be regarded by posterity, they preserved their bonds with each other, as Freeman observes, in the letters they exchanged. Gordon-Reed discusses a friendship that was much more narrowly political than the one between Adams and Jefferson. She notes that Jefferson and Madison, if not always in perfect agreement, were always on the same page with each other. The more moderate and emotionally restrained Madison checked occasional Jeffersonian rhetorical excesses, as in his proposal to write a new constitution every nineteen years. Their correspondence also reveals a shared "Virginianness," for example in their lack of any serious discussion about slavery and the attitudes they implicitly shared about race. Their letters also differ from those exchanged between Adams and Jefferson because they were supplemented by far more frequent and extensive face-to-face meetings.

Douglas Anderson's concluding chapter, "Jefferson and the democratic future," speculates about Jefferson's concerns for what the future might hold for the democratic project in America. On the occasion of Jefferson's 250th anniversary in 1993, a conference in Virginia and a subsequent publication of the papers addressed *Jeffersonian Legacies*.[4] Jefferson was himself concerned about his legacy, designing his own tombstone, which inscribed the achievements by which he especially wished to be remembered. Ambivalent to the last, he also included verses in Greek that translated as

"And small we must lie, / A dust of loosened bones." Memory and forgetfulness thus inscribed on different faces of the stone perhaps describe the nature of Jefferson's legacy as Anderson presents it. Jefferson was on the one hand committed to handing down a historical record of the republican experiment, yet he was equally concerned that the past not impose its dead hand on the lively future. If democracy meant the possibility of independent thought to Jefferson, then he was obliged not to impose on the independence of the future, not least because he hoped the future might be able to move beyond the mistakes and misconceptions of his own generation. For Jefferson, democracy was less something to be handed down in an embalmed form than a process of possibly endless improvement. He recognized, as Anderson puts it, "We are not yet what we mean to be." Jefferson's real importance to us is not as the source of a political bible but as a challenge to assumptions and an endless invitation to debate.

NOTES

1. Quoted in Merrill Peterson, *The Jefferson Image in the American Mind* (New York: Oxford University Press, 1960), 162, 216.
2. For a good account of Jefferson's reputation in the years since Peterson's 1960 study, see Francis D. Cogliano, *Thomas Jefferson: Reputation and Legacy* (Charlottesville: University Press of Virginia, 2006).
3. See, for example, Paul Finkleman, *Slavery and the Founders* (Armonk, NY: M. E. Sharpe, 1996); Anthony F. C. Wallace, *Jefferson and the Indians* (Cambridge, MA: Harvard University Press, 1999); Leonard W. Levy, *Jefferson and Civil Liberties* (Cambridge, MA: Harvard University Press, 1963); Conor Cruise O'Brien, *The Long Affair* (Chicago: University of Chicago Press, 1996).
4. Peter S. Onuf (ed.), *Jeffersonian Legacies* (Charlottesville: University Press of Virginia, 1993).

I

ERIC SLAUTER

The Declaration of Independence and the new nation

On July 2, 1776 the news that "the CONTINENTAL CONGRESS declared the UNITED COLONIES FREE and INDEPENDENT STATES" appeared in the *Pennsylvania Evening Post* beside a notice about a local man who had declared his own independence. Ishmael, "twenty-five years of age, above six feet high, strong made, his colour between a Mulatto and a Black," ran away from his Philadelphia owner despite being "somewhat lame, occasioned by his having his thigh bone broke when a boy."[1] The newspapers and state papers of the American Revolution made impassioned declarations about liberty and property, setting the stage for a civil war in the language of rights acted out by and upon unfree individuals like Ishmael. Modern readers cannot miss the proximity of liberty to slavery in the new nation, but would contemporaries have connected a slave's escape with the resolution that Congress passed on July 2 or with the Declaration explaining that resolution approved on July 4, published in the same newspaper on July 5, and celebrated in Philadelphia and elsewhere on July 8?[2] More importantly, would Ishmael?[3]

To ask such questions is to confront a powerful narrative about the changing meaning of the Declaration of Independence. Scholars once confidently equated the Declaration with the statements that "all Men are created equal, that they are endowed by their Creator with certain unalienable Rights, that among these are Life, Liberty, and the Pursuit of Happiness." But since the 1960s, and with increasing persuasiveness in book-length studies by historians Pauline Maier and David Armitage, scholars have contended that the self-evident truths of the second paragraph, so familiar to modern readers, did not constitute the core of the Declaration to contemporaries.[4] The earliest domestic and foreign commentators passed over those truths in favor of the long list of charges against the king and especially the final paragraph, which reproduced (and in early printed versions typographically emphasized) the congressional resolution of July 2. For these readers, the Declaration was the statement that:

these United Colonies are, and of Right ought to be, FREE AND INDEPENDENT STATES; that they are absolved from all Allegiance to the British Crown, and that all political Connection between them and the State of Great-Britain, is and ought to be totally dissolved; and that as FREE AND INDEPENDENT STATES, they have full Power to levy War, conclude Peace, contract Alliances, establish Commerce, and to do all other Acts and Things which INDEPENDENT STATES may of right do.

The capitalized words of the final paragraph of the printed Declaration were the only ones in the body of the text, which was, after all, a declaration of national independence and not a declaration of individual rights.[5]

Nineteenth-century readers transformed the Declaration from an assertion of sovreignty to a charter of rights, elevating the significance of the self-evident truths of the second paragraph. Indeed, Abraham Lincoln's explanation that the "assertion that 'all men are created equal' was of no practical use in effecting our separation from Great Britain; and it was placed in the Declaration, not for that, but for future use" stands as a characteristic mid-nineteenth-century acknowledgement that the document meant something different as a bequest than it had to those who bequeathed it.[6] The nature of that inheritance was contested – even Lincoln reduced the "truth" of equality to an "assertion" and (more famously, in the Gettysburg Address) a "proposition." For antebellum abolitionists the hypocrisy of slavery in a land of liberty was obvious, as was the irony that a text associated with liberty had been principally authored by a slaveholder; apologists for slavery, on the other hand, claimed that African-descended people, if they were truly human, were not included within the rights-bearing "Men" of the Declaration and that the authors of the Declaration had not meant to include them.[7] Despite this interpretive divide, all parties agreed on the centrality of the second paragraph, and this fact distinguishes the text's meaning to subsequent generations from its meaning in 1776.

A careful reading of the contemporary production and reception, however, suggests we need to revise the story of how the new nation understood its Declaration. We should not return to older interpretations that mistook nineteenth-century understandings for eighteenth-century meanings, but nevertheless the now-dominant narrative that emphasizes dynamic change over time unduly homogenizes original meanings and does not account for a particular kind of contemporary reader. Beginning in 1776, when a young Massachusetts man of mixed racial identity named Lemuel Haynes – he had a black father and a white mother, identified himself as a "Mulatto," and had been an indentured servant but never a slave – took the Declaration's self-evident truths of equality and rights as an epigraph for an essay on the "illegality of Slave-keeping," black and white antislavery activists seized upon the first part of the second paragraph and insisted it was the central fact of the text. Writers like Haynes constituted a minority of early readers, but his citation of the second paragraph was significant: for, following others who had taken the rhetoric of colonial rights as an opportunity for questioning the hollowness of commitments to individual liberty, Haynes hoped to personalize that paragraph and he hoped to identify unfree blacks as the potential and actual subjects of the Declaration's political philosophy.[8] To understand the Declaration from the perspective of its congressional authors involves abandoning the comfort of a singular historical meaning. Early readers like Haynes also invested the text with a significance that Congress may not have anticipated. The Declaration is a radical text further radicalized by its readers, who learned to critique the new nation as early as 1776 by appealing specifically to the document Jefferson helped to draft.

****

Historians have often told the story of the drafting of the Declaration with the unspoken assurance that it was the most important text produced in Congress in June or July 1776; for members of Congress, it probably wasn't. John Adams would seem to have preferred to confederate first and then to declare independence, but explained to Patrick Henry on June 3, 1776, that he really did not think it made much difference.[9] The Declaration was one report prepared by a congressional committee in response to a bundle of resolutions proposed on June 7, 1776, by Richard Henry Lee of Virginia. Lee proposed (and John Adams of Massachusetts seconded) that Congress resolve:

> That these United Colonies are, and of right ought to be, free and independent States, that they are absolved from all allegiance to the British Crown, and that all political connection between them and the State of Great Britain is, and ought to be, totally dissolved.

> That it is expedient forthwith to take the most effectual measures for forming foreign Alliances.

> That a plan of confederation be prepared and transmitted to the respective Colonies for their consideration and approbation.[10]

The prospect of independence was intimately tied to securing foreign alliances and forming a domestic government, both of which entailed complicated acts of political construction with agents beyond Congress. In contrast, Lee made declaring independence sound easy. His phrasing was significant: the first resolution stated a simple fact; the other two outlined congressional priorities that should follow on that fact. In an effort to build support among anxious delegates, Lee, Adams, and George Wythe of Virginia told colleagues during the debate on Lee's motion that a declaration would not *do* anything, for to declare the colonies independent was only to "declare a fact which already exists."[11] Adams believed his own congressional resolution of May 15, which instructed individual colonies to organize new governments, was a positive assertion of de facto independence; and besides, as a preface he wrote for the publication of that resolution indicated, if anyone was the author of independence it was the king.[12] Given the deterioration of British authority, and the fact that the king had removed the colonists from his protection, a declaration of independence would be a descriptive rather than a performative utterance: it would not change what was already true. Or so they argued. But, as the ordering of resolutions made manifest, some believed a formal declaration would smooth the way for a treaty with France and was perhaps a prerequisite for forming a new government. Others thought the ordering was backwards – after all, shouldn't the states confederate first and then declare independence?[13] And, of course, though independence had been looming ever larger in public and private discussions since the military phase of the American Revolution began in April 1775, some delegates vigorously opposed it. Congress debated Lee's resolutions, then decided on June 10 to postpone discussion for three weeks so delegates could receive instructions from their home governments about how to proceed. The next day, anticipating that the votes would favor independence, delegates elected three committees charged with preparing three texts tied to Lee's resolutions: a declaration, a plan of treaties, and a form of confederation.[14]

Jefferson may have drafted the Declaration because better-known writers were tied up with other committees. The delegates, sensing the formal creation of a national government would prove most complicated and controversial, placed one member from each of the thirteen colonies on the confederation committee; the other two committees had five members. The job of drafting the confederation plan went to the best-known political writer in Congress, someone who did not even support Lee's resolution on independence: John Dickinson of Delaware, whose *Letters from a Farmer in Pennsylvania* from 1768 was one of the most reprinted political pamphlets of the period.[15] The delegates placed John Adams, Benjamin Franklin of Pennsylvania, Thomas Jefferson of Virginia, Robert R. Livingston of New York, and Roger Sherman of Connecticut on the "committee to prepare the Declaration" (known to history and to historians as the Committee of Five, though the treaty committee also had five members). Significantly, delegates elected all of these men except Jefferson to one of the other two committees as well. Adams later recalled that he had asked Jefferson to draft the Declaration because he felt it important that the text come from a Virginian; and indeed, Jefferson was the only committee member from the South. To be sure, Jefferson also had an emerging reputation. He was the principal author of two congressional state papers and had written – though not intending it for public consumption – a pamphlet which, in the form of proposed congressional resolutions, constituted the first sustained published attack on the king.[16] But probably just as crucial as his literary abilities was the fact that Jefferson was the only member of the declaration committee without other duties directly tied to the Lee resolutions.[17] Adams and Franklin, the other established political writers in Congress, also served on the treaty committee. Both played crucial roles in the report Jefferson drafted, but Adams was the primary author of the plan of treaties and Franklin spent much of the season ill and out of Congress.

As the committee reports came in, Congress treated them with different degrees of editorial care, and even material differences in the way members encountered the reports tell us that the Declaration was a different kind of document. After voting in favor of Lee's first resolution on July 2, delegates spent two days editing the Declaration committee's draft manuscript before sending the final version to printer John Dunlap on July 4. Most likely, Jefferson or Secretary Charles Thomson read the text aloud and representatives made suggestions for revision. But when the other two texts came in, Congress resolved to print the draft reports of the confederation and treaties committees in editions of eighty copies, one for each member to use during discussion. These texts were to be printed, not published: Congress insisted that Dunlap swear an oath not to disclose the reports or to reprint them in his newspaper, and members agreed not to share copies with anyone outside of Congress. Dunlap produced draft documents with ample space in the left-hand margin for changes, and surviving copies show that delegates filled this space with numerous revisions. Without evidence, scholars have sometimes suggested that Congress printed draft copies of the Declaration as well, that Secretary Thomson failed to note the resolution in the journal, and that all copies were destroyed. This is unlikely. Congress had not taken this kind of care with similar papers that were issued in their voice or name, and delegates spent much longer with the draft reports from the other committees than with the draft of the Declaration. The reason for the care with these other texts stemmed from the fact that they were not congressional statements but were designed to be legal documents entered into by at least two parties (in the case of the treaties) and by as many as thirteen (in the case of the confederation plan, a different kind of treaty). The Declaration, though delivered in the voice of Congress, did not seem to demand comparable expense or editorial energy.[18] Unlike the other reports, the Declaration was about dissolving rather than building connections, and it was a unilateral statement that required agreement only among a majority of delegations in Congress. Despite the legalism of form and language, the Declaration was not a legal text or a legislative act.[19]

The document Congress agreed to on July 4 materialized some of the confusion delegates must have felt about what they were doing; it is no wonder that future readers have come to different understandings. On the one hand, the text portrayed Congress as essentially reactive and George III as the primary author of Independence.[20] On the other, it seemed curiously to tack back and forth between claims that independence had already happened and claims that independence was happening through the process of the congressional resolution – or even more radically, by virtue of the text itself. In addition, it was not always clear who was speaking in the text, a fact made even more obscure when Congress officially changed the title of the document two weeks after publication. On the top of his own copy of the Rough Draft of the Declaration (a copy that contains the form of the text the committee presented to Congress on July 2, along with congressional changes), Jefferson wrote that it was "A Declaration of" before changing it to "A Declaration by the Representatives of the United States of America"; the minor shift from "of" to "by" was meant presumably to signal that the representatives did not speak for themselves but for the states they represented.[21] The journals of Congress during the debates of the first days of July refer to the committee's report as "the declaration respecting independence," "the declaration on independence," and as simply "the Declaration"; but crucially, it was not called the Declaration *of* Independence. John Dunlap printed the approved text on July 4 as *A Declaration By the Representatives of the United States of America, In General Congress Assembled*. On July 19, after New York's delegates belatedly received authorization empowering them to vote for independence (New York abstained on July 2), Congress ordered the text to be engrossed with a new title to reflect that it was now *The Unanimous Declaration of the Thirteen United States of America*.[22] The Declaration was printed and published six weeks before it was written in manuscript on parchment and signed. The title and material change put delegates in an awkward position. The "Representatives" who had clearly been the speakers in the title of the printed text of July 4 – the "WE" who resolved on independence – now further subordinated themselves to the states they represented even as the text was for the first time specifically made available to be signed by those representatives.[23]

Though the now-common title suggests the text declares independence, it is perhaps better understood as a declaration of reasons or causes for why the United States of America are (or were) already independent. At the very least, this is how a majority in Congress understood the text. Passing references in private and public letters suggest that, to its earliest congressional readers, the Declaration rationalized and publicized rather than performed an action.[24] Further evidence can be found in an edit Congress made to the final paragraph of the text itself. The Rough Draft shows that Jefferson and the Declaration committee wished Congress to say "we do assert and declare these colonies to be free and independent states," but Congress preferred to say "WE … solemnly Publish and Declare, That these United Colonies are, and of Right ought to be, FREE AND INDEPENDENT STATES." Jefferson and the committee may have thought of independence as a textual event. But other members of Congress clearly wanted to document the precise language of the resolution they approved on July 2 (which was the language Lee introduced on June 7). The change also signaled that Congress distinguished the textual Declaration of July 4 from the resolution of July 2. The Declaration was the publication of the resolution for independence, not the assertion of independence itself. In the closest thing to an internal self-description, the first paragraph of the Declaration states that what is required and what is offered is less a declaration of independence than a declaration of "the causes which impel them to the Separation" from Great Britain; this too was the product of intense revision.

Jefferson and the committee heavily revised the first paragraph during the drafting process and the revisions reveal two distinct understandings of why independence was being declared. Two early drafts, one in Jefferson's and one in Adams's hand, suggest what literary scholar Jay Fliegelman has termed a "generational or morphological argument": the dependency of one people on another was in all cases a temporary status and so (as those early drafts put it) "in the course of human events it becomes necessary for a people to advance from that subordination in which they have hitherto remained, & to assume among the powers of the earth the equal & independent station to which the laws of nature & of nature's god entitle them." When an advance from subordination happened, a people should "declare the causes which impel them to the change." Jefferson's original language resonated with Thomas Paine's *Common Sense*, a pamphlet that had electrified readers in early 1776 with a strong critique of monarchy and a sustained attack on political metaphors that seemingly implied colonial subordination. Paine argued that talk of a mother country with colonies as children ultimately served the interests of the figural children, since it was only natural to advance from minority status to independence. It was perhaps no accident that Jefferson would adopt a similar rhetorical strategy. But the final version of the Rough Draft that the Declaration committee reported, and ultimately the document Congress signed off on, did not argue in this vein. Instead Congress spoke of political necessity and of moments when "it becomes necessary for one People to dissolve the Political Bands which have connected them with another, and to assume among the Powers of the Earth, the separate and equal Station to which the Laws of Nature and Nature's God entitle them." Gone was the appeal to the inevitability of independence as a natural fact of growing up: indeed, the revision removed the notion of "subordination" and it completely rid the paragraph of reference to a prior dependent status. The "one People" were now to assume a station that was "separate" (the word preferred to "independent"); and this was to be a political "separation" (the more precise word substituted for "change") that required declaring causes. The revisions eliminated the concept of prior dependency entirely from the first paragraph, effectively removing any residue of generational language.[25] Arguably, no other editing of the Rough Draft was as important as this one: it made the text about the severing of "political" rather than natural bonds. And there was nothing natural about politics.

Because the connections between the colonies and Britain were political rather than natural, the colonies did not become states by virtue of the Declaration; they were states within the British Empire all along. According to the logic of the second paragraph, the "Political Bands" being dissolved had been rooted in the "Consent of the Governed," a consent that children or other dependents could not be expected to give. In the penultimate paragraph, the representatives alluded to prior messages to the British people that "reminded them of the Circumstances of our Emigration and Settlement here"; these circumstances did not include an internal legislative subordination to Parliament. Jefferson first elaborated this argument in a proposed congressional resolution published in 1774 under the title (it was not his) *A Summary View of the Rights of British America*. Jefferson wanted the king to know that "these his states" had been encroached upon "by the legislature of one part of the empire" and "that our ancestors, before their emigration to America, ... possessed a right, which nature has given all men, of departing from the country in which chance, not choice has placed them, of going in quest of new habitations, and of there establishing new societies, under such laws and regulations as to them shall seem most likely to promote public happiness." "These states," erected at the expense of individuals and not the British public, had never been under the jurisdiction of Parliament but had submitted themselves for protection "to the same common sovereign, who was thereby made the central link connecting the several parts of the empire."[26] Here, then, was Jefferson's substantive prior articulation of the narrative of "choice" rather than "chance" (and even the keywords of nature, rights, and happiness) that would underwrite the revision to the first paragraph and which he would later incorporate into the second paragraph of the Declaration.

The theory of government in the second paragraph is rooted in a right that the Declaration is at most pains to define, but about which the *Summary View* was wholly silent: while the individual rights of "all Men" were only loosely acknowledged, Jefferson and Congress described the collective "Right of the People" to alter governments as the central right of the text.[27] The Declaration barely enumerates the "certain unalienable Rights" announced at the opening of the second paragraph (the final draft states simply that "among these" rights are "Life, Liberty, and the Pursuit of Happiness") but it rises to explain more precisely that governments are "instituted among men" to "secure these rights," that they derive "their just Powers from the Consent of the Governed," and that "whenever any Form of Government becomes destructive of these Ends, it is the Right of the People to alter or abolish it, and to institute new Government, laying its Foundation on such Principles, and organizing its Powers in such Form, as to them shall seem most likely to effect their Safety and Happiness." This last point was the central premise of the text and, significantly, it was the only part of a long paragraph in which Jefferson's original language passed unaltered through the editing process. The final draft (like Jefferson's original) even stated this right twice, explaining that "when a long Train of Abuses and Usurpations ... evinces a Design to reduce them under absolute Despotism" – the reference to despotism was an addition of Franklin's in preference to Jefferson's "absolute power" – then "it is their Right, it is their Duty, to throw off such Government and to provide new Guards for their future Security." Jefferson clinched the point by verbalizing the key noun: Congress would acknowledge that many suffer silently when they should "right themselves" by abolishing their governments.

The problem, endlessly debated in the centuries before and after the publication of Locke's *Second Treatise* in 1690, was how a people knew they were employing their right to alter government legitimately.[28] The Declaration massaged the issue. On the one hand, representatives said the king abdicated and had declared his independence of them; on the other, they sketched "a Design to reduce them under absolute Despotism." The body of the Declaration presented this sketch as a list of "Facts ... submitted to a candid World." As the literary and legal scholar Robert A. Ferguson has shown, the Declaration employed the "language and forms of legality" to mimic common-law pleading, playing the people as "plaintiff" against the king as "defendant."[29] In 1774, the First Continental Congress decided to restrict discussion to acts passed under the current monarch, George III.[30] The theory of empire advanced over the previous two years and the decade-long denial of Parliamentary power meant George would stand alone in the indictment. Some of the "facts" perplexed early readers: what were the "wholesome and necessary" laws the king had refused or the "Laws of immediate and pressing Importance" he would not allow governors to pass?[31] As historian Woody Holton has shown, some charges reflected Virginia's experience; inevitably they did not register with readers elsewhere.[32] The major unifying indictment against the king was not simply that he was currently "waging War against us" – plundering "our Seas," ravaging "our Coasts," burning "our Towns," destroying the lives of "our People," and impressing "our fellow Citizens"; it was that he had interfered with colonial self-government. It did not matter what the laws were, the important thing was that they were "our Laws," "our most valuable Laws." Even the charge that Parliament taxed colonists "without our consent," which appeared at the dead center of the broadside printing of the Declaration, became the king's crime because he had assented to those bills; in essence he had preferred "their Acts of pretended Legislation" to "our Laws." Importantly, representatives said that Americans were not yet living "under absolute Despotism" but rather under a king who had that "Design" or "Object" in mind. Seventeen of the final eighteen charges were historical ("HE has ... HE has ... HE has"); the exception was that "HE is, at this Time, transporting large Armies of foreign Mercenaries to compleat the Works of Death, Desolation, and Tyranny, already begun." The specter of incomplete despotism, rather than despotism as such, allowed Congress to maintain they were still "a free People" and not simply (as Jefferson had originally put it, in a phrase that could imply servitude) "a people who mean to be free."

Meaning to be free was obviously crucial, for the Declaration committee wanted to indict the king for the slave trade and for inciting slave rebellions in Virginia, but both charges failed to make the final draft. Jefferson intended the list to crescendo outward in its final indictments, bringing in the full range of the king's purchased accomplices in his war on the colonists: the king had conspired with "large Armies of foreign Mercenaries," with "merciless Indian savages," with traitors among "our fellow-subjects," and ultimately with black slaves. In the draft the Declaration committee presented to Congress, the final charge was that:

> he has waged cruel war against human nature itself, violating it's most sacred rights of life & liberty in the persons of a distant people who never offended him, captivating & carrying them into slavery in another hemisphere, or to incur miserable death in their transportation thither. this piratical warfare, the opprobrium of *infidel* powers, is the warfare of the *Christian* king of Great-Britain. determined to keep open a market where MEN should be bought & sold, he has prostituted his negative for suppressing every legislative attempt to prohibit or to restrain this execrable commerce: and that this assemblage of horrors might want no fact of distinguished die, he is now exciting those very people to rise up in arms among us, and to purchase that liberty of which *he* has deprived them, by murdering the people upon whom *he* also obtruded them; thus paying off former crimes committed against the *liberties* of one people, with crimes which he urges them to commit against the *lives* of another.

Adams and Franklin let this passage stand, but the bombastic nature of the claim was too easy to disprove, for slavery had been sanctioned and supported by every colonial government, and specious claims called into question the validity of others. Jefferson grumbled that it had been eliminated to appease certain southern states as well as the northerners who profited off the slave trade.[33] It was no accident that Jefferson, in what Julian Boyd called his "Original Rough Draught," waited until this final charge to name the king (Adams revised this in committee), that Jefferson held the king responsible for the perpetuation of New World slavery, that he continued throughout his lifetime to send correspondents versions of the Declaration as it had been originally reported to Congress, or that his slaveholding correspondents in Virginia approved of the sentiment.[34] The economy of rights was at its barest point here, illustrated and personified by the stolen liberties of black slaves and the now-threatened lives of white colonists. The king, Jefferson believed, had brought this situation to a point of combustion, but the reality was more complicated. Virginia legislators had tried for decades to impose a tariff that would curb the open market of the international slave trade, not because of antislavery sentiment but because an open market lowered the value of slaves in the domestic trade in Virginia. It is easy and right to highlight Jefferson's hypocrisy and the obscurity of his motives, his denial of other agents in the perpetuation of slavery, and his contradiction in condemning the king for freeing slaves, but it is also possible that a declaration with an explicit antislavery statement might very well have founded a nation with a very different history.

Jefferson described the rights violated by slavery as "sacred," an adjective he had also employed in his "Original Rough Draught" of the second paragraph. Though articulating a secular theory of the state and acknowledging a secular timeline ("the Course of human Events"), Congress appealed to "the Supreme Judge of the World" in the final paragraph. The religious language of the Declaration has made some later commentators uncomfortable, but it had an important function. The most significant immediate predecessor document was the Virginia Declaration of Rights, drafted principally by George Mason in late May 1776. Like the Declaration itself, the Virginia Declaration of Rights went through several drafts. Jefferson probably knew the committee draft, which circulated widely in print and appeared in a Philadelphia newspaper in June 1776. This draft stated "That all men are born equally free and independent, and have certain inherent natural rights, of which they cannot, by any compact, deprive or divest their posterity; among which are, the enjoyment of life and liberty, with the means of acquiring and possessing property, and pursuing and obtaining happiness and safety." Virginia legislators revised the committee draft so that its expansive language excluded slaves: it was only when men "entered into society," which slaves had not done, that rights had any meaning.[35] But in both the committee and final drafts Virginia had not named the source of the "natural rights" enumerated – indeed, when Mason suggested in his original draft that "Power is, by God and Nature, vested in and consequently derived from the People," the committee edited out "by God and Nature."[36]

In late May, the Virginia committee edited a reference to God out of their Declaration of Rights; a few weeks later the congressional Declaration committee edited one into the Declaration of Independence. Like the committee draft of the Virginia Declaration of Rights, Jefferson's "Original Rough Draught" avoided an explicit reference to God. According to a version of the Rough Draft in John Adams's handwriting, Jefferson originally wrote "that all men are created equal & independant, that from that equal creation they derive rights inherent & inalienable." At some point before Adams made his transcription of the text, and perhaps at the urging of a fellow committee member, Jefferson changed "We hold these truths to be sacred & undeniable" to "We hold these truths to be self-evident."[37] Jefferson's "Original Rough Draught," then, described the truths held as "sacred" and the rights enumerated as derived from "equal Creation" and inhering in "all men"; but Jefferson had not explicitly named an agent, except insofar as "Creation" implied a creator. The shift from Mason's "all men" as "born equally free and independent" to Jefferson's "all men" as "created equal" perhaps begged the question of agency, for, at some point after discussions with Franklin and Adams, Jefferson replaced the phrase about derivation of rights from "equal Creation" in favor of the sense that "all men ... are endowed by their creator with certain [inherent &] inalienable rights."[38] By choosing "created" rather than "born" equal, Jefferson had perhaps painted himself into a verbal corner, but in reality the issue was more fundamental than the choice of a transitive over an intransitive verb. The final Declaration simply made explicit what was implicit in other declarations of rights: the sense that appeals to the rights of men were guaranteed by pointing to God as the author of rights and as the ultimate arbiter of rights claims. Like the Declaration, the congressional Declaration of Causes that Jefferson had drafted with John Dickinson in 1775 referred to God as "the supreme and impartial Judge and Ruler of the universe."[39] The Massachusetts Constitution of 1780 drafted by John Adams called God the "Great Legislator of the Universe"; in 1785 James Madison called God the "great Governour of the Universe" in his Memorial and Remonstrance in favor of religious liberty. In an age committed to the separation of powers, God was variously and simultaneously described in terms of unified legislative, executive, and judicial authority. God was thus the mirror image of that other authorizing agent of the second paragraph: the individual person in a state of nature; or rather, the collection of individuals who constituted the people, either in the state of nature or after it. Both God and the people stood outside of government, if not outside of politics.

The question of political authorization was played out by references to God, by the theory of pre-political people, and more mundanely by various strategies of endorsing the document. In a brief but intriguing reading of the Declaration, philosopher Jacques Derrida highlighted the paradoxes and instabilities that inhere in a signed text that created the authority by which it could be signed, for Derrida held that the United States and the people had been created through the text.[40] Most in Congress did not understand the function of the document in this way; indeed, to them it was not a founding text. The paradoxes of performativity that made the Declaration theoretically interesting to Derrida tend to evaporate on closer scrutiny, but others multiply. The question of authorization, of the authority upon which the Declaration was based, was a vexed one, and the problems of legitimacy ran deep. Congress acted on instructions from the colonial governments, but in 1775 and 1776 these governments were extra-legal conventions and committees that claimed to represent the people but were not in most cases constituted by them. And the issue of signatures was also a complicated one. Congress had generated and abandoned different material practices relating to the way in which they endorsed documents issued in their name. The first state paper issued by Congress in 1774 was printed on special paper in an edition of 120 copies (10 for each colony) and the delegates signed each copy in manuscript.[41] Almost immediately, delegates abandoned this practice, preferring simply to let the president put his printed name to state papers and to let the secretary of Congress attest them with his name. Congress first published the Declaration in this way: it appeared as a broadside printed by John Dunlap and then in newspapers without the signatures of the representatives. President John Hancock "Signed by Order and in Behalf of the Congress" and Secretary Charles Thomson attested, but they did not sign in manuscript any of the surviving copies of the Dunlap broadside. Though delegates abandoned the practice of putting their names on state papers, the final line of the Declaration perhaps suggested (belatedly) that signatures were necessary: "And for the support of this Declaration ... we mutually pledge to each other our Lives, our Fortunes, and our sacred Honor." Though a number of delegates later said they signed the Declaration on July 4, it seems to have been signed almost a month and a half later.[42]

Delegates signed the parchment copy, which bore the new title of *The Unanimous Declaration of the Thirteen United States of America*, in geographic groupings by state delegation, another indication that they now wished to represent the states rather than themselves as the authors of the text.

Congress commissioned a second official printing, with the new title and the names of signers, from Baltimore printer Mary Katherine Goddard in January 1777; and though she attempted to reproduce the pattern of signatures the underlying geography was lost. The resolution of July 19 that changed the name and called for engrossment also provided (as John Adams later recalled with disdain) for a kind of continuous re-authorization: it suggested not simply that members who had been present and voted for independence should sign the parchment, but "that all *future* members should sign the *original parchment*."[43] The idea, even if it struck Adams as preposterous, had resonance in other material practices: since the late 1760s, colonists equated signing one's name to agreements not to buy imported British goods to swearing allegiance to the cause; and, since 1775, rebellious colonists subscribed their names on loyalty oaths to the extra-legal committees and conventions of the individual colonies. It was thus fitting that some congressmen believed the document required future signatures. The parchment copy eliminated from the title the agents of the Declaration, the "WE" who actually resolved on independence in the final paragraph, in favor of a vision of the United States of America as the authors of independence. But even as Congress tried to downplay its agency, and even as the document itself suggested that independence had already happened (not that it was happening through the text), the notion that future representatives should affix their names to the parchment copy demonstrated just how unresolved members of Congress were about the declaration of their resolution on independence.

***

If the "WE" who had authored the Declaration was purposefully ambiguous within Congress, in the streets of Philadelphia and elsewhere in the new nation local committees and conventions, in league with patriot newspapers, worked to represent, as historian David Waldstreicher has put it, the people who celebrated its publication less as auditors than as "the authors of Independence, if not of the Declaration of Independence."[44] More people may have heard the Declaration proclaimed than read printed versions. In a dazzling book-length contextualization of the Declaration's place in a larger culture of political performance, Jay Fliegelman has demonstrated that Jefferson specifically drafted the text for oral delivery; and Congress certainly encouraged military officers to read it aloud as a recruiting tactic. Twenty-nine newspapers also reprinted the full Declaration before July 26, and fifteen printers issued broadside copies of the text between the official Dunlap and Goddard printings in July 1776 and January 1777. A paper copy could become an icon of allegiance; the radical printer John Holt of New York encouraged readers to "fix it up, in open view, in their Houses, as a mark of their approbation of the INDEPENDENT SPIRIT of their Representatives." The corners of surviving copies from New York and Massachusetts suggest such display, but, since no copy bore the names of signers until January 1777, this meant individual readers in occupied cities like New York and Boston exposed themselves more than the unidentified representatives whose independent spirit was being celebrated.[45] Sympathetic owners of paper copies truly could think of it as their Declaration.

But after the flurry of printings, the document went underground: it was rarely reprinted or even cited until the 1790s, when it became a text embroiled in party politics. In the early nineteenth century, Democratic Republicans celebrated the Declaration as the work of President Thomas Jefferson. Federalists, a party in decline, did not surrender wholesale; they offered critical parodies and found ways to tie the text to the party of Washington and Adams.[46] By the end of the second decade of the nineteenth century, however, entrepreneurs offered several decorative engravings of the text; and by the early 1820s Congress authorized a facsimile of the engrossed copy, giving that forgotten and little-seen document a new iconic status. During that decade, the jubilee of the Declaration made the text better known, even as revolutions in Latin America and elsewhere gave the genre itself new significance and stability.[47] Quite suddenly the text became meaningful and appropriable in ways it had not been before.

Beginning in the late 1820s, radical groups adopted the form that Jefferson and Congress employed fifty years earlier in order to publicize their own grievances. Radical readers in the middle of the nineteenth century looked to the second paragraph of the Declaration for confirmation of a set of core rights and values – the truth that "all Men are created equal" and endowed with the rights of "Life, Liberty, and the Pursuit of Happiness" – and as a benchmark against which to test current inequalities. It is telling that, in all of what historian Philip S. Foner called the "alternative" Declarations drafted in the antebellum period, the one paragraph largely unaltered was the second. Indeed, in perhaps the most famous new-modeling of the text, drafted by Elizabeth Cady Stanton in 1848, a women's rights convention declared that "all men and women are created equal," but Stanton left the rest of the sentence untouched. Congress's use of "man" in the Declaration of Independence, as historian Linda Kerber has observed, "was in fact literal, not generic"; Stanton's revision suggested that it was better to clarify by addition than by redefinition. Even still, radical revisors needed a stable second paragraph, since it was that paragraph that suggested the harmony between what was being newly declared and what the founders took to be self-evident. The point of many of these alternative Declarations, of course, was to give new meaning to that paragraph, to hold it up as a foundational creed even if it had never seemed so to the so-called founders themselves.[48] Indeed, what they insisted was that the Declaration was a founding text.

But in reality, though historians have not paused over it, some contemporaries of the Revolution quickly embraced the utility and radical potential for social change of the second paragraph. Beginning with Lemuel Haynes in Massachusetts, whose 1776 antislavery tract "Liberty Further Extended" was not published in his lifetime but served as the basis of a speech, abolitionists in the new nation pointed specifically to the second paragraph of the Declaration. "If liberty is one of the natural and unalienable rights of all men," said the white antislavery advocate Jacob Green of New Jersey in a gloss on the second paragraph in a 1778 sermon, "if 'tis self-evident, i.e. so clear that it needs not proof, how unjust, how inhuman, for Britons, or Americans, not only to attempt, but actually to violate this right?" In an essay published in Pennsylvania that same year, the Quaker Anthony Benezet invoked the second paragraph of the Declaration, as well as the first article of the Virginia Declaration of Rights, and predicted that a people who could make such public declarations of equality and rights and still maintain slavery deserved whatever punishment they received during wartime. Three years later, Benezet again singled out the second paragraph of the Declaration, this time along with the Congressional Declaration of the Causes of Taking Up Arms (penned in part by Jefferson in 1775); Benezet wanted Americans to "consider how far they can justify a conduct so abhorrent from these sacred truths as that of dragging these oppressed Strangers from their native land, and all those tender connections we hold dear." In 1783, David Cooper offered an address on the inconsistency of slavery in a land committed to liberty; on the pages of his printed text he placed the words of American state papers on the left with his comments on the right. Across from the second paragraph of the Declaration, Cooper wrote:

> If these solemn *truths* uttered at such an awful crisis, are *self-evident*: unless we can shew that the African race are not *men*, words can hardly express the amazement which naturally arises on reflecting, that the very people who make these pompous declarations are slave-holders, and, by their legislative conduct, tell us, that these blessings were only meant to be the *rights* of *white-men* not of *all men*.[49]

That same year, the Rhode Island legislature passed an Act for the Abolition of Slavery that mentioned in its preamble that "all men are created equal, and endowed with the unalienable rights of life, liberty, and the pursuit for happiness."

And slowly, as war gave way to peace, writers and activists made sure that audiences understood that the Declaration was not simply the statement of slaveholders and others in Congress, but was in fact "the voice of all America, through her representatives in solemn Congress uttered." Though the Constitution of the United States made no claims about the equality of men and sanctioned slavery, the Constitution of the Pennsylvania Society for Promoting the Abolition of Slavery, drafted in 1788, invoked the language of the second paragraph of the Declaration; so did abolitionists in Maryland in 1791. A similar society in New Jersey placed the sentence on the title page of their 1793 Constitution.[50] By 1792, when African American almanac maker Benjamin Banneker quoted the "true and invaluable doctrine ... 'that all men are created equal'" back to Secretary of State Thomas Jefferson in an exchange of letters reprinted in papers across the new nation, antislavery activists had worked for a decade and a half to make Americans identify the Declaration of Independence specifically with the cause of enslaved African Americans.[51] This identification would intensify in the next decade and a half, even as the Declaration was coming to look like the property of the Democratic Republican political party. When, in the middle of Jefferson's second term as president, a convention of abolitionists reminded its affiliates that "nearly one fifth of the nation drag the galling chain of slavery," it also told them not to abandon the cause "until the rulers of the land shall practice what they teach, that they 'hold these truths to be self-evident, that all men are created equal; that they are endowed by their Creator with certain unalienable rights: that among these are life, liberty, and the pursuit of happiness.'" At the next meeting of the same group, after the passage of an 1807 law prohibiting citizens of the United States from participating in the international slave trade, the abolitionists hoped "our hearts will still be enlarged, and our hands still strengthened in the work, till the rulers, and the ruled, shall practice what the sacred charter of our liberty declares": "that all men are created equal" with "certain unalienable rights."[52] When Frederick Douglass in 1852 famously asked an audience in Rochester, New York, "What, to the American slave, is your 4th of July?," the question was not based on a wholesale revision of the meaning of the text but was as old as the Declaration itself.[53] Though for most the Declaration had not taken on its modern meaning as a charter of rights, a small group of black and white readers beginning in 1776 asserted that it should and, in doing so, made the Declaration their own and helped to make it modern.

NOTES

This essay includes, in revised form, some material previously published in Eric Slauter, *The State as a Work of Art: The Cultural Origins of the Constitution* (Chicago: University of Chicago Press, 2008).
1. *Pennsylvania Evening Post*, July 2, 1776.

2. It is of course impossible to know just how white readers connected independence and Ishmael's escape. Some runaway advertisements from this period mention Virginia governor Lord Dunmore's promise of freedom for slaves who escaped to the British side, and it is probable that some white readers who learned of Ishmael's escape treated it as further evidence of Britain's campaign to rob the colonists of their rightful property. Other readers, such as the Quakers who had been manumitting slaves in large numbers or the Philadelphia reformers who had founded the world's first abolition society in 1775, perhaps identified Ishmael's cause with America's; they routinely worried that Americans compromised claims for rights (and for God's protection) by enslaving human beings. See Cassandra Pybus, *Epic Journeys of Freedom: Runaway Slaves of the American Revolution and their Global Quest for Liberty* (Boston: Beacon Press, 2006). On the formation of the Pennsylvania Society for the Abolition of Slavery in 1775, see Richard S. Newman, *The Transformation of American Abolitionism: Fighting Slavery in the Early Republic* (Chapel Hill: University of North Carolina Press, 2002), 16.

3. A much harder question to address, but it is clear that the number of runaways was on the rise in pre-revolutionary Philadelphia even as the institution of slavery was on the decline; see Gary B. Nash and Jean R. Soderlund, *Freedom By Degrees: Emancipation in Pennsylvania and Its Aftermath* (New York: Oxford University Press, 1991), 94–5, 138–9. On runaway slaves and the Revolution in Philadelphia, see Billy G. Smith and Richard Wojtowicz, *Blacks who Stole Themselves: Advertisements for Runaways in the Pennsylvania Gazette, 1728–1790* (Philadelphia: University of Philadelphia Press, 1989), 123–33; and David Waldstreicher, "Reading the Runaways: Self Fashioning, Print Culture, and Confidence in Slavery in the Eighteenth-Century Mid-Atlantic," *William and Mary Quarterly*, 3rd. ser., 56 (1999): 243–72.

4. Unless otherwise stated, references to the Declaration are to the first broadside printing of July 4 or 5, 1776: *In Congress, July 4, 1776. A Declaration By the Representatives of the United States of America, In General Congress Assembled* (Philadelphia: John Dunlap, [1776]).

5. For accounts of original meaning, changing meaning, and uses of the text over time, see Merril D. Peterson, *The Jefferson Image in the American Mind* (New York: Oxford University Press, 1960); Philip F. Detweiler, "The Changing Reputation of the Declaration of Independence: The First Fifty Years," *William and Mary Quarterly*, 3rd ser., 19:4 (October 1962): 557–74; John Philip Reid, "The Irrelevance of the Declaration," in *Law in the American Revolution and the Revolution of the Law*, ed. Hendrick Hartog (New York, 1981), 46–89; and, more recently, Pauline Maier, *American Scripture* (New York: Knopf, 1997); David Thelen, "Reception of the Declaration of Independence," in *The Declaration of Independence: Origins and Impact* (Washington, DC: CQ Press, 2002), 191–212. For an account of the original meaning of the text to international readers, see David Armitage, "The Declaration of Independence and International Law," *William and Mary Quarterly*, 59:1 (January 2002): 39–64.

6. Robert M. S. McDonald, "Thomas Jefferson's Changing Reputation as Author of the Declaration of Independence: The First Fifty Years," *Journal of the Early Republic*, 19:2 (Summer 1999): 169–95; Lincoln, "Speech at Springfield, Illinois," June 26, 1857, cited in Armitage, "The Declaration of Independence and International Law."

7. Indeed, if Benjamin Towne of the *Pennsylvania Evening Post* saw no disjunction in the advertisement for a runaway slave on the same page as the news of Independence, by 1805 newspaper editors in Philadelphia would specifically highlight the irony that their counterparts in Charleston, South Carolina, could unhesitatingly print the Declaration of Independence's claim "that all men are created equal" side-by-side with advertisements for slaves just imported from Africa; see, for instance, "From Poulson's *Daily Advertiser*," *Pennsylvania Correspondent, And Farmer's Advertiser*, June 4, 1805.

8. For Haynes's text, see Ruth Bogin, "'Liberty Further Extended': A 1776 Antislavery Manuscript by Lemuel Haynes," *William and Mary Quarterly*, 3rd. ser., 40:1 (January 1983): 85–106. For the background of the text, see John Saillant, *Black Puritan, Black Republican: The Life and Thought of Lemuel Haynes, 1753–1833* (New York: Oxford University Press, 2003).

9. Julian P. Boyd, *The Declaration of Independence*, ed. Gerard W. Gawalt (1943; Washington, DC, and Charlottesville: Library of Congress and Thomas Jefferson Memorial Foundation, 1999), 18. For histories of the composition of the text, see John H. Hazelton, *The Declaration of Independence: Its History* (New York: Dodd, Mead, and Co., 1906), 306–42; Carl L. Becker, *The Declaration of Independence* (1922; New York: Knopf, 1942), 135–93; and Boyd, *Declaration of Independence*.

10. *Journals of the Continental Congress, 1774–1789*, ed. Worthington Chauncey Ford, 34 vols. (Washington, DC: Government Printing Office, 1904–37), V: 425–31 (June 7–11, 1776).

11. TJ's "Notes of Debates," cited in Maier, *American Scripture*, 42. Throughout the notes, the name "Thomas Jefferson" is abbreviated as "TJ" in citations of his letters.

12. John Adams to Abigail Adams, May 17, 1776, cited in Boyd, *Declaration of Independence*, 18.

13. Adams also seems to have thought that the confederation draft might come first; see Adams to Cotton Tufts, June 23, 1776, in *Letters of Delegates, to Congress, 1774–1789*, ed. Paul H. Smith *et al.*, 26 vols. (Washington, DC: Library of Congress, 1976–2000), IV: 297. In late July, Joseph Hewes thought that the treaty plan and confederation articles "ought to have been setled before our declaration of Independence went forth to the world"; see Hewes to Samuel Johnston, July 28, 1776, in *Letters of Delegates*, IV: 555.

14. *Journals of the Continental Congress*, V: 425–31 (June 7–11, 1776).

15. For Dickinson's potential authorship of state papers before he joined Congress, see James H. Hutson (ed.), *A Decent Respect to the Opinions of Mankind: Congressional State Papers, 1774–1776* (Washington: Library of Congress, 1975), 34, 50–2.

16. Maier, *American Scripture*, 112.

17. *Journals of the Continental Congress*, V: 431, V: 433.

18. See ibid., V: 556 (July 12, 1776), V: 594 (July 20, 1776), and V: 674 n. 1. For printed drafts of the reports of the confederation and plan of treaties committees, see *Articles of Confederation* [Philadelphia: Dunlap, 1776]; and *There shall be a firm, inviolable and universal peace, and a true and sincere friendship between A. and B. ...* [Philadelphia: Dunlap, 1776]. In the only extended study of governmental printing practices in the early United States, John H. Powell sides with Boyd and Hazelton and rejects the idea that Congress printed draft copies of the Declaration;

see Powell, *The Books of a New Nation; United States Government Publications, 1774–1814* (Philadelphia: University of Pennsylvania Press, 1957), 55. For the conjecture that Congress printed copies of the Declaration for members to read in debates, see Wilfred J. Ritz, "From the Here of Jefferson's Handwritten Rough Draft of the Declaration of Independence to the There of the Printed Dunlap Broadside," *Pennsylvania Magazine of History and Biography*, 116:4 (October 1992): 499–512. Pauline Maier follows Ritz on this point: see Maier, *American Scripture*, 144. On the small amount of time Congress devoted to the editing of the Declaration, see Jack N. Rakove, *The Beginnings of National Politics: An Interpretive History of the Continental Congress* (New York: Knopf, 1979), 80–1.

19. For a reading of the Declaration attentive to legal form and language, see Robert A. Ferguson, *The American Enlightenment, 1760–1820* (Cambridge, MA: Harvard University Press, 1997), 126–30. Technically, the Declaration was not a legal enactment. Congress had enacted laws, such as the Tory Act in January 1776, but the Declaration is simply a state paper issued by Congress. Nevertheless, President Hancock referred to the Declaration as "the Ground & Foundation of a future Government" (he probably meant state government) when he sent copies of the Dunlap broadside printing of the text to the states in July 1776, and as the "Act of Independence" when he sent copies of the Goddard broadside printing (now with the names of the signers) to the states in January 1777; see John Hancock to Certain States, July 5, 1776, and Hancock to the States, January 31, 1777, in *Letters of Delegates*, IV: 393, 396, and VII: 171. Congress also clearly promoted the view of the Declaration as a quasi-legal and foundational act when it included the Declaration alongside the Articles of Confederation, the individual state constitutions, and the Franco-American Treaty in an anthology it ordered published in late 1780; see *The Constitutions of the Several Independent States of America; the Declaration of Independence; the Articles of Confederation between the said states; the Treaties between His Most Christian Majesty and the United States of America. Published by order of Congress* (Philadelphia: Francis Bailey, 1781).

20. Maier, *American Scripture*, 38, 27; and for a similar understanding of the king as the author of independence, see South Carolina Delegates to John Rutledge, July 9, 1776, in *Letters of Delegates*, IV: 420.

21. Boyd, *Declaration of Independence*, 59–71. For edited versions of the text, from the "Original Rough Draught," see *Papers of Thomas Jefferson*, ed. Julian P. Boyd et al. (Princeton: Princeton University Press, 1950–), I: 413–33. For a line-by-line comparison of seven versions of the Declaration, see Hazelton, *The Declaration of Independence*, 306–42.

22. *Journals of the Continental Congress*, V: 506 (July 1), V: 507 (July 2), V: 509 (July 3); Elbridge Gerry to General Warren, in *Letters of Delegates*, V: 516 n. 1; and see the reference to the "Declaration of Independence" in the official edition issued by Massachusetts and printed by Ezekiel Russell in Salem in 1776.

23. Note also that the engrossed Declaration presents the words "of the Thirteen United" in a much smaller size than the words preceding ("The Unanimous Declaration") or following them ("States of America"). It seems likely that the scribe may have first blocked out "The Unanimous Declaration of the States of America," perhaps because the name of the new nation was so novel and because to say that the states were "United" and "Unanimous" seemed redundant.

24. Josiah Bartlett to John Langdon, July 1, 1776, in *Letters of Delegates*, IV: 351; John Adams to Abigail, July 3, 1776, in *Letters of Delegates*, IV: 374; Samuel Adams to John Pitts, c. July 9, 1776, in *Letters of Delegates*, IV: 417; John Hancock to the States, January 31, 1777, in *Letters of Delegates*, VII: 171.

25. Jay Fliegelman, *Prodigals and Pilgrims: The American Revolution against Patriarchal Authority* (New York: Cambridge University Press, 1982), 4. Fliegelman finds residues of the generational ideology in the final version of the Declaration, but this seems to me to be exactly what Jefferson and the Declaration committee edited out.

26. Jefferson, "Draft of Instructions to the Virginia Delegates in the Continental Congress (MS Text of *A Summary View*, &c.)," in *Papers*, I: 121–3.

27. Indeed, though the Declaration stresses the priority of individual rights, Dror Wahrman has recently suggested that this was profoundly more experimental than has been previously noticed; in Wahrman's reading, claims of individual rights historically preceded the advent of modern individualism upon which those claims seem to rest. See Wahrman, *The Making of the Modern Self: Identity and Culture in Eighteenth-Century England* (London: Yale University Press, 2004), 309–10. For the significance of collective rights in the eighteenth century, see Akhil Reed Amar, *The Bill of Rights: Creation and Reconstruction* (New Haven: Yale University Press, 1998).

28. Historians continue to debate the sources for the theory of government in the Declaration. For the classic statement of the Declaration as a Lockean text, see Becker, *Declaration of Independence*. For a brilliant revision, stressing the importance of Scottish moral sense philosophy and its continental counterparts on Jefferson's thinking, see Garry Wills, *Inventing America: Jefferson's Declaration of Independence* (New York: Doubleday, 1978).

29. Ferguson, *American Enlightenment*, 128–9.

30. Hutson (ed.), *Decent Respect*, 4–5.

31. For the reactions of Thomas Hutchinson, former governor of Massachusetts, in his *Strictures upon the Declaration of the Congress at Philadelphia* (London, 1776), see Maier, *American Scripture*, 106; for the views of John Lind and Jeremy Bentham (the response of the British administration) in their *An Answer to the Declaration of the American Congress* (London: Cadell, Walter, and Sewell, 1776), see Armitage, "The Declaration of Independence and International Law."

32. Woody Holton, *Forced Founders: Indians, Debtors, Slaves, and the Making of the American Revolution in Virginia* (Chapel Hill: University of North Carolina Press, 1999).

33. On resonances between the rejected slavery charge and Franklin's ideas, see David Waldstreicher, *Runaway America: Benjamin Franklin, Slavery, and the American Revolution* (New York: Hill and Wang, 2004), 212–14.

34. See TJ to Richard Henry Lee, July 8, 1776, in *Papers*, I: 445–46; and see Boyd, *Declaration of Independence*, 25.

35. For the alteration between draft and approved text, see Jack N. Rakove, *Declaring Rights: A Brief History with Documents* (Boston: Bedford / St. Martin's, 1998), 77. Boyd and Maier agree that Mason's draft had little effect on Jefferson's phrasing; see Boyd, *Declaration of Independence*, 24–5, and Maier, *American Scripture*, 126.

36. See George Mason, "First Draft of the Virginia Declaration of Rights," *c.* May 20–26, 1776, in *Papers of George Mason*, ed. Robert A. Rutland (Chapel Hill: University of North Carolina Press, 1970), 1: 277.

37. *Papers*, 1: 423 and 427 n. 2.

38. Boyd, *Declaration of Independence*, 67.

39. Rough Draft in ibid., 27; Declaration of Causes of Taking Up Arms in *Decent Respect*, ed. Hutson, 91, 96.

40. On the question of signing, see Jacques Derrida, "Declarations of Independence," *New Political Science*, 15 (1986): 7–17; and on the more crucial issue of legitimating law, see Michael Warner, *The Letters of the Republic: Publication and the Public Sphere in Eighteenth-Century America* (Cambridge, MA: Harvard University Press, 1990), 97–117, esp. 104–6. David Armitage suggests that Derrida's ruminations are very much in line with those of theorists of the law of nations in the two generations after the Declaration: "how could independence be declared, except by a body that was already independent, in the sense understood by the law of nations? A mere declaration could not constitute independence; it could only announce what had already been achieved by other means"; see Armitage, "The Declaration of Independence and International Law."

41. See Hutson (ed.), *Decent Respect*, 10.

42. A single copy of the second state of the Dunlap broadside (now held by the American Philosophical Society) is printed on parchment, a fact that suggests that Revolutionaries were thinking that diffusion through print was not enough and that printed copies might need to be preserved on traditional materials; see Whitfield J. Bell, Jr., *The Declaration of Independence: Four 1776 Versions* (Philadelphia: American Philosophical Society, 1976), [n.p.].

43. For an argument that the Declaration was signed on July 4, 1776, see Wilfred J. Ritz, "The Authentication of the Engrossed Declaration of Independence on July 4, 1776," *Law and History Review*, 4:1 (Spring 1986): 179–204. Ritz cites the letter from John Adams to Caeser A. Rodney, April 30, 1823, establishing that the July 19, 1776 resolution implied that future members should sign the text and notes that Goddard failed to reproduce the geography of signatures properly; see Ritz, "Authentication," 191, 193 n. 38.

44. David Waldstreicher, *In the Midst of Perpetual Fetes: The Making of American Nationalism, 1776–1820* (Chapel Hill: University of North Carolina Press, 1997), 32; for a study focusing on the evolving uses of festivity to mask partisan differences, see Len Travers, *Celebrating the Fourth: Independence Day and the Rites of Nationalism in the Early Republic* (Amherst: University of Massachusetts Press, 1997).

45. Jay Fligelman, *Declaring Independence* (Stanford: Stanford University Press, 1993); Michael J. Walsh, "Contemporary Broadside Editions of the Declaration of Independence," *Harvard Library Bulletin*, 3:1 (Winter 1949): 31–43; Maier, *American Scripture*, 155–60; Fischer, *Liberty and Freedom: A Visual History of America's Founding Ideas* (New York: Oxford University Press, 2005), 123.

46. For early nineteenth-century printings of the Declaration, see François Furstenburg, *In the Name of the Father: Washington's Legacy, Slavery, and the Making of a Nation* (New York: Penguin, 2006), Appendix.

47. See David Armitage, "The Declaration of Independence in World Context," *Magazine of History*, 18:3 (2004): 61–6.

48. For Stanton's Declaration of Sentiments (1848) and other revisions to the Declaration, see *We, the Other People: Alternative Declarations of Independence by Labor Groups, Farmers, Woman's Rights Advocates, Socialists, and Blacks, 1829–1975,* ed. Philip S. Foner (Urbana: University of Illinois Press, 1976).

49. Bogin, "'Liberty Further Extended': A 1776 Antislavery Manuscript by Lemuel Haynes," 94; Jacob Green, *A Sermon Delivered at Hanover, (in New-Jersey) April 22d, 1778. Being the Day of Public Fasting and Prayer Throughout the United States of America* (Chatham: Shepard Kollock, 1779), 13; Anthony Benezet, "Observations on Slavery," in *Serious Considerations on Several Important Subjects ... [with] Observations on Slavery* (Philadelphia: Joseph Crukshank, 1778), 28–9; Anthony Benezet, *Short Observations on Slavery, Introductory to some Extracts from the writing of the Abbe Raynal, on that Important Subject* ([Philadelphia: Crukshank, 1781?]), 1–2; [David Cooper], *A Serious Address to the Rulers of America on the Inconsistency of their Conduct respecting Slavery: Forming a Contrast Between the Encroachments of England on American Liberty, and, American Injustice in tolerating Slavery* (Trenton: Isaac Collins, 1783), 12–13.

50. [Cooper], *Serious Address,* 13; "Justice," "From the *Freeman's Journal* (Philadelphia)," *New-Hampshire Gazette,* July 22, 1785; *Constitution of the Pennsylvania Society for Promoting the Abolition of Slavery* (Philadelphia: Francis Bailey, 1788), 19, 21; for the Maryland Society, see a report in the *Providence Gazette,* May 7, 1791; *The Constitution of the New-Jersey Society, for Promoting the Abolition of Slavery* (Burlington: Isaac Neale, 1793); for the 1783 Rhode Island law, see *Providence Gazette,* September 20, 1783.

51. *Copy of a Letter from Benjamin Banneker to the Secretary of State, With his Answer* (Philadelphia: Daniel Lawrence, 1792), 7–8; for other printings of the exchange, see *Baltimore Evening Post,* October 13, 1792; *Virginia Gazette,* October 31, 1792; and, with a preface suggesting that the exchange affirmed Jefferson's antislavery credentials, *Gazette of the United States,* November 17, 1796.

52. *Minutes of the Proceedings of the Eleventh American Convention for Promoting the Abolition of Slavery and Improving the Condition of the African Race: Assembled at Philadelphia* (Philadelelphia: Kimber, Conrad, 1806), 29; *Minutes of the Proceedings of the Twelfth American Convention for Promoting the Abolition of Slavery ...* (Philadelphia: J. Bouvier, 1809), 19.

53. Frederick Douglass, *Oration, Delivered in Corinthian Hall, Rochester, July 5th, 1852* (Rochester, 1852), in *The Frederick Douglass Papers, Series 1: Speeches, Debates, and Interviews, 1845–1891,* ed. John W. Blassingame (New Haven: Yale University Press, 1979–), II: 359–88.

2

ARI HELO

Jefferson's conception of republican government

Thomas Jefferson freely admitted that "the term *republic* is of very vague application in every language," while, in its most simple meaning, it denoted but "a government by its citizens in mass, acting directly and personally, according to rules established by majority."[1] James Madison defined this same ancient city-state-inspired model of participatory democracy as "consisting of a small number of citizens, who assemble to administer the government in person," even if only to contrast it with the properly modern, republican government as representative democracy.[2] It was equally clear to Jefferson that, in the modern world, "numbers, distance, or force oblige" people "to act by deputy." Hence, "their government continues *republican in proportion only* as the functions they still exercise in person are more or fewer and, as in those exercised by deputy."[3]

As to this conspicuously indeterminate "ideal" republic, it is notable that, in their Declaration of Independence, the American Revolutionaries were not opposing any specific form of government, be it monarchy, aristocracy, democracy, or the classic mixed regime that offered a more or less balanced blend of all the former elements. Rather, their argument was that, in order to secure their "Life, Liberty and ... pursuit of Happiness," they were, like any free people, entitled to abolish the now obviously corrupt British government and to "institute new Government, laying its foundation on such principles and organizing its powers in such form, as to them shall seem most likely to effect their Safety and Happiness."[4] Perhaps more importantly, no particular form of government was claimed to be the only one capable of fulfilling the only historical condition set for all such governments, namely "the consent of the governed."

The necessity of securing and eliciting the consent of the governed was central to Jefferson's political thinking, even if he limited it to the population of adult white males. His persistent, though ultimately unsuccessful, attempts to reform the Virginia 1776 constitution, which still excluded approximately half of white male citizens from the right to vote, clearly speak to his commitment to modern democratic ideals. Indeed, according to his later definition, a "pure republic" comprised "a state of society in which every member of mature and sound mind has an equal right of participation, personally, in the direction of the affairs of the society."[5] Regarding any branch of the modern, representative government, whether judicial, executive, or legislative, its "independence of the will of the nation," Jefferson proclaimed, "is a solecism, at least in a republican government."[6]

From this concern to protect the independence of the people also arises Jefferson's much-discussed skepticism about particular political constitutions as permanent guarantees of free government. As his famous doctrine of generational independence held, "Each generation is as independent as the one preceding [and has] a right to choose for itself the form of government it believes most promoting its happiness." Most important, it was for no less a goal than "the peace and good of mankind that a solemn opportunity of doing this every nineteen or twenty years" should have been guaranteed.[7]

Focusing on Jefferson's own understanding of republicanism, this chapter will begin with special consideration of his well-known tenet that self-government is a natural right of man. This right appears to have been naturalistic rather than moral in character, derived from historically valid experience and political practice rather than from any assumed universal moral truth, such as human equality. This is best discernible in Jefferson's revolutionary writings, where we find him forcefully arguing that the British colonies were civil societies prior to the Revolution and were therefore unwilling to be reduced to the state of nature. In essence, Jefferson's naturalist conception of self-government entailed viewing some political ordering of society as a basic necessity of human life.

Secondly, it is worth considering how the moral ideal of equal rights was supposed to be reconciled with the naturalist, or at least historically verifiable, concept of self-government in the post-revolutionary American republic. To fully grasp Jefferson's understanding of the just division of powers between the federal and state governments, one needs to consider the philosophical basis of the Lockean civil government as a juridical construction. Deep down, every human government was but an instrument for the people to peacefully exercise the law of nature and nations within the framework of the universal standard of equal rights.

Thirdly, since a just government could be achieved only within the limits of the consent of the governed, extending responsibility for governmental action to each and every free man was a natural goal for all Jeffersonian republicanism. This is also to argue that Jefferson's democratic ideals need to be understood in the context of his own belief that reconciling contemporary American society with genuine majority rule still called for thorough democratic reforms in every state of the Union.

"The first principle of republicanism"

While Jefferson had "but one code of morality for man whether acting singly or collectively," his statecraft represented an almost unconditional surrender to the temporally variable will of the people.[8] The will of the majority being not only "the Natural law of every society," but also "the only sure guardian of the rights of man,"[9] it was evident that the statesman's wisdom must yield to that will.[10] Nor could genuine republicanism be found in constitutions "but merely in the spirit of our people."[11] Hence we arrive at Jefferson's "first principle of republicanism," being: "*lex majoris partis* is the fundamental law of every society of individuals of equal rights."[12]

This at least apparently naturalist conception of majority rule shaped Jefferson's historiography of the Revolution in fundamental ways. To begin with the mythic, Teutonic origins of American freedom, it is notable that, even when subscribing to the claim that Anglo-Americans' "Saxon ancestors" had once upon a time moved to Britain from "their native wilds and woods in the North of Europe," Jefferson insisted that they had done so under a "universal law." By that same law – or, conspicuously, simply by the "right" – of "all men of departing from the country in which chance, and not choice, had placed them," the British colonists had, in turn, gone to America and established there "new societies, under such laws and regulations as to them" had seemed most likely to promote their happiness.[13]

By the same token, Jefferson held that only when forming themselves "into a nation" had the Virginians voluntarily "manifested by the organs we constituted, that the common law was to be our law." Specific legal and political forms were of secondary importance regarding the natural right to self-government of all nations on the earth, expressed as "the will of the nation."[14] From its beginnings, the British common law itself had been "altered from time to time by proper legislative authority," regardless of whether that authority could truly devolve from something other than the ancient customary law, or *jus commune*, the Saxon equivalent of which was the "folc-right," translatable, as Jefferson found it, simply as "the people's right."[15]

That the natural right to self-government was independent of any precise governmental forms can best be inferred from Jefferson's statements concerning Native Americans. His famous contention that Indian nations could attain more happiness without permanent governments than could the Europeans was not to say that Indians were independent of the rule of majority as the genuine basis of popular sovereignty. Jefferson claimed simply that, among them, "public opinion is in the place of law, & restrains morals as powerfully as laws ever did anywhere."[16] By 1812 he saw the most "advanced" of these nations already developing regular representative governments for themselves.[17]

Let us proceed to take a brief look at how deeply Jefferson's Virginia-centered history of the American founding was constructed upon the simple continuity of "acts of national will" within and among the revolutionary colonies. Being already civil societies with various constitutions, none of the colonies had been or could be "reduced to a state of nature" by the imperial government.[18] Regarding his home state of Virginia, Jefferson traced the proper beginnings of civil society there back to the year of 1621, when an agreement was achieved that "after the government of the colony should be well framed and settled, no orders of council in England should bind the colony unless ratified" by the colony's own government.[19] In 1776, accordingly, the Virginia people "chose to abolish their former organs of declaring their will," i.e. the old colonial legislature, whereas their "acts of will already formally & constitutionally declared, remained untouched. For the nation was not dissolved, was not annihilated; it's will, therefore, remained in full vigor."[20]

For Jefferson, there was a nation of Virginia, which, throughout the War of Independence and the consequent changes in its form of government, remained untouched and un-dissolved, just as it had been from 1621 onwards. Nor did the situation essentially change when the nation joined the Union. The "states composing" the federal association did so, in Jefferson's words, solely "for the management of their concerns with one another & with foreign nations, and the states composing the association chose to give it powers for those purposes & no others."[21]

The legal origins of the Union thus rested on the continuous flow of expressions of the will of its member states, or, indeed, of the nations of those states. Elaborating on this, Jefferson declared: "the law being law because it is the will of the nation, is not changed by their changing the organ through which they chuse to announce their future will." As to the universal application of this principle, it is notable that, according to Jefferson, the Americans would offer the French republic in 1793 a legitimate cause of war if they precipitately dismissed the treaties once made with the pre-revolutionary French government. The formal changes in the French government could not nullify the treaties with that "nation."[22] With respect to individual rights, all this meant that "Every man, & every body of men on earth, possesses the righ[t] of self-government," which the individuals "exercise by their single will" and the "collections of men by that of their majority."[23]

Just governmental powers in the federation

To fully grasp how far Jefferson's naturalist conception of self-government could be reconciled with the moral ideal of equal rights of all men, one needs to consider the Declaration of Independence as also a declaration of just war. Its justification devolved from the Lockean right to overturn any government violating the natural liberties of the people. Yet, stripped to its essence, this crucial notion of justified violence amounted to every man's right to punish those who violate his rights in the state of nature. John Locke's response to this anomaly in all contemporary natural jurisprudence held that an individual's consistent attempt to hold such a stance would eventually dissolve society into the Hobbesian war of every man against all others. Civil society, by contrast, was simply about entrusting one's rights to the hands of the civil government.[24] In short, the grand concept of the state of nature, as Jefferson came to know it from his reading, concerned men as sinful, selfish creatures in need of a juridical, law-based notion of human morality with which only the civil government could provide them.

Thus, the Lockean commonwealth itself evolved from the maxim that, since "it is unreasonable for Men to be Judges in their own Cases," as was the situation in the state of nature, "God hath certainly appointed Government to restrain the partiality and violence of Men."[25] Or, as one of Jefferson's favorite authorities in natural law, Emerich de Vattel, put the case, "as there does not exist in mankind a disposition voluntarily to observe towards each other the rules of the law of nature, they have had recourse to a political association," which the moral law of nature "itself approves of."[26]

Justified violence, in turn, remained something to which only nations could resort. Otherwise, the juridical, governmental monopoly to regulate human behavior, with respect to a more or less shared commitment to justice and equality on the part of the governed, could at any moment be challenged by just rebellion on some part of the population. The early American republic hardly epitomized absolute human equality in the eyes of any Virginia slaveholder and was thus susceptible to violence from individuals or groups who judged themselves to be aggrieved.

To be sure, Jefferson could occasionally hail the uprisings of discontented war veterans as healthy reminders for the administrators to cling to the notion of common good as equivalent to true common interests[27] and could even distinguish slave rebels from common criminals.[28] But he never imagined that republican government could permanently comply with any other citizen activity than constant, "peaceful deliberation," which he hoped would reflect "the voice of the whole people." In other words, all questions of justice and equality were to be "fairly, fully and peaceably expressed, discussed, and decided by the common reason of the society," in order to prevent any utopian notion of equality from turning society into a stage of justified violence.[29] None of this was to claim that nations, once organized into civil societies, could not resort to just violence, endowed as they were with police force in response to internal disturbances and an army for national self-defense. Nor did the concept of just war vanish from studies on the law of nature and nations by such renowned authorities in the field as Jean-Jacques Burlamaqui, Hugo Grotius, Samuel Pufendorf, and Emerich de Vattel, all of them frequently quoted in Jefferson's diplomatic memoranda and other statements. Under international law, Jefferson had no scruples about waging war in the name of "national morality," whenever practicable. His incessant problems with securing American access to Atlantic trade justified the American war measures against the Barbary nations, as well as those against the British during the war of 1812. After all, as early as in 1774, Jefferson had claimed that the Americans were in possession of the natural right to free trade with the rest of the world.[30]

The enforcement of the law of nature and nations remained a government monopoly also in the American federative republic in so far as "the consent of the governed" prevailed. In this respect, Jefferson held that the states were to remain the sole executive power of the civil law (*jus civile*) except in the few cases specifically listed in the Constitution, and the federal government as that of international law (*jus gentium*), with its special prerogative of settling disputes between the member states.[31] And, as Jefferson never ceased arguing, mixing these two functions could not be done without rendering all local democratic institutions mere subjects to the rule of the few federal Supreme Court justices, all of them nominated for life. No wonder he flatly denounced Chief Justice John Marshall's maxim that, since "there must be an ultimate arbiter somewhere," the arbiter of civil law predicaments should be Mr. Marshall's court. Instead, Jefferson invoked the authority of the constitutional convention: "The ultimate arbiter is the people of the Union, assembled by their deputies in convention, at the call of Congress or of two-thirds of the States."[32] In this respect, the standard political tenet of checks and balances meant that, in practice, each branch of the federal government checked the constitutionality of each other's actions continuously. Moreover, in the draft of the Kentucky Resolutions which Jefferson wrote in 1798, he asserted that the individual states had the right to judge the constitutionality of laws not based on powers specifically delegated to Congress by the Constitution.[33] The ultimate repository of political power for Jefferson was in the consent of the governed, the people.

Jefferson could fully embrace the Constitution as the permanent basis of the American government, particularly as its civil rights amendments guaranteed the individual's right to disagree with that government. But, regardless of Jefferson's attempts to change the Constitution in order to legitimate the Louisiana Purchase in 1803, no purely jurisdictional concern could prevent him from relying on the fact that neither the Congress nor the states seemed willing to question the right of the nation to peaceably expand to the west.

As noted earlier, regarding the issues of civil law and citizen rights in general, the representative function of the federal government had to remain in the states. As Jefferson explained the issue to Samuel Kercheval, a correspondent working to reform Virginia's constitution, the 3/5 ratio of representation of each Virginia slave in the federal congress was a mere compromise, for, besides being taxed according to the same ratio, the voting constituency of the state represented not only slaves but also women and children, as well as those free, male Virginia citizens who did not qualify for suffrage. In this sense, the whole population of the state counted as free men with regard to the Union as well as to any foreign state.[34]

The representative, democratic republic of Virginia

As historian Herbert Sloan insightfully put it, the federal Constitution did not violate Jefferson's principle of generational sovereignty, whereas "the Virginia constitution was another matter."[35] And the crucial difference between the two did not arise as much from the federal constitution's clause that authorized change through amendments as from the fact that such issues as citizenship and the exact political rights of men were left to be defined by the states. As each of the states moved closer to democratic government, their common republic would more closely reflect true, national will, so as to be capable of "deliberating peacefully" all questions of justice and equality.

Jefferson's hopes of radically extending democracy in his home state pre-date his authorship of the Declaration of Independence. In his draft constitution of Virginia from the spring of 1776 – to which the state legislation paid little attention – he suggested not only the appropriation of fifty acres of land to "every person of full age neither owning nor having owned" such property, and the law of religious freedom, but also the adoption of general male suffrage in the election of the Virginia house of representatives and the consequent election of the state senate by that lower house.[36]

Most importantly, Jefferson's seemingly conventional, republican commit-ment to bicameral legislatures did not arise from any pretension to divide the citizenry of free white men into different political orders and different classes. His bicameralism drew solely on the idea of making the representatives of the majority think twice: such "double deliberation," Jefferson explained, was obtainable "either by requiring a greater age in one of the bodies, or by electing a proper number of representatives of persons, dividing them by lots into two chambers."[37] But, when depicting the contemporary Virginia's legislative system as the one in which "wealth and wisdom have equal chance for admission into both houses," Jefferson's point was that, unfortunately, the constituency consisted of the wealthy alone.[38]

The commonplace rationale for excluding the poor from the electorate can be traced to Blackstone's classic tenet – cited, for example, in Alexander Hamilton's *The Farmer Refuted* (1775) – that "the true reason of requiring any qualification, with the regard to property, in voters, is to exclude such persons as are in so mean a situation that they are esteemed to have no will of their own."[39] By comparison, Jefferson thundered, in any country where "only one man in ten has a right to vote," all nominees inclined to buy their way to the assembly simply "get nine-tenths of their price clear."[40]

It is equally notable that, even with his outspoken "moral and physical preference of the agricultural, over the manufacturing, man," Jefferson did not aim at excluding the latter from the ballots.[41] His general wish to have as few artisans as possible among Virginia yeomen drew on the commonplace wisdom of the times that mechanics and manufacturers were too dependent on their employers to be fully independent in their voting decisions, the point also brought up by such an outright Federalist as Gouverneur Morris in the Philadelphia Convention.[42]

Nor could Jefferson agree with John Adams's obsession that the republic would gain some extra stability by devoting the senate to the natural aristocracy of "a few in whom all advantages of birth, fortune, and fame are united."[43] Such a tenet resembled British bicameralism, which, according to Jefferson, made sense only "if honesty were to be bought with money, and if wisdom were hereditary."[44] Elites were unlikely to disappear from even American society, but an elite without any other than socio-economic qualifications was, in Jefferson's terms, an "artificial aristocracy ... founded on wealth and birth without either virtue or talents, for with these it would belong to" the natural aristocracy.[45]

Contrary to Adams's republicanism, Jefferson's democratic idealism could well include those lucky few who were genuinely "good and wise"[46] as well as rich and well-born. They could qualify to any government office, provided that the public deemed them worth their trust. Moreover, given that the simple majority of the people would occasionally err in such judgment, the constant rotation of offices would keep every representative aware of being bound to "return into the mass of the people" and become one of the governed in turn.[47]

Majority democracy, however, remained an association between genuinely different individuals. It was inconceivable for Jefferson's thought that human differences in talents and inclinations – which indeed could be viewed as that which made people individuals – would somehow disappear with equal access to education. Public, elementary education was supposed to guarantee only that "Worth and genius would [be] sought out from every condition of life, and completely prepared by education for defeating the competition of wealth and birth for public trusts."[48] When elaborating his contention that the Americans were "constitutionally and conscientiously democrats," Jefferson made it fully clear that, by and large, the general public was "unqualified for the management of affairs requiring intelligence above common level."[49] This is why his political program consisted of the idea of "distributing to every one exactly the functions he is competent to."[50] Among the less competent in political science, their personal participation in government could be carried out only at the local level.

Jefferson's famous doctrine of dividing counties into small "ward republics" or townships, even though devised only in his retirement years, was clearly related to his life-long goal of extending democracy in Virginia. Soon after the Revolution, he opined that, by excluding half of the white male population from the ballots, the state essentially failed to make them genuinely responsible for "all public expenses, whether of the general treasury, or of a parish, or county, (as for maintenance of the poor, building bridges, court-houses &c.)."[51] Given that the issue covered all the levels of the state, the county, and the parish equally, it seems evident that Jefferson's later ward system was supposed eventually to replace the old Anglican parishes altogether, so as to secularize the whole administrative apparatus of the state. The list of the tasks now ascribed to the wards included not only the maintenance of the court, "a constable, a military company, a patrol, a school," but also "the care of their poor."[52]

None of this was to exclude the simplest farmer from the government as a whole, for he remained the elector of those few directing "the county republics, the States republics, and the republic of the Union."[53] From 1776 onwards, Jefferson had aimed at "extending the right of suffrage (or in other words the rights of a citizen) to all who had a permanent interest of living in the country," regardless of whether that meant "having a family, or having property" there.[54] To qualify for full citizenship, it sufficed that a man paid taxes or served in the army or in a state militia. Even a tenant could do this.

Conclusions

Jefferson's notion of democratic republicanism was thoroughly historicized: judging who truly belonged to the aristocracy of "good and wise" and who were worthy to represent them was to be in the hands of all free men, as a single constituency, naturally doing so generation after generation. "The earth belongs in usufruct to the living," he famously wrote in 1789 to James Madison, in commenting on the new federal Constitution. From that simple principle also stemmed Jefferson's consistent demand to change the Virginia constitution so as to allow "General Suffrage" and "Periodical amendments."[55] No constitution could be enacted as unchangeable, for nothing was "unchangeable but the inherent and unalienable rights of man."[56] Nor could an individual statesman set norms for the general will of his people without subscribing to some tyrannical form of government. Thus, equal elementary education was an obvious necessity in the modern republic, so as to help the people "to understand their rights, to maintain them, and to exercise with intelligence their parts in self-government."[57]

Finally, let us keep in mind that, regardless of Jefferson's incessant advice to the opposite, his home state did not become even the white man's mass democracy during his life, which explains a good deal of his anxious pressing for constitutional reform as to the most urgent social issue to be settled for his country. As he told Samuel Kercheval, "I know also, that laws and constitutions must go hand in hand with the progress of the human mind."[58] In the decades after his death in 1826, abolitionists would quote his criticism of slavery, and the Seneca Falls Convention would revise the Declaration of Independence to specifically include women as rights holders. Even if Jefferson in many ways grew more out of touch with the progressive indications of the Revolution in his later years, it is good to bear in mind that he publicly subscribed to a number of racial prejudices throughout his life. As for women's rights, his excuse for not appointing a woman into a political office was only that, for such an innovation, the contemporary American "public is not prepared, nor am I."[59]

NOTES

The author wishes to thank Jeffrey Meikle, Peter S. Onuf, and Eran Shalev for their valuable critical advice, and to acknowledge the financial support of the Academy of Finland.

1. TJ to John Taylor, May 28, 1816, in *Thomas Jefferson: Writings* (hereafter cited as *TJW*), ed. Merrill D. Peterson (New York: Library of America, 1984), 1392.
2. James Madison, Federalist No. 10, *The Federalist Papers*, ed. Clinton Rossiter (New York: New American Library, 1961), 81.
3. TJ to Isaac H. Tiffany, April 4, 1819, in *Thomas Jefferson, Political Writings*, ed. Joyce Appleby and Terence Ball (Cambridge: Cambridge University Press, 1999), 224 (emphasis added.)
4. Jefferson, The Declaration of Independence, in *Papers of Thomas Jefferson*, ed. Julian P. Boyd *et al.* (Princeton: Princeton University Press, 1950–), 1: 429.
5. TJ to Isaac H. Tiffany, April 4, 1819, in *Political Writings*, 224.

6. TJ to Thomas Ritchie, December 25, 1820, in *TJW*, 1446.
7. TJ to Samuel Kercheval, July 12, 1816, in *TJW*, 1402.
8. TJ to James Madison, August 28, 1789, in *Papers*, XV: 367.
9. TJ, Response to the Citizens of Albemarle, February 12, 1790, in *TJW*, 491.
10. TJ to P. S. Dupont de Nemours, April 24, 1816, in *TJW*, 1388.
11. TJ to Samuel Kercheval, July 12, 1816, in *TJW*, 1397.
12. TJ to Alexander von Humboldt, June 13, 1817, in *Political Writings*, 221.
13. Jefferson, *A Summary View of the Rights of British America* (1774), in *TJW*, 105–6.
14. TJ to Edmund Randolph, August 18, 1799, in *TJW*, 1068.
15. On alterations in common law, see TJ's so-called Legal Commonplace Book: *The Commonplace Book of Thomas Jefferson. A Repertory of His Ideas on Government*, ed. Gilbert Chinard (Baltimore, MD: Johns Hopkins University Press, 1926), "Entry 873," 354; for the etymology of *jus commune* as "*folcright*", see "Entry 896," 348.
16. TJ to Edward Carrington, January 16, 1787, in *TJW*, 880.
17. TJ to John Adams, June 11, 1812, in *TJW*, 1263–4.
18. See Jefferson's "Composition Draft" of the Declaration of the Causes and Necessity for Taking Up Arms (June–July, 1775), in *Papers*, I: 193; see also *A Summary View of the Rights of British America* (1774), in *TJW*, 111.
19. *Notes*, Query XIII, in *TJW*, 237–8.
20. TJ to Edmund Randolph, August 18, 1799, in *TJW*, 1068–9.
21. Ibid.
22. See "Opinion on the French Treaties," April 28, 1793, in *TJW*, 423–9.
23. "Jefferson's Opinion on the Constitutionality of the Residence Bill," July 15, 1790, in *Papers*, XVII: 195; for a book-length philosophical background for this statement, see Knud Haakonssen, *Natural Law and Moral Philosophy from Grotius to the Scottish Enlightenment* (Cambridge: Cambridge University Press, 1996).
24. Jefferson could go as far as to claim that no man had "a natural right to be the judge between himself and another." TJ to Francis W. Gilmer, June 7, 1816, in *The Works of Thomas Jefferson*, ed. Paul Leicester Ford (New York: G. P. Putnam's Sons, 1904–5), XI: 534.
25. See *The Second Treatise*, §13, in John Locke, *Two Treatises of Government, A Critical Edition*, ed. Peter Laslett (Cambridge: Cambridge University Press, 1994), 275–6.
26. Emerich de Vattel, *The Law of Nations; or the Principles of the Law of Nature applied to the Conduct and Affairs of Nations and Sovereigns*, 6th American edn., trans. from the French edn. of 1797 by Joseph Chitty (Philadelphia: T. & T. J. Johnson Law Booksellers, 1811), xi.
27. TJ to James Madison, January 30, 1787, in *TJW*, 881–7.
28. TJ to James Monroe, November 24, 1801, in *TJW*, 1388.
29. Quotations, TJ to Samuel Kercheval, July 12, 1816, in *TJW*, 1401–3.
30. Jefferson, *A Summary View of the Rights of British America* (1774), in *TJW*, 108.
31. See, for example, TJ to Edmund Randolph, August 18, 1799, in *TJW*, 1068–9.
32. TJ to William Johnson, June 12, 1823, in *TJW*, 1476.
33. "Draft of the Kentucky Resolutions," in *TJW*, 449–56.
34. TJ to Samuel Kercheval, July 12, 1816, in *TJW* 1398; September 5, 1816, in *Political Writings*, 220.

35. Herbert Sloan, *Principle and Interest. Thomas Jefferson and the Problem of Debt* (Charlottesville: University of Virginia Press, 2001), 280, n. 30.
36. Jefferson's third draft of the Virginia Constitution, in *Papers*, I: 358–63.
37. TJ to Major John Cartwright, June 5, 1824, in *TJW*, 1492.
38. *Notes*, Query XIII, in *TJW*, 245.
39. For the Blackstone quotation as cited by Hamilton, see Morton White, *The Philosophy of the American Revolution* (New York: Oxford University Press, 1978), 259.
40. *Notes*, Query XIV, in *TJW*, 275.
41. TJ to Jean Baptiste Say, February 1, 1804, in *TJW*, 1144.
42. See Morris's statement on August 7, 1787 in *Notes of Debates in the Federal Convention of 1787 reported by James Madison*, ed. Adrianne Koch (New York and London: W.W. Norton & Company, 1984), 402.
43. John Adams's *A Defense of the Constitution of Government in the United States of America*, in *The Political Writings of John Adams: Representative Selections*, ed. George A. Peek, Jr. (New York: The Liberal Arts Press, 1954), 138–9.
44. *Notes*, Query XIII, in *TJW*, 245.
45. TJ to John Adams, October 28, 1813, in *The Adams–Jefferson Letters*, ed. Lester J. Cappon (Chapel Hill: University of North Carolina Press, 1959), 388.
46. For this alternative of "virtue and talent," see ibid., 389.
47. TJ to Edmund Pendleton, August 26, 1776, in *TJW*, 755.
48. TJ to John Adams, October 18, 1813, in *Adams–Jefferson Letters*, 390.
49. TJ to P. S. Dupont de Nemours, April 25, 1816, in *TJW*, 1385.
50. TJ to Joseph C. Cabell, February 2, 1816, in *TJW*, 1380.
51. *Notes*, Query XIV, in *TJW*, 263.
52. TJ to Samuel Kercheval, July 12, 1816, in *TJW*, 1399–400; see also TJ to John Tyler, May 26, 1810, in *TJW*, 1226–7.
53. TJ to Joseph C. Cabell, February 2, 1816, in *TJW*, 1380.
54. TJ to Edmund Pendleton, August 26, 1776, in *TJW*, 756; for Jefferson's "later" view that the state should "let every man who fights or pays, exercise his just and equal right" to vote, see TJ to Samuel Kercheval, July 12, 1816, in *TJW*, 1398.
55. TJ to Samuel Kercheval, July 12, 1816, in *TJW*, 1399–400.
56. TJ to James Madison, September 6, 1789, in *TJW*, 959; to Major John Cartwright, June 5, 1824, in *TJW*, 1494.
57. *Autobiography* (1821), in *TJW*, 44.
58. TJ to Kercheval, July 12, 1816, in *TJW*, 1401.
59. TJ to Albert Gallatin, January 13, 1807, in *The Works of Thomas Jefferson*, ed. Paul Leicester Ford, 12 vols. (New York, 1904–5), X: 339.

3

THOMAS HALLOCK

Notes on the State of Virginia and the Jeffersonian West

In spring 1784, first-term Congressional delegate Thomas Jefferson chaired the committee that drafted a plan for western government. At stake was the dimly defined territory past the Appalachians, ceded in the 1783 Peace of Paris that ended the war with England, and contested between several former colonies. The "Report of a Plan of Government for the Western Territory" defined boundaries; set liberal terms for "free males of full age" to meet and establish a "temporary government"; banned slavery after 1800; zoned and named future states; and established a timetable for entering the union on "equal footing" with the existing thirteen. Congress made some revisions and adopted the committee's plan as the Ordinance of 1784 that April. The most significant changes were dropping the "hard names": Cherronesus in what is now Michigan, Assenisipia for today's northern Illinois and southern Wisconsin, and Pelisipia in eastern Kentucky.[1]

Over the next three years Congress passed a series of measures designed to bring revenue-bearing settlement and stability to a region that policy makers regarded as both dangerously fractious and rife with potential. A Land Ordinance of 1785 charged the geographer Thomas Hutchins with marking thirteen "ranges" (or columns) of property along the Ohio River. Angry squatters, Native Americans, and the "mirey swamps," however, allowed Hutchins to complete only seven of the thirteen and the survey failed to generate the much needed revenue. In 1787 Congress passed the Northwest Ordinance, which tightened the channels of speculation and government control in the Ohio Valley. The Boston-based Ohio Company had lobbied for the revised Ordinance, and settlers migrated from New England the following year. The Company's promotional literature described a landscape of pure possibility: swamps were "natural meadows," staple crops would reach "great perfection," and the "raw materials" for manufacture awaited "an enlightened people." The motto on the seal of the Northwest Territory outlines what was essentially a program of ecological imperialism: *meliorem lapsa locavit*, a better one has taken its place.[2] The environmental changes that accompanied settlement, unsurprisingly, drew hostility from the existing inhabitants. Although the Northwest Ordinance assured that "property shall never be taken" without the consent of Native Americans, the government dealt arrogantly with the Ohio Indians. A series of treaties signed in 1789 led only to wars, which continued until 1794 – ending only after England cut off supplies to the resisting groups.

This invasion of Ohio provided the backdrop to one of the most important literary works of the Revolutionary period, Jefferson's *Notes on the State of Virginia*. Much as the legislation leading to the Northwest Territory was a combination of bureaucracy and force, so too did the *Notes on Virginia* issue a blueprint for national expansion. Jefferson started the book in 1781 after receiving a set of Queries (or questions) from François Marbois, secretary to the French legation, and he made his most significant changes to the manuscript in 1783–84, right before taking his seat in Congress. The book appeared as a limited edition in 1785 and was published for a general audience two years later. The topical relevance was inevitable, and at least one settler perused its pages during his first winter in the Northwest Territory. Solomon Drowne, while waiting for the ice to melt on the Ohio, read Virgil's *Georgics*, Le Page du Pratz's *History of Louisiana*, and "Dr. Jefferson's Notes on Virginia." He pronounced the latter "*Opus omnigena literatura imbutuns*," a work imbued with every species of literary genius. The following spring, Drowne gave an Address to the settlers of Marietta, the first federal town in Ohio, which drew heavily from his winter reading. He praised that "firm band" of settlers who braved "the great business of unbarring a secluded wilderness," and he likened the nation's expansion to the course of the sun. Taking a direct cue from the *opus omnigena*, Drowne intoned that "no foul blot [may] stain the important volume" which "time is unfolding in this western world."[3]

An equation between nationhood and the West runs through much of Jefferson's literary and political work. It was no coincidence that official pronouncements from the Ohio Valley echoed the language of *Notes on the State of Virginia*. Not only did the book's composition and publication parallel the Ohio Ordinances, but it provided the conceptual basis for how the United States should expand. Secretary of War Henry Knox based the "benevolent plan," a federal Indian policy that shaped native–white relations over the next three decades, upon Jeffersonian thought. Anticipating progress across space, Knox maintained that Native Americans eventually would adopt European methods of land use. Once they saw the better way, they would "improve" in culture and no longer need their traditional hunting grounds, making violent usurpation unnecessary. During Jefferson's presidency, one of his lasting legacies was the Louisiana Purchase, which extended the boundaries of the United States threefold, and, with preparations for the 1804–6 expedition led by Meriwether Lewis and William Clark, Jefferson returned to the preoccupations of *Notes on the State of Virginia*. Even in his waning years, Jefferson held fast to the vision of a civilization expanding across the continent. "Let a philosophical observer" travel "from the savages of the Rocky Mountains" east to the Atlantic seaboard, he wrote to William Ludlow in 1824:

> These he would observe in the earliest stage of association living under no law but that of nature, subsisting and covering themselves with the flesh and skins of wild beasts. He would next find those on our frontiers in the pastoral state, raising domestic animals to supply the defects of hunting. Then succeed our own semi-barbarous citizens, the pioneers of the advance of civilization, and so on in his progress he would meet the gradual shades of improving man until he would reach his, as yet, most improved state in our seaport towns.[4]

Popular culture has dipped into Jefferson's own writings, making it impossible to disentangle his words from the history of the American West. His is one of the four faces that peers out at us from Mount Rushmore. The letter to William Ludlow presents the "stage theory," a common eighteenth-century idea that cast the interior as a future Europe and that is read today as an unsubtle rhetoric of empire. Wrestling with the legacy of Frederick Jackson Turner, a generation of historians have noted that the republican prospect led to arrogant usurpation in the next century. Yet "improvement" was just one keynote in Jefferson's writings; so too did he understand that a westering nation would incorporate existing knowledge of the land, its flora and fauna, waterways, and natural riches. How then to situate Enlightenment principles against nineteenth-century calls for Indian removal? This chapter reviews three modes of Jeffersonian thought: improvement, incorporation, and disappearance – from the years of *Notes on the State of Virginia* to the period when Knox's "benevolent plan" corroded into more aggressive policies.[5] The purpose is not to pin the legacy of an entire culture upon one person. Nor should the chronological structure of this chapter be interpreted as the inexorable march towards Indian removal. Jeffersonian thought becomes all the more compelling, indeed, when we attend to the overlap between these three modes.

Improvement (*Notes on the State of Virginia*)

Although difficult to classify, *Notes on the State of Virginia* may be read as the product of and blueprint for an expanding republic. It belongs on the same shelf as westering texts like Jedediah Morse's *American Geography* (1789),

John Filson's *Discovery, Settlement and present State of Kentucke* (1784), or Hector St. John de Crèvecoeur's *Letters from an American Farmer* (1784). Its argument engages the Comte de Buffon's *Histoire naturelle* (1749–1804), the Abbé Raynal's *Philosophical and Political History of the ... East and West Indies* (1772), and pamphleteering on both sides of the Atlantic about the promise of the Revolution. Yet the book was also a product of the legislation being framed at that time. The opening sentence directs readers straight into the Northwest Territory. "Virginia is bounded on the East by the Atlantic," the Query "Boundaries" begins,

> on the North by a line of latitude, crossing the Eastern Shore through Watkins's Point ... from thence by a streight line to Cinquac, near the mouth of Patowmac; thence by the Patowmac, which is common to Virginia and Maryland, to the first fountain of its northern branch; thence by a meridian line, passing through that fountain till it intersects a line running East and West ... which divides Maryland from Pennsylvania, and which was marked by Messrs. Mason and Dixon.[6]

The remaining twenty-two Queries (or chapters) fill in this cartographically defined space. To lend the argument coherence, Jefferson rearranged the order of Marbois's questionnaire, so that the discussion moves from Boundaries, to physical features of the land, to natural productions ("Productions, Mineral, Vegetable and Animal"), to "Climate," and lastly to civic and cultural institutions. The effect is what Solomon Drowne likened to the unbarring of a wilderness (or if one prefers classifying the book as natural history, to the completion of an old-fashioned museum diorama).

The same thematic tensions found in the literature describing Ohio, where future prospects were imagined over the real terrain, also shape the book. Jefferson's ideological geography appears to be constantly on the verge of overtaking the physical landscape. The Query "Rivers" offers a ready example. Marbois asked for a "notice" of the state's "rivers, rivulets, and how far they are navigable."[7] Jefferson responded with accounts of the Roanoke, the James, the Potomac, and their tributaries, emphasizing length, current, and potential for navigation. Toggling between physical properties and trade, however, would lead to an expansion of boundaries. The topic shifts from one waterway to another – and well beyond the legal jurisdiction of Virginia. Without a single line of explanation, Jefferson writes:

> The Shenandoah branch interlocks with James river about the Blue ridge, and may perhaps in future be opened.
>
> The *Missisipi* will be one of the principal channels of future commerce for the country westward of the Alleghaney. From the mouth of this river to where it receives the Ohio, is 1000 miles by water, but only 500 by land, passing through the Chickasaw country.[8]

The prerogatives of trade allow the "notice" to move from the Shenandoah, to the Ohio, to the Chickasaw territories of current-day Mississippi. The remainder of the Query ranges still further, reviewing trade posts at Santa Fe and New Orleans, as well as the Ohio River and *its* tributaries.

Here and elsewhere, imagined prospects eclipse material fact – despite the book's nominally empirical basis. This tension between improvement and disappearance most dramatically shapes Query Six, "Productions, Mineral, Vegetable and Animal," where a review of animals leads to a challenge of eighteenth-century scientific thought. At issue was the heliotropic theory, most famously propounded by the Comte de Buffon, which maintained that the earth dried at different rates after the biblical flood. Consequently different quadrants of the globe were more developed than others. In short, Buffon argued that "something" in the American climate "opposes the aggrandizement of animal nature." French philosophes extended Buffon's hypothesis to explain a cultural lag: Americans who lived "in a state of nature" were "incapable of progress" and "but little advanced in the arts of civilization."[9]

To refute these arguments, Jefferson looked West. He sent for the bones and teeth of a mastodon, which had been recently exhumed from a tar pit south of Fort Pitt, and recounted a Delaware legend about a mammoth living in the continental interior. The mastodon should suffice to "have rescued the earth it inhabited"; what Jefferson wanted, in short, was a *big* animal – whether living or not. The mammoth appeared at the head of a table of weights, comparing animals from Europe and America, that meant to stifle Buffon's hypothesis "that nature is less active, less energetic on one side of the globe than on the other."[10] A visual juxtaposition displays the European cow (763 pounds) next to the Rhode Island bullock (2,500 pounds), the wild boar next to the tapir, and so on down to the shrew mouse and flying squirrel. The weight for the mammoth, for obvious reasons, is left blank.

Patriotism allows that omission, and, as Jefferson shifts from the natural to the human realm, cultural achievements are tallied in the same manner as the weights of a bullock and boar: "We produce a Washington, a Franklin, a Rittenhouse," he writes. Where the Abbé Raynal saw stunted human cultures in the New World, Jefferson would see potential; Native Americans are brave and "affectionate," and they have demonstrated their capacity for refinement in oratory. The case for Indians follows the same logic as that brought to the land – they awaited the "improving" influence of Europeans. "Before we condemn the Indians of wanting genius," Jefferson counters,

we must consider that letters have not yet been introduced among them. Were we to compare them in their present state with the Europeans North of the Alps, when the Roman arms and arts first crossed those mountains, the comparison would be unequal, because at that time, those parts of Europe were swarming with numbers; because numbers produce emulation and multiply the chances of improvement, and one improvement begets another.[11]

To clinch his case, Jefferson would offer evidence that was questionable at best: a well-traveled speech by a western Seneca named Logan, or Tahgahjute, who lived and earned his living as a trader on the Ohio River. The history of the speech merits review, because it reveals how the figures of "improvement" overtook facts in accounts of the trans-Appalachian West. The story had its origins in a territorial conflict during the late colonial period. After a British–Iroquois Treaty of 1768, white settlers and speculators flooded into the trans-Appalachian West. This hostile milieu produced a crisis between Tahgahjute, a surveyor named Michael Cresap, and a Daniel Greathouse. After a spat of violence, Cresap and Greathouse sought vengeance against Tahgahjute's family; the heretofore innocent Tahgahjute retaliated with thirteen scalps – equaling the number of his losses. News of these murders gave pretense for the colonial governor of Virginia, John Murray, the Earl of Dunmore, to lead an army into Kentucky. And from the fallout came Logan's speech, which was purportedly delivered after Dunmore's War and which first appeared in the *Pennsylvania Journal* as an implicit criticism of land grabbing under British rule. Jefferson later included the address in *Notes on the State of Virginia*, where he would compare Logan to Demosthenes and Cicero. In a stirring conclusion that recalls the cadences of the King James Bible (not to mention the figure of the Noble Savage), Logan justifies his revenge: "I have killed many: I have fully glutted my vengeance. For my country, I rejoice at the beams of peace. But do not harbour a thought that mine is the joy of fear. Logan never felt fear. He will not turn on his heel to save his life. Who is there to mourn for Logan? – Not one" (*Notes*, 63). That the speech turned out to be the fabrication of local journalists never troubled Jefferson.

Drafted into a trans-Atlantic debate with the Comte de Buffon, the Logan of *Notes on Virginia* came to exist primarily as metaphor. His speech offered a possible equivalent to classical sources, a strike against the theory of degenerative climes, the embodiment of bad government under Lord Dunmore, and a foundation for Knox's "benevolent plan." But Logan was no longer an actual person. The implications were severe. Using *Notes on the State of Virginia* as a pilot, Knox saw Native Americans as figures for "improvement," which complicated the life of any real individual who was forced to inhabit this "plan."

Incorporation (the Lewis and Clark *Journals*)

If Jefferson's westering vision has an epitome, it is the Louisiana Purchase and reconnaissance expeditions that followed. One of several, the mission led by Meriwether Lewis and William Clark provided an opportunity to expand the trade network tested in the Query "Rivers." The instructions given to Lewis were to find a Northwest Passage, by tracing the Missouri River, as well as "it's course & communication with the waters of the Pacific Ocean [to] offer the most direct and practicable water communication across the continent, for the purposes of its commerce." Again following the model of *Notes on the State of Virginia*, Lewis was to take note of the climate, geography, soil, mineral wealth, flora and fauna, and people of the Louisiana Territory. The Corps of Discovery (the name for the roughly forty trappers, traders, soldiers, one slave, and a Shoshone woman who made the journey) left a base camp at St. Louis in 1804, wintered among the Mandan and Hidatsa Indians in 1804–5, reached the Pacific and spent the following winter in the Columbia River basin, recrossed the mountains in summer 1806, and returned to St. Louis the following autumn. Along the way Lewis, Clark, and the members who could write assembled an archive that totals over a million words and thirty bound volumes; they have been called "the writingest explorers of their time." Afficionados and scholars liken the journey to everything from a national "epic" to the nation's "bedtime story."[12]

Nearly every account emphasizes the movement from east to west (although the explorers traveled in both directions). And the same accounts advance a well-worn plot: realizing Jefferson's vision, the Corps of Discovery initiated a nation's history over the interior of the continent. It was a story that Lewis himself encouraged. He did not enter the expedition's daily log until April 7, 1805, when he crossed into territory that "the foot of civilized man had never trodden."[13] What holds this figurative language together (with civilization reduced to the metonymic "foot") is an implied narrative of progress across space. That the claim was inflated almost seems unnecessary to state; Lewis casts himself as the Enlightenment Prometheus who brings "civilization" into darkness. Yet this story is remarkably enduring, and one that even serious scholars will occasionally indulge. In a blurb excerpted for a US Forest Service brochure, James Ronda (author of the definitive study of native–white relations during the expedition) suggests that: "Jefferson's Captains went up the Missouri into the West in search of ideas shaped by imagination and born of desire. The idea of a western wonder land – all these seemed waiting to be found in shapes of earth, rock and weather just over the horizon."[14] Popular as well as scholarly histories follow the same trajectory as Jefferson's letter to William Ludlow, where an ideological geography is consummated by "earth, rock and weather." But there is a catch to Ronda's tactile prose. Despite its elemental bearing, the sentence hinges grammatically upon the word "seemed," which locates the "idea" in fuzzy mythology rather than fact. A western "wonder land" *seems* to await the arrival of Lewis and Clark. Even in the words of an accomplished ethnohistorian, Native Americans appear as secondary figures.

By virtue of its sheer size, however, the archive does offer other approaches. And so narratives of "improvement" may often sit alongside examples of incorporation. One such episode (predictably overlooked in popular history) occurs on the return journey. From late May through June 1806, Lewis and Clark camped on the upper Clearwater River, in the heart of Nee-Mee-Poo or Nez Perce country.[15] Snow in the Bitterroot Mountains had forced them to wait; the *Journals* change tack as a result, showing increased attention to nature and to native knowledge of the place. Action yields to astute observations on blooming flowers, fish runs, bird life, animal population, and the ways of harvesting these resources. On May 27 and 28, the captains would identify their signature species: Lewis's woodpecker and Clark's nutcracker. The entry for June 16 notes the blooming glacier lily, orange honeysuckle, mountain huckleberry, columbine, bluebell, mountain thermopsis, and an angelica that was probably licorice root. A running essay on bears allowed for the distinction of grizzlies and a second species, noting a difference that native observers recognized already. An entry on May 11 describes salmon fishing. And so on.

Little of this information receives mention in popular accounts. Nature simply fails to offer the same gripping plot as the heroic march to the sea, and the stay among the Nee-Mee-Poos consequently appears to be little more than an interruption. Lewis likened the six weeks on the Clearwater to torture, cursing "that icy barier which seperates me from my friends and Country, from all which makes life esteemable." He offered self-counsel and, in a passage that guidebooks invariably cite, wrote: "patience, patience" (May 17, 1806). The Nee-Mee-Poos register in this story, if at all, as glorified stable hands. Lewis and Clark had left horses with them the previous fall, in 1805, and most histories dwell upon a trivializing intratribal conflict that kept the white explorers from retrieving their herd. The high drama of the 1805 (westering) journey overshadows the 1806 (return) leg. In fall 1805, the company had relied upon the geographically limited Shoshone Sioux, who got the explorers lost and led them down a path where Clark was as "wet and cold in every part as I ever was in my life" (September 15, 1805).

It bears asking, what insight is lost behind the epic charge to the sea? In contrast to the previous year's journey, the 1806 crossing of the Bitterroots occurred almost without incident. (The company did depart earlier and was forced to backtrack once.) The Corps of Discovery owed its success to excellent guides. And the reason why becomes intelligible only by considering a history *before* Lewis and Clark. The Nee-Mee-Poos are a loosely organized nation, whose economy has traditionally operated within seasonal flows. Hunting and war parties regularly traveled to the Great Plains. Their traditional lore contains dozens of stories that involve mountain crossings, and, following the acquisition of horses in the 1730s, the Nee-Mee-Poos increased their geographic range still further.[16] This happy convergence of factors resulted in an unremarkable leg of the expedition. The guides took the Corps of Discovery through one of the three routes to the Great Plains, following a trail that keeps the ridge to the left and the river to the right, along a string of blazes and massive boulder cairns. They returned to the headwaters of the east-flowing Missouri without serious incident.

The self-aggrandizing literary persona of a hero-naturalist, meanwhile, leads to conspicuous amazement about the Nee-Mee-Poo guides. Anticipating his metropolitan audience, Lewis emphasizes the skill of his "pilots" through a maze of mountains:

> we were entirely surrounded by those mountains from which to one unac-
> quainted with them it would have seemed impossible ever to have escaped; in
> short without the assistance of our guides I doubt much whether we who had
> once passed them could find our way to Travellers rest in their present situation
> for the marked trees on which we had placed considerable reliance are much
> fewer and more difficult to find than we had apprehended. these fellows are
> most admireable pilots; we find the road wherever the snow has disappeared
> though it be only for a few hundred paces.   (June 27, 1806)

The language revealingly distances the author from his immediate locale. To one "unacquainted" with the terrain, the trail assuredly would be lost. Yet it was Lewis alone who was unacquainted; the perspective of the heroic traveler in near-impossible straits trumps the very real factors that made the Nee-Mee-Poos such excellent guides.

Here and elsewhere, the expedition's success or failure depended upon productive Native American relations. After crossing the Bitterroots, Lewis split from Clark (who led a reconnaissance of the Yellowstone River) and met hostile Blackfeet Sioux. Pre-existing rivalries between the Blackfeet and Shoshones, who hosted the party the previous fall, culminated with Lewis taking a bullet in his rear end. He survived, met Clark downriver, but did not write again until their return to St. Louis. The lesson is clear: despite nods in the *Journal* to the imagined audience, the expedition depended upon an ability to read knowledges about the land as well as the pre-existing histories there. One of the challenges that the literature of the early republic poses to contemporary readers is in this strong patina of mythology. The voice of Meriwether Lewis – or Thomas Jefferson, for that matter – overtakes a broader sense of the encounter, so that an easy explanation of the Bitterroot crossing becomes impossible or simply not worth commentary. The problem is an overwhelming sense of national importance that begins with the authors themselves. Much as the need for an American Cicero turned Tahgahjute into an exemplum, Lewis's master plot of endurance and triumph obfuscated the obvious. In reality the Corps of Discovery crossed the mountains, bade fare-well to the Nee-Mee-Poo guides, and "proceeded on." For an audience primed for the high drama of an expanding civilization, what kind of story is that?

Disappearance

The distancing from initial points of contact, as noted, was not simply an aesthetic concern. Similar cases of intellectual blindness bore consequences in public policy. As Jeffersonian principles warped with the next century, the same pretense of benevolence came to justify demands for Indian removal. The speech allegedly by Tahgahjute most notably took on new meanings. In *Notes on the State of Virginia*, it served as proof of Indians' excellence in oration: "Who is there to mourn for Logan? – Not one." The later history of the speech, however, illustrates the tenuous role that (even idealized) Native Americans played as US power consolidated without an opposing European empire.

In 1797 politically motivated attacks led then Vice President Jefferson to revisit the case involving Tahgahjute, Cresap, and Greathouse. Jefferson published an appendix to *Notes on Virginia* in 1801 with several affidavits that reviewed the murders in tedious detail. Little about this controversy bears discussion today, except for a short comment that reveals a jarring indiffer-ence towards authenticity. Jefferson conceded that Logan's famous speech was probably fake. Against allegations of forgery, or claims that the words were his own, Jefferson countered:

> wherefore the forgery? Whether Logan's or mine, it would still have been American. I should indeed consult my own fame if the suggestion, that this speech is mine, were suffered to be believed. He would have a just right to be proud who could with truth claim that composition. But it is none of mine; and I yield it to whom it is due. (*Notes*, 230)

The words mattered only as an example of what an American could produce, and whether they were by a Native or British American did not matter. Yet the 1801 Appendix lays bare an important pattern of appropriation: as

Tahgahjute on the Ohio Valley was drafted into a trans-national historical debate, so too did literary usurpation anticipate real ones.

The speech's continued circulation makes it a valuable marker for understanding how literary projects intersected with a broader history. That history sank to a new low in 1814, when Andrew Jackson led the United States against the divided Creek nation. Ostensibly part of the war of 1812, the battle nonetheless led to demands for 23 million acres of Creek land. Logan's words entered into these controversial events in specific ways. A young Washington Irving published a long essay in the *Analectic Magazine* that criticized US involvement in Creek affairs. Even while Irving expressed sympathy for "misguided" Indians, however, he also advanced the patronizing stereotype of an innocent and easily duped people. Later versions of the same essay show that the sympathies did neither the Creeks nor other native groups any favors. The same essay appeared in Irving's *Sketch Book of Geoffrey Crayon* six years later, but without the topical references. Pointed criticisms in the later version dissolve into vague reflections on the "Indian Character" and melancholy predictions about their fate. "There is something in the character and habits of the North American savage," Irving writes, "that is, to my mind, wonderfully striking and sublime." He posits a view, then fashionable in England, that the United States should not "stigmatize the Indians" lest they "vanish like a vapour from the face of the earth."[17] The crux of his argument was the need to protect the good character of native people. Southern politicians who coveted Indian lands justified usurpation on the grounds that natives should be protected from backcountry whites, and so too Irving echoed a concern that corrupted Indians would not be able to "reclaim" their innate nobility. As evidence of that nobility, Irving cited Logan's speech. The case for betterment from *Notes on the State of Virginia* in this way came to serve the proponents of removal.

But the story does not end there. Logan's spurious speech took yet another turn when it was adopted in the 1830s by the Cherokee journalist, Elias Boudinot. The product of a missionary education, Boudinot exemplified the difficulties that Native Americans faced as they struggled over whether and/or upon what terms they should incorporate a colonizing culture. On one hand, Boudinot represented the republic's best hope for "improvement." Born Buck Waitie in 1804 to partially assimilated parents, he attended a Christian school in New England around the time that his contemporary, Sequoyah, developed a syllabary (like an alphabet but based on syllables) for the Cherokee language. Boudinot founded the *Cherokee Phoenix*, a bilingual newspaper that was published in English and in Cherokee. Siding with federal policies, Boudinot used the *Phoenix* to advance the image of a "civilization" that was being "redeemed from a savage state."[18] He tallied and celebrated local "progress" in agriculture, trade, and culture. On the other hand, sympathies with the United States contributed to Boudinot's alienation among his own people. In 1835, he signed the Treaty of Echota, the infamous agreement that ceded lands in Georgia and led to the Trail of Tears. His views led to a forced march west, and eventually to his murder at the hands of a kinsman.

Boudinot's signature essay, "Address to the Whites," illustrates the difficulty of inhabiting a Jeffersonian vision. Written in 1826 to raise funds for a Cherokee school and purchase supplies for the *Phoenix*, this speech incorporated the republican language of progress across space to advance Native American civilization. Much like *Notes on the State of Virginia*, it begins by situating boundaries, reviews the quality and commercial potential of his nation's territory, predicts the day when waste lands will become "one of the Garden spots of America," and uses all the conventional markers of Enlightenment geography, tallying heads of cattle, looms, spinning wheels, mills, plows, smiths, schools, roads, "good books," and redeemed souls. As he turns Euroamerican conceptions of the environment and culture to his own people and place, however, he must acknowledge the prejudices of his audience. He observes that "the term *Indian* is pregnant with ideas" that strike listeners as "repelling and repugnant," and, to the same ends that Jefferson used Logan, Boudinot offers a bit of literary polish to evidence his humanity. Even though the Cherokees need "not the display of language," the editor of the *Phoenix* drops allusions to *The Merchant of Venice*, the Bible, and Washington Irving. "They will vanish like a vapour from the face of the earth," Boudinot exclaims; must they "perish" and "go down in sorrow to their grave?" Drawing from a line of influence that passed from *Notes on the State of Virginia* to Irving's "Traits on the Indian Character," Boudinot would argue that the fate of a nation must "hang upon your mercy as to a garment. Will you push them from you, or will you save them? Let humanity answer."[19]

The phrasing echoes Logan's. A rhetorical question is followed by a short concluding phrase. And the adaptation rounds out the three modes charted in this essay: from a language of "improvement," to melancholy thoughts on "disappearance," to "incorporation." Because these three modes interlock and switch back, it would be a mistake to suggest the inevitability of chronology; that is, it simplifies matters to imply that literary disappearances led to real removals and that there was no other story to tell. Rather, Euroamerican and Native American worlds came together as a nation moved west, and the terms of this westering nation were being renegotiated constantly. This leaves several lessons that can be drawn from the Jeffersonian legacy. First, curiosity (even in the form of admiration) was not the same as adopting another's interests. Patronizing charity was as brutal as usurpation in the end. Second and more broadly, American culture is both permeable and imbricated by uneven distributions of power. Lastly, the United States was (and is) a place where people from a variety of backgrounds try to figure each other out. Blinded by his own prejudices, Jefferson becomes particularly instructive in this process. He remains relevant to the study of colonial (or post-colonial) nations, where authors must struggle to situate themselves amidst human differences. The literature of intercultural contact is, as it also was for Jefferson, difficult, painful, unfair, and enormously rich.

NOTES

1. *Thomas Jefferson: Writings*, ed. Merrill D. Peterson (New York: Library of America, 1984), 376–8.
2. William Perkins Cutler and Julia Perkins Cutler (eds.), *Life, Journals and Correspondence of Manasseh Cutler* (Cincinnati: Clarke, 1888), 393–7, 401–5; Edgar C. Reinke, "*Meliorem lapsa locavit*: An Intriguing Puzzle Solved," *Ohio History*, 94 (1985): 68–74.
3. Solomon Drown[e], *An Oration Delivered at Marietta, April 7, 1789, In Commemoration of the Commencement of the Settlement formed by the Ohio Company* (Worcester: Isaiah Thomas, 1789), 7, 10, 15; Solomon Drowne's journal is at the John Hay Library, Brown University.
4. *Thomas Jefferson: Writings*, 1496.
5. I develop these ideas further in *From the Fallen Tree: Frontier Narratives, Environmental Politics, and the Roots of a National Pastoral, 1749–1826* (Chapel Hill: University of North Carolina Press, 2003).
6. *Notes on the State of Virginia*, ed. William Peden (Chapel Hill: University of North Carolina Press, 1954), 3–4.
7. Ibid., 5.
8. Ibid., 7.
9. Georges Louis Leclerc, Comte de Buffon, *Natural History* (London, 1797), VII: 30, 39–40, 47–8; Antonello Gerbi, *The Dispute of the New World: The History of a Polemic, 1750–1900* (Pittsburgh: University of Pittsburgh Press, 1973), 53; Guillaume Thomas François Raynal, Abbé Raynal, *A Philosophical and Political History ... of the East and West Indies* (London, 1783), VII: 150–1.
10. *Notes*, 47.
11. Ibid., 65.
12. Larry McMurtry, "The First American Epic," *New York Review of Books*, 48 (February 8, 2001); Kris Fresonke, *Lewis and Clark: Legacies, Memories, and New Perspectives*, ed. Fresonke and Mark Spence (Berkeley: University of California Press, 2004), 20; *Letters of the Lewis and Clark Expedition, with Related Documents, 1783–1854*, ed. Donald Jackson (Champaign: University of Illinois Press, 2000), 7.
13. *Journals of the Lewis and Clark Expedition*, ed. Gary E. Moulton (Lincoln: University of Nebraska Press, 1983–2004), April 7, 1805. Because there are several editions, entries will be cited by date.
14. Ronda's *Finding the West: Explorations with Lewis and Clark* is quoted in the USDA Forest Service pamphlet, *Enduring Stories, Dynamic Landscapes: The*

Lewis and Clark Expedition on National Forests and Grasslands (Washington, DC: USDA, 2004), n.p.

15. The camp is the only extended site that does not have a name: nineteenth-century historians labeled it "Camp Chopunnish" (a corruption of the native language, Sahaptin?), and it is described today as "The Long Camp."

16. Allen P. Slickpoo emphasizes mobility in a published tribal history, *Noon Nee-Me-Poo (We, the Nez Perces): Culture and History of the Nez Perces* (Lapwait, ID: Nez Perce Tribe of Idaho, 1973), 24–31.

17. Irving, "Traits of Indian Character," *Analectic Magazine*, 3 (1814): 145; *Selected Writings of Washington Irving*, ed. William P. Kelly (New York: Modern Library, 1984), 299–301, 306, 311.

18. *Cherokee Editor: The Writings of Elias Boudinot*, ed. Theda Perdue (Athens: University of Georgia Press, 1996), 94.

19. Ibid., 72–3, 65, 79.

4

GORDON M. SAYRE

Jefferson and Native Americans: policy and archive

For many students and teachers who read Jefferson's *Notes on the State of Virginia*, one of the most striking or disturbing passages in the text may be the description of Jefferson's experiments as an archaeologist, in Query XI, "Aborigines." Native American burial mounds, or "Barrows ... are to be found all over this country" of Virginia, he wrote.[1] Local legends offered various accounts of which, why, or how many individuals were buried beneath these mounds, and so "There being one of these in my neighbourhood, I wished to satisfy myself whether any, and which of these opinions were just. For this purpose I determined to open and examine it thoroughly. It was situated on the low grounds of the Rivanna, about two miles above its principal fork," within the modern city of Charlottesville, but also near the site of the Monacan town of Monasickapanough.[2] Although archaeology as a science had not yet developed by 1780, Jefferson nonetheless described in great detail the size and shape of the barrow, and the depth and arrangement of the bones he found in it. His systematic description of "part of the jaw of a child, which had not yet cut its teeth" employed anatomical terminology and reads much like a modern archaeological monograph: "The processes, by which it was articulated to the temporal bones, were entire: and the bone itself firm to where it had been broken off, which, as nearly as I could judge, was about the place of the eye-tooth."[3] Here as elsewhere in the *Notes*, Jefferson was trying to demonstrate scientific methods of inquiry and a learned vocabulary that would place him in the company of British and French anatomists such as John Hunter and Louis Jean Marie Daubenton, whom he had already cited in Query VI in writing of the elephant or mammoth bones found in the Ohio Valley.

Jefferson's science was impressive, but it is because of later United States policies towards Native Americans (some of which Jefferson himself initiated) that the "Barrows" passage is haunting to many modern readers. Jefferson did not attempt to get permission from the kinfolk or descendants of the people buried in the mound before he began excavating the graves, as he would be required to do under the Native American Graves Protection and Repatriation Act (NAGPRA) of 1990. Nor did he make any effort to rebury the bones after he examined them, nor to restore the mound to its original appearance, as NAGPRA has stipulated for many archaeological digs. The mound "had been of about twelve feet altitude, though now reduced by the plough to seven and a half, having been under cultivation about a dozen years. Before this it was covered with trees of twelve inches diameter."[4] Anglo-Virginians' agriculture had supplanted Native American peoples, and the mounds sank and shrank in a process that may have appeared to be as natural as erosion, but in fact was a consequence of European colonization.

The large trees atop the mounds not only gave them a "natural" appearance, they also proved that the bodies must have been buried there at least sixty or seventy years earlier.[5] In fact the Monacan peoples of piedmont Virginia had been forced to move to the south and west before the 1720s, when William Byrd wrote briefly of them in his *History of the Dividing Line*. But from his own childhood Jefferson did recall "a party passing, about thirty years ago, through the part of the country where this barrow is, [who] went through the woods directly to it, without any instructions or enquiry, and having staid about it some time, with expressions which were construed to be those of sorrow, returned to the high road."[6] The anthropologist Anthony F. C. Wallace, in his study of Jefferson and the Indians, suggests that these Indians may have been Tutelos or Saponis, Siouan speakers who in the early 1700s became refugees among the larger Tuscarora or Catawba tribes, and that this scene took place in the late 1740s or early 1750s, when Jefferson was less than 10 years old.

The gap between these two scenes in *Notes*, the grown man's systematic excavation, mensuration, and examination of bones, and his misty memory of a childhood encounter with a group of mourning Indians, captures conflicting impulses not only in Jefferson but in modern US attitudes towards native peoples. It suggests a division between heart and head, between a sense of melancholy or regret, and a refusal on the part of those feeling the sentiments to recognize their own responsibility for them.

Query XI goes on to pose a question that American anthropologists have debated for more than three centuries and still not answered: "whence came these aboriginal inhabitants of America?" Jefferson proposed answering the question by using a linguistic method now called glotto-chronology: "for two dialects to recede from one another till they have lost all vestiges of their common origin, must require an immense course of time"; and he believed there were "twenty ... of those radical languages in America ... for one in Asia."[7] However, today's anthropologists (as well as some of Jefferson's best-informed predecessors such as Pierre François-Xavier de Charlevoix) identify only three or four families of Native North American languages: Iroquoian, Algonquian, Siouan, and, further west, Uto-Aztecan. Jefferson seemed to know that his linguistics was not as accurate as his archaeology, and he appealed for further research: "It is to be lamented then, very much to be lamented, that we have suffered so many of the Indian tribes to extinguish, without our having previously collected and deposited in the records of our literature, the general rudiments at least of the languages they spoke."[8] Jefferson made this research one of his many scientific projects; he began compiling lists of transcriptions of up to 250 different words in various Native American languages, either by copying from published ethnographies or by soliciting the help of Indian agents, missionaries, and frontier explorers such as Lewis and Clark, who collected several lists during their expedition. In 1801 he wrote to William Dunbar, who had sent from Natchez, Mississippi, word lists from three southern tribes, that "I have it much at heart to make as extensive a collection as possible of the Indian tongues. I have at present about 30, tolerably full, among which the number radically different, is truly wonderful."[9] The American Philosophical Society has a manuscript list of such vocabularies in twenty-two languages from 1802 or 1803. But unfortunately, in 1809, Jefferson's collection, which by then included some fifty languages, was stolen and destroyed during his move back to Monticello at the end of his presidency.

Given his dedication to the word list project, one senses that Jefferson may have profoundly regretted that, as a child, he had failed to take the opportunity to speak to the "party" of mourners who detoured from the "high road" to visit their ancestors' remains in the "Barrows." As a boy he did not or could not ask them who was buried in the mound. Now as an adult he would belatedly pose the questions anew even as he desecrated the graves. In like manner, in the early twentieth century, US policies of forced assimilation separated Indian children from their parents and sent them to boarding schools where they were forbidden to speak their native languages. But towards the end of the century, the US government was awarding grants to help tribes preserve some of the same languages it had previously tried to exterminate. As if to make up for his lost opportunity, Jefferson wants to somehow make Indian languages as tangible, storable, and searchable as a collection of bones or archaeological artifacts. The speech of living people would be frozen and "deposited in all the public libraries," not as audio recordings, of course, but as alphabetic transcriptions, even if the speakers did not use alphabets and would not have access to the libraries.[10] He would like to turn word into object, living mortal peoples into an inanimate permanent archive. Jonathan Elmer has analyzed Jefferson's "effort to archive the Native American both materially and discursively," that is to say, both archaeologically and linguistically: "If the barrow is no monument, but merely an 'accustomary collection of bones,' then this is because the 'custom' involved in such a 'collection … and deposition' seems too rudimentary and unelaborated as commemorative impulse."[11] The Indians themselves failed to create a "monument" or an archive of their past, but Jefferson believes that he can do so. Bones reveal the secrets of past Indian cultures in an apparently objective manner that does not require the researcher to learn native languages, or to protect the lives and cultures of those who speak those languages. Jefferson observed that "The sculls were so tender, that they generally fell to pieces on being touched," yet though his own hands destroyed the evidence he so highly valued, he did not hold himself responsible for their deaths, nor the demise of the village nearby, nor the loss of the languages that these people spoke while alive.[12]

What might Jefferson have learned or heard if he had spoken with these mourners? Another formative experience in Jefferson's youth was meeting Outacite, a Cherokee leader who in 1762 had traveled with explorer Henry Timberlake to London, one of a series of widely publicized visits by Indians to European capitals.[13] Writing to John Adams in 1811, Jefferson recalled that:

> The great Outassete, the warrior and orator of the Cherokees … was always the guest of my father on his journeys to and from Williamsburg. I was in his camp when he made his great farewell oration to his people the evening before his departure for England. The moon was in full splendor, and to her he seemed to address himself in his prayers for his own safety on the voyage, and that of his people during his absence; his sounding voice, distinct articulation, animated actions, and the solemn silence of his people at their several fires, filled me with awe and veneration, altho' I did not understand a word he uttered.[14]

Neither Jefferson nor other Virginia "founding fathers" spoke the Cherokee language, and so Outacite could expect little help from them in response to his address; it might as well have been the moon to whom he pleaded for the safety of his people. In fact, in the letter, Jefferson goes on to write of how the United States will deal with tribes who ally with the enemy English in the impending war of 1812: "we shall be obliged to drive them, with the beasts of the forest into the Stony mountains."[15] As Jay Fliegelman has described in *Declaring Independence*, his book on Jefferson and theories of oratory and performance in the eighteenth century, eloquent speech was believed to consist as much in its emotive tone and theatrical gesture as in the rhetorical skill of its argument. Jefferson believed he could sympathize with native peoples and their plight without having to actually listen to their leaders' demands. Hence the title of Bernard Sheehan's 1973 book, *Seeds of Extinction: Jeffersonian Philanthropy and the American Indian*, which argued that "the Jeffersonian brand of philanthropy could be justly accused of treating the native more like a precious abstraction than a living human being. For the Indian it wanted only the best, but that meant ultimately the elimination of the tribal order."[16]

Some of the guiding principles of US Indian policy, policies that would prove disastrous for tribes in the nineteenth and early twentieth centuries, began with Jeffersonian philanthropy: his idea that, in order to move ahead in the process of history, the tribes had to shift from hunting to agriculture, and that this shift could come about only through a forced assimilation that would necessitate the elimination of tribal languages and self-governance. This grand anthropological concept cloaked the self-interest of the colonizers. As Jefferson wrote to the Seneca leader, Handsome Lake, in 1802, justifying the appropriation of lands in western New York: "While they [the Indians] depended on hunting, the more extensive the forest around them, the more game they would yield. But going into a state of agriculture, it may be advantageous to a society, as it is to an individual, who had more land than he can improve, to sell a part" and "The right to sell is one of the rights of property."[17] In his addresses to Indians, Jefferson used some of the conventionally florid language of treaty councils, promising to "pray to the Great Spirit who made us all and planted us in this land," but his focus was on instructing his audience in patriarchal capitalism à la John Locke and Adam Smith. Thus, in a speech to Cherokee chiefs during his presidency, he advised:

> When a man has enclosed and improved his farm ... he will wish when he dies that these things shall go to his wife and children, whom he loves more than he does his other relations ... You will therefore find it necessary to establish laws for this. When man has property, earned by his own labor, he will not like to see another come and take it from him ... You will find it necessary then to appoint good men, as judges.[18]

As Betsy Erkkila has written, "In Jefferson's Indian policy, history – 'the natural progress of things' – moves in only one direction."[19] But while it is fairly easy to perceive the imperialist motives in Jefferson's later remarks to and about Indians, in *Notes on the State of Virginia*, not only in Query XI, "Aborigines," but throughout, Jefferson's discourse about Native Americans was informed by philosophical issues of the eighteenth century that can be harder to recover. There were two overarching goals which may not be evident to first-time readers, and which were each undermined by contradictory beliefs.

The first goal concerned natural history. When students reading *Notes* first encounter the tables in Query VI, "A Comparative View of the Quadrapeds of Europe and America," many quickly sense the point. As Wayne Franklin put it: "the great blank space under Europe is a coyly graphic reminder of Jefferson's conclusion that America is far more lavish in its forms of life than the Old World," or, as Erkkila summarizes, *Notes* is "an early nationalist narrative of New World sexual virility, or 'MINE'S BIGGER THAN YOURS.'"[20] The Indians of Virginia do not appear in the table of animals, but in another in Query XI which, although it lists nearly forty tribes' names, severely underestimated the total population of Algonquian Indians in the tidewater region at the time.[21] But just as large animal species, beginning with the mammoth, refute Buffon's assertion "That the animals common to both the old and new world, are smaller in the latter," the diversity of aboriginal peoples of Virginia prove that it is a place capable of supporting a thriving civilization. In his polemic with Buffon, Jefferson concedes that the density of the Native American population was never as high as the population in Europe: "Were we to compare them in their present state with the Europeans North of the Alps, when the Roman arms and arts first crossed those mountains, the comparison would be unequal, because, at that time, those parts of Europe were swarming with numbers," but he argues that the many separate polities and languages among the Indians proves that they have lived here as long as any peoples on earth.[22] The twenty radical languages of "the red men of America, proves them of greater antiquity than those of Asia."[23]

Like many other Enlightenment thinkers writing about the pre-history of mankind, Jefferson endorsed a stadial historiography, whereby human societies proceeded through a sequence of stages, for example from hunting to herding to agriculture, and from spoken to written language. The precise time between the stages could vary according to local conditions, but the order could not be altered. However, unlike many early anthropologists, Jefferson did not endorse any of the popular diffusionist theories which sought to identify the origins of Native American populations by identifying similarities between their customs, languages, or appearance and those of Eurasian peoples. A few years before Jefferson wrote the *Notes*, James Adair published in London his *History of the American Indians*, an account of the Cherokee that asserted, as Jefferson put it in the same letter to Adams quoted above: "all the Indians of America to be descended from the Jews; the same laws, usages, rites, ceremonies, the same sacrifices, priests, prophets, fasts and festivals, almost the same religion, and that they all spoke Hebrew."[24] Today, many Native American intellectuals are angered by scientists' assertions that Indians migrated to America across a Bering Straits land bridge some 12,000–20,000 years ago.[25] They see this as an ideological tool to undermine Indians' claims to sovereignty. Jefferson, however, did not endorse a theory such as that one of the ten lost tribes of Israel had departed eastward from the holy land in Old Testament times and migrated to North America, losing on the journey all but the vestiges of their language and religion. This theory became increasingly influential during the nineteenth century, with the support of Adair, Elias Boudinot, and others.[26] However, it implied both that human societies could move backwards on the scale of progress, from pastoralism to hunting and from revealed religion to paganism, and a biblical chronology that dated the earth as 6,000–7,000 years old. Jefferson's Enlightenment deism rejected both of these principles.

Much recent critical attention to Jefferson has focused on the profound contradictions between the democratic principles articulated in his *Declaration of Independence* and the genocide of Native Americans, or on his relationship with Sally Hemings and his status as a slaveholder.[27] The fact that Query VI discusses Natives and African Americans as animals only seems to confirm suspicions of Jefferson's racism. Yet it should be recognized that the entire polemic with the Comte de Buffon centered on the effects that the climate, soil, and atmosphere of America had on the humans and animals who lived there. Buffon, although he never traveled to America, maintained that it was cooler and moister than the Old World, and hence had fewer and smaller animals. During the second half of the eighteenth century, the "Dispute of the New World" preoccupied many intellectuals in Europe and Latin America.[28] The Dutchman Cornelius De Pauw, even more than Buffon, championed the argument that the American environment was harmful to native species and to humans of European ancestry, and this argument was used to justify the Spanish policy of appointing European-born Iberian *peninsulares*, not American-born *criollos* or creoles, to colonial administrative posts. Jefferson recognized himself as a creole and tied his own identity to that of the Indians, and this explains the nature of his racism. To malign the Indians as weak or stupid would be to impugn himself as an American. Thus he argued that "the speech of Logan, a Mingo chief" was superior to "the whole orations of Demosthenes and Cicero, and of any more eminent orator, if Europe has furnished more eminent." On the other hand, later in the book he wrote, "never yet could I find that a black had uttered a thought above the level of narration," and that Phyllis Wheatley's writing was not worthy of being called poetry. Yet Logan probably could not even speak English, much less write it, whereas Wheatley, born in Africa and carried across the Atlantic as a slave, had as a teenager mastered written English and the Augustan poetic style so prestigious at that time.[29]

In Logan's speech, Jefferson may again have imagined he could offer a substitute for the lost words of the sorrowful visitors to the Barrow he later excavated, or a translation of the farewell oration of Outacite which he had heard at Williamsburg. The speech demonstrates the complex dialectic of assimilation and difference, translation and incomprehension in Jefferson's understanding of Native Americans. Query VI offers Logan alongside "a Washington, a Franklin, a Rittenhouse" (70) as evidence of American genius in war, physics, astronomy, and oratory. Logan's oration was not a public address, however; it was delivered to an audience of just one man, a then-obscure Pennsylvania trader named John Gibson, and the speech itself says Logan has no living kin, and that no one will mourn him or sympathize with his grief.

Jefferson's motives for reprinting the speech of Logan lead us to the second goal of the writings about Indians in *Notes*. Jefferson wanted to defend the claims of Virginia (whether as a province or as one of the thirteen states in the new republic) to sovereignty over all the land within the boundaries he traced in Query I. After its victory in the Seven Years War, Britain wished to reward the Indian allies who had fought against the French, and issued a Royal Proclamation of October 7, 1763, which decreed that "the several Nations or Tribes of Indians with whom we are connected ... should not be molested or disturbed in the Possession of such Parts of our Dominions and Territories as, not having been ceded to, or purchased by Us, are reserved to them."[30] Accompanying maps drew a boundary line along the crest of the Allegheny Mountains, limiting Pennsylvania and Virginia to around half of their modern size. During the next decade, however, many "backsettlers" defied the proclamation by moving west of the mountains, which provoked a series of raids and retaliations, including Cresap's attack and Logan's vengeance. The elite men of Philadelphia and Williamsburg were angered by the violence against Indian tribes with whom they had engaged in trade and treaty councils, and reluctant to send costly military expeditions to defend renegade backsettlers, the type of lower-class insurgents who continued to cause headaches for the US government with the Whiskey Rebellion in the 1790s. However, in 1774 the British governor of Virginia, Lord Dunmore, did send an expedition led by Colonel Andrew Lewis to attack the Shawnee Indians who, like Logan, had sought to defend their land along the Ohio River. In the Battle of Point Pleasant at the confluence of the Kanawha and Ohio Rivers on October 10, 1774, the "decisive battle" Jefferson refers to, the Shawnee attacked Lewis's force of 1,100 men and killed 75 of them before being turned back north of the Ohio. Some historians suspect that Dunmore's true motive was not so much to exact vengeance on Logan and the Shawnees as to secure control over the south bank of the Ohio. As governor of Virginia from 1779 to 1781, Jefferson was Dunmore's Revolutionary usurper, but he shared with Dunmore an interest in controlling western Virginia in order to profit from selling lands there.

In modern US politics, a frenzy of media attention can give certain individuals or events a symbolic importance far beyond their intrinsic power. The same was true in the early republic. Logan was "Swift Boated" by Jefferson's political opponents, and to defend his political reputation Jefferson had to defend the veracity and authenticity of the speech. Since its publication in a number of newspapers in 1775, Logan's speech had come to be used as an oral recitation in schools and public performances, and, after a 1797 performance by British actor James Fennel, a Federalist attorney general of Maryland named Luther Martin took it up as a club against the then vice president. Martin was the husband of Michael Cresap's daughter, and he published his essay in the satiric arch-Federalist periodical *Porcupine's Gazette*. Jefferson's interest in scientific research had already been the focus of political satire, but Martin was only peripherally concerned with whether the quality of Logan's oration matched that of Demosthenes and Cicero. He focused instead on the accusation that Cresap was singly responsible for killing Logan's family. Martin made Cresap a martyr-hero for two groups of anti-Jeffersonians who otherwise had little in common: reactionary Federalists and anti-Indian backsettlers.

In 1800 Jefferson published in Philadelphia a pamphlet intended to answer Martin's charges without stooping to his level. It was entitled *Relative to the Murder of Logan's Family*, and was included as an appendix in subsequent editions of *Notes*. Much of it is a series of legal depositions from witnesses, including John Gibson, the man who alone had heard Logan's speech and translated it from a Native language (most likely the Cayuga of Logan's father, Shickellamy). Gibson acknowledged that Logan's accusation against Cresap was mistaken, that the murderous party had instead been led by a man named Daniel Greathouse, but insisted that the text of the speech was authentic. In the other depositions an important fact emerged, however. One of the victims of the notorious attack was Logan's sister, who had borne a child by John Gibson. Gibson never openly admitted his paternity, but he "educated the child, and took care of it, as if it had been his own."[31]

The repressed truth of the liaison between Gibson and Logan's family suggests larger patterns of appropriation and expropriation between Jefferson and Native America, and in later US Indian policy. We've seen how Jefferson's motive in using the speech was to champion not so much the genius of American Indians as the eloquence and virility of creole settlers. Now we must acknowledge that the text of Logan's speech was most likely composed by its translator Gibson, and, if we read it as Gibson's speech, further motives emerge. We can sense Gibson's frustration at having to follow orders to attack Indians, and his outrage that Cresap or his allies murdered "my wom[a]n and children," even if one child was spared. This crossblood offspring, whose age and sex differ in the various sources, Gibson felt he could not recognize as legitimate, and it was raised in ignorance of its mother's culture, as children later were raised in the Indian boarding schools. Gibson/Logan's speech expresses the alienation of a vigilante who has been betrayed by Anglo friends yet refuses to cooperate with Indian warriors. Recent work by historians such as Richard White and James Merrell has emphasized that relations between Indians and Euro-Americans in eighteenth-century Pennsylvania and Ohio were not dominated by vengeance, and that there were many bi-lingual and intercultural negotiators, including many crossblood or *métis* individuals. Yet Logan's speech and legend obscures the fact that many such diplomats tried to prevent Logan's vigilantism, and the ensuing Battle of Point Pleasant, by arranging for payments to compensate for the murders at Baker's Bottom.[32] The speech is an ideological tour de force insofar as it invites us to believe things that are not true. Logan's speech claims no one will mourn for him even as we repeat his elegy. Logan claims to have no kin even though Gibson was his brother-in-law and father to his niece or nephew. The speech insists that vengeance is the only recourse, even as many worked to secure peace.

The scientific polemic that Jefferson was pursuing in *Notes on the State of Virginia* led him to embrace Native American identity as bound up with his own status as an Anglo-American creole. Later, when, as US secretary of state, vice president, and president, he had responsibility for policies towards Native Americans, he continued to promote a fantasy of assimilation and incorporation: American Indians could become just like Anglo-Americans if they abandoned their own culture and language. But before, in between and behind Jefferson's writings, a process of *métissage* was happening, one that did not extinguish native culture and was not commonly recognized since it did not square with official policy. The Logan speech, once its full context is known, opens a small window on this process.

NOTES

1. *Notes on the State of Virginia*, ed. Frank Shuffelton (New York: Penguin Putnam, 1999), 104.
2. Ibid., 104. Anthony F. C. Wallace, *Jefferson and the Indians* (Cambridge, MA: Harvard University Press, 1999); 87.
3. *Notes*, 105, 104. William Peden, the editor of the 1954 North Carolina Press edition of the text, commented that Jefferson "anticipated by a century the aims and methods of modern archaeological science" (281 n. 8).
4. Ibid., 104.
5. On the perception of Indian mounds as natural and cultural, see Gordon Sayre, "The Mound Builders and the Imagination of American Antiquity in Jefferson, Bartram, and Chateaubriand," *Early American Literature*, 33.3 (1998): 225–49.
6. *Notes*, 106.
7. Ibid., 107, 108. By "radical" Jefferson meant "root" or "original."

8. Ibid., 107.
9. TJ to Dunbar, January 12, 1801, in *Thomas Jefferson: Writings*, ed. Merrill Peterson (New York: Library of America, 1984), 1083. See also Sheehan, *Seeds of Extinction* (Chapel Hill: University of North Carolina Press, 1973), 54–7.
10. *Notes*, 108.
11. Jonathan Elmer, "The Archive, the Native American, and Jefferson's Convulsions," *Diacritics*, 28.4 (1998): 7.
12. *Notes*, 105.
13. See *The memoirs of Lieut. Henry Timberlake (who accompanied the three Cherokee Indians to England in the year 1762) containing whatever he observed* ... (London, 1765). The most sensational such visit was that of four Mohawk leaders in 1710. See Richmond P. Bond, *Queen Anne's American Kings* (Oxford: Clarendon, 1952).
14. *Thomas Jefferson: Writings*, 1263. Jefferson's father died when he was 14, so Outacite's travels with Peter Jefferson must have taken place at least five years before the speech paraphrased here. Jay Fliegelman proposes that "the memory of the Cherokee orator's departure speech seems to have served Jefferson as a way of addressing, mourning, and ennobling the death of his father, a deeply traumatic event." *Declaring Independence: Jefferson, Natural Language, and the Culture of Performance* (Stanford: Stanford University Press, 1993), 99.
15. *Thomas Jefferson: Writings*, 1264.
16. Sheehan, *Seeds of Extinction*, 12.
17. *Thomas Jefferson: Writings*, 556. In a letter to Indian agent Benjamin Hawkins around the same time, Jefferson wrote: "The promotion of agriculture, therefore, and household manufacture, are essential in their preservation, and I am disposed to aid and encourage it liberally. This will enable them to live on much smaller portions of land ... While they are learning to do better on less land, our increasing numbers will be calling for more land, and thus a coincidence of interests will be produced." Ibid., 1115.
18. Ibid., 562, 561.
19. Erkkila, *Mixed Bloods and Other Crosses: Rethinking American Literature from the Revolution to the Culture Wars* (Philadelphia: University of Pennsylvania Press, 2005), 42.
20. Franklin, *Discoverers, Explorers, Settlers: The Diligent Writers of Early America* (Chicago: University of Chicago Press, 1979), plate 2. Erkkila, *Mixed Bloods*, 40.
21. Wallace, *Jefferson and the Indians*, 83–4.
22. *Notes*, 48, 68.
23. Ibid., 108.
24. *Thomas Jefferson: Writings*, 1261. He also ridiculed the *Mœurs des Sauvages Américains comparées aux mœurs des premiers temps* of Joseph-François Lafitau, translated by Iroquois ethnohistorians William Fenton and Elizabeth Moore as *Customs of the American Indians Compared with the Customs of Primitive Times*, 2 vols. (Toronto: Champlain Society, 1974). Adair's 1775 book has been republished with an introduction and notes by Kathryn E. Holland Braund (Tuscaloosa: University of Alabama Press, 2005).
25. See, for example, Vine Deloria, *Red Earth, White Lies: Native Americans and the Myth of Scientific Fact* (Golden, CO: Fulcrum, 1997), 67–82.

26. Boudinot, *A star in the west; or, A humble attempt to discover the long lost ten tribes of Israel, preparatory to their return to their beloved city, Jerusalem* (Trenton, NJ, 1816).

27. For a good overview, see David Waldstreicher's introduction to *Notes on the State of Virginia, with Related Documents* (Boston: Bedford St. Martins, 2002), 1–38.

28. See Antonello Gerbi, *The Dispute of the New World: The History of a Polemic, 1750–1900*, trans. Jeremy Moyle (Pittsburgh: University of Pittsburgh Press, 1973), 52–79, 252–68.

29. *Notes*, 67, 147. For a fuller account of Logan and his speech see Gordon Sayre, *The Indian Chief as Tragic Hero: Native Resistance and the Literatures of America, from Moctezuma to Tecumseh* (Chapel Hill: University of North Carolina Press, 2005), 162–202.

30. Quoted in Francis Jennings, *Empire of Fortune: Crowns, Colonies, and Tribes in the Seven Years War in America* (New York: Norton, 1988), 462.

31. John Sappington, in a statement obtained after the 1800 pamphlet, and printed in the appendices to later editions. *Notes*, 264.

32. White, *The Middle Ground: Indians, Empires and Republics in the Great Lakes Region, 1650–1815* (New York: Cambridge University Press, 1991), 361–3. Merrell, *Into the American Woods: Negotiators on the Pennsylvania Frontier* (New York: Norton, 1999), includes a wealth of information about Shickellamy, Logan's father.

5

DOUGLAS R. EGERTON

Race and slavery in the era of Jefferson

Thomas Jefferson's earliest memory was being carried on a pillow by a slave, and when he died in 1826, he was buried in a coffin built by an enslaved carpenter. More than any other member of the founding generation, Jefferson exemplified the inconsistent outlook and behavior of the post-revolutionary republic. He consistently and eloquently professed to despise slavery, yet he freed only those bondpeople who were related to him. And while many contemporaries regarded Jefferson as a disciple of the Enlightenment, his comments on Africans and their descendants were founded upon his labor needs, not on rational observation, and were reactionary even by eighteenth-century standards.

Even more than other planter-politicians of his day, Jefferson was especially adept at shifting the blame for slavery onto others – as well as avoiding the responsibility for ending it. In his most celebrated formulation, put forth in the Declaration of Independence, Jefferson held Britain and King George III responsible for both the slave trade and the creation of unfree labor in Virginia, as if eager Chesapeake planters had played no role in the purchase of captured Africans. Denouncing the Atlantic traffic in humans as "piratical warfare," Jefferson insisted that it was only the British monarch who was "[d]etermined to keep open a market where Men" were sold into slavery.[1] As a young politician, Jefferson insisted that abolishing slavery was the task of senior statesmen, but even after retiring from the presidency, when he had nothing left to lose apart from his reputation among Virginia planters, he rebuffed Edward Coles's request to endorse a plan to liberate slaves in the West. Jefferson now insisted that it was the duty of "the younger generation" to advance "the hour of emancipation." By 1814, he claimed that he had "ceased to think" about black liberation, as it was "not to be the work of my day."[2]

Jefferson did have his antislavery moments, but they were invariably modest for a professed revolutionary, and they diminished in frequency as he grew older and more politically successful. As a new member of the House of Burgesses in 1769, Jefferson crafted a bill that would have allowed for private manumissions, as the current law required the approval of the royal governor before liberating even a single bondperson. Being a freshman legislator, Jefferson approached Richard Bland, "one of the oldest, ablest, & most respected members" of the House, to submit the act, while he seconded the motion. Angry planters denounced Bland as "an enemy" of Virginia and "treated [him] with the grossest indecorum." The bill failed. From that debacle Jefferson drew the lesson that, if he desired a career in politics, he would have to take care never to get too far in front of public opinion, or to labor quietly behind the scenes.[3]

Even so, the following year found the youthful Jefferson in court representing Samuel Howell, a mixed-race servant held to bondage until the age of 31. The 1705 Virginia slave code required mulatto children born to white women outside of marriage to be bound out by county churchwardens. In court, Jefferson appealed to natural rights, arguing that "under the law of nature, all men are born free." Here too, the young attorney learned a lesson about the harsh reality of racial politics, as the court ruled against Howell even before the other side could present its case. Some historians suggest that this incident and Jefferson's early appeal to the notion that "every one comes into the world with a right to his own person" reveal his hidden antislavery ideals. Yet Howell was neither a slave nor an African, and one wonders if Jefferson would have taken the case had his client not been light-skinned.[4]

Perhaps more typical of Jefferson's conflicted views regarding slavery were his ruminations on Africans and unwaged labor in his *Notes on the State of Virginia*. Drafted first in 1781 and revised several times before being published in France, the book included a proposed amendment to the Virginia constitution for gradual emancipation and mandatory colonization for the former bondpeople. The plan called for all slaves born after December 31, 1800, to be "declared free." The stipulation, however, was that these children, after being trained as apprentices, would be forced to leave the state upon reaching maturity, which meant that freed adolescents would be forever separated from their still-enslaved parents. Unlike St. George Tucker's realistic 1796 *A Dissertation on Slavery*, which proposed to gradually transform Virginia's bonded into a free but politically powerless class of agricultural proletarians, Jefferson's plan of compulsory colonization would remove Virginia's labor force. Jefferson's planter brethren, of course, would never support a plan that eliminated the state's working class. As French critic Duc de La Rochefoucauld-Liancourt observed, Jefferson added "so many conditions to [emancipation] to render it practicable, that it is thus reduced to the impossible."[5]

When asked to explain why black Virginians could only be freed if they were sent out of the state, he fell back on racism. "Deep rooted prejudices entertained by the whites," Jefferson wrote in *Notes*, "ten thousand recollections, by the blacks, of the injuries they have sustained" rendered it essential that African Americans be colonized outside Virginia.[6] On that score, Jefferson was to be proven right, as racism remained a barrier against black advancement for more than a century after his death. Yet as St. George Tucker discovered through his correspondence with northern reformers, white animosity was not an insurmountable obstacle in passing legislation for gradual emancipation in Pennsylvania and New York. Virginia, of course, with its sizeable black minority, was hardly Quok Walker's Massachusetts, but in Jefferson's day New York City was demographically the second most black city in the United States, yet the burden of white racism there had not kept the New York Assembly from passing legislation for measured manumissions without resorting to colonization. Tucker was a realist enough to understand that Virginia planters would never permit an end to slavery unless they could somehow retain their black labor force. Under Tucker's plan, unlike Jefferson's vague scheme, "the earth cannot want [black] cultivators."[7]

This ambiguity was found also in the act that Jefferson's modern defenders regard as his crowning achievement of antislavery activism, the draft law that formed the basis for the Northwest Ordinance of 1787. As a member of the Articles Congress in 1783, Jefferson proposed a "Plan of Government for the Western Territory." The bill banned unfree labor in the entire western region, south as well as north of the Ohio River. But the ban was not to take effect until 1800. Slaves already worked the land in what would become Tennessee and Kentucky, and Jefferson's plan gave southern planters sixteen years to settle the West and lobby Congress to repeal the prohibition. The clause banning slavery failed; with one exception, every southern delegate to Congress voted to reject the exclusion, which failed by a single vote. The compromise finally reached in 1787 banned slavery only in the region north of the Ohio and east of the Mississippi River. After obtaining the Louisiana territory in 1803, Jefferson, then president, did nothing to prohibit slavery in the state, and the purchase treaty with France, negotiated in part by his protégé James Monroe, explicitly recognized the security of French and Spanish slave property in the region. As one historian has aptly observed, although Jefferson is widely regarded "as the father of exclusion in the Old Northwest," he is rarely "labeled as the father of slavery in Louisiana."[8]

If Jefferson was resolute on any point, it was regarding his fear that slave rebelliousness in the Caribbean might spread to the southern mainland. He was particularly concerned that "black crews & missionaries" from the French colony of Saint-Domingue could spread word of the uprising under Toussaint Louverture to Virginia. When Napoleon Bonaparte questioned what the American position would be should he attempt to re-enslave the

Haitian people, President Jefferson assured a French diplomat that "nothing would be more simple than to furnish your army and your fleet with everything and to starve out Toussaint." When the French invasion proved disastrous, Virginia Congressman John W. Eppes, Jefferson's son-in-law, pledged "the Treasury of the United States, that the Negro government should be destroyed," lest the contagion of liberty "bring immediate and horrible destruction on the fairest portion of America."[9]

Although the subsequent Louisiana Purchase is typically regarded as the crowning achievement of Jefferson's first term as president, the truth is that it was Louverture's black army that made the purchase possible. There was a crucial connection in Bonaparte's diplomacy that Jefferson utterly failed to perceive. The *premier consul* desired the Mississippi valley as a breadbasket to feed the re-enslaved Dominguans, all of whom were to be employed in producing sugar, not grains. Far from obtaining Louisiana by conciliating Bonaparte, Jefferson's tragic willingness to "starve out Toussaint" nearly cost the president his western prize. Had the French military succeeded in recapturing Saint-Domingue, Bonaparte would have refused to sell the mainland region. Only when his dream of a re-enslaved island lay in ashes did the French dictator discover that he no longer needed Louisiana. Jefferson's greatest accomplishment came not because of adroit diplomacy, but – just the reverse – because of the courage of half a million black rebels who refused to be subjugated.[10]

Late in life, Jefferson abandoned even his habit of procrastination on slavery. He responded to the Missouri debates, which began in 1819 when Congressman James Tallmadge drafted an amendment to the statehood bill that prohibited slavery in the new state. Although the crisis over the frontier prompted several Virginia legislators, including Jefferson's other son-in-law, Thomas Mann Randolph, to renew calls for gradual emancipation combined with removal to Haiti or Africa, the former president instead abandoned his previous desire to restrict slavery from the West. Jefferson began to champion the idea of allowing unfree labor to spread west, on the grounds that its dispersal would result in eventual extinction. "[D]iffusion over a greater surface would make [the slaves] individually happier," he insisted, "and proportionally facilitate the accomplishment of their emancipation, by dividing the burden on a greater number of coadjutors." Although James Madison also embraced diffusion theory, when the Marquis de Lafayette heard this news he regarded it as sad evidence that his old friend's once brilliant mind had dimmed with age.[11]

As John W. Eppes's incendiary rhetoric and the southern vote on territorial restriction in 1783 indicated, the slaveholding south was determined to maintain their bonded laborers. It is also true that, as most of Jefferson's biographers have observed, the president lacked both the constitutional power and the political clout to move decisively against slavery in the republic. But decisions made on his hilltop plantation of Monticello were quite a different matter, and there Jefferson was equally cautious. During the course of his long life, Jefferson freed only three slaves, or approximately 2 percent of his total bond population; upon his death, he freed five others through his will. All of those liberated were Hemings family members who were connected to Jefferson by kinship or marriage.[12]

In an effort to assuage his embattled conscience, Jefferson tried to convince himself that, tragic as slavery was, it was preferable to releasing his childlike black wards into a harsh world for which they were ill prepared. "[N]ever yet," he wrote, "could I find a black [who] had uttered a thought above the level of plain narration; never see even an elementary trait of painting or sculpture." Refusing to concede that his overworked, unpaid laborers had little opportunity to hone their artistic or intellectual skills, Jefferson precipitated a vicious circle of illogic. The alleged inferiority of blacks was used to justify their enslavement, yet the resulting inability of his weary slaves to comprehend "the investigations of Euclid" was in turn used to prove that they were indeed inferior beings.[13] As one historian has suggested, the sage of Monticello was "intellectually undone" by the racist arguments his guilt induced him to generate. Jefferson's determination to live off of the labor of others (including his own mixed-race relatives) forced him not only to abandon and qualify his belief in natural rights, but also to retreat into ancient distinctions between the races that tarnished his reputation as a man of science.[14]

In pondering the nature of humankind, Jefferson had two traditions to draw upon, one of them ancient and hierarchical, the other more recent and horizontal in nature. The former was the Great Chain of Being, a pyramid-like scale that indicated the God-given ranking of all creatures, from the lowest insect up to the deity. Africans, who formed a separate race in this model, were below Europeans but above great apes. More recent was the monogenist model of Swedish botanist Carolus Linnaeus, who argued instead that all of humankind was of a single biological species. But if the deeply religious Linnaeus could not accept the pre-Christian Chain of Being, he still affirmed that all creatures received their ranking from the hand of God. Despite his denial that Africans were of a different origin from Europeans (which would raise troubling questions about the biblical version of creation), the description of blacks in Linnaeus's *Systema naturae* (1758) owed much to Chain philosophy. *Homo Sapiens afer* (the African) was cunning yet indolent, phlegmatic yet "ruled by caprice." Given this common melding of the two traditions, it is not surprising that Jefferson drew from both. He filled his

Notes with animals listed by Linnaean categories, yet also wrote of humans being assigned a "rank in the scale of beings [by] their Creator."[15]

Although Linnaeus lacked a Darwinian sense of nature's adaptability, both his followers and adherents of the Chain of Being assumed a flexibility in nature. Influenced by the optimism of the Enlightenment, which found its way into both religious and scientific literature, western intellectuals began to argue that the natural order mandated few fixed categories. By altering the cultural environment, society might transform the Chain of Being into a ladder which humankind – indeed, all creatures – might ascend. Despite his Linnaean proclivities, Jefferson found this idea most attractive. "Animals transplanted into unfriendly climates, either change their nature and acquire new [de]fences against the new difficulties, in which they are placed," he observed, "or they multiply poorly and become extinct."[16] In his defense of the New World's indigenous inhabitants, who had been derided by Georges Louis Leclerc, the Comte de Buffon, and other French naturalists as backward and puny, Jefferson relied upon environmental theories of cultural change. "Before we condemn the Indians of this continent as wanting genius," he lectured, "we must consider that letters have not yet been introduced among them." Native Americans, he suggested, might well be compared to northern Europeans prior to the advancement of Roman culture. All that was required to "place [Natives] on a level with Whites" was time and technology. There was little doubt that "in body and mind" Native Americans were fully "equal to the Whiteman."[17]

When it came to slaves and Euclid, however, Jefferson refused to apply the same environmental principles. By arguing that Natives were little more than Europeans in rustic clothing, President Jefferson was able to pursue assimilationist policies that steadily reduced Indian land holdings. But if the same theory were used to explain his slaves' alleged lack of artistic or intellectual ability, planter Jefferson would be forced to abandon the only justification he had for their enslavement. Although he often promised European correspondents that he would "be delighted" to find that the "want of talents" in his slaves was due to "their degraded condition," his insistence that light-skinned Roman slaves had risen above their bondage contrasts sharply with his belief that "blacks, whether originally a distinct race, or made distinct by time and circumstances, are inferior to the whites in the endowments both of body and mind." In short, whether judged against the standards of monogenists like Linnaeus, who largely attributed distinctions among humans to chance and environment, or against the ideas of polygenist Chain theorists who postulated that the many separate races could all advance up the scale by altering their cultural world, Jefferson trailed far behind the prevailing philosophers of his day. His static, racialist views of African Americans belonged to an earlier century, before Enlightenment ideas of progress began to erode the hierarchical assumptions that informed older views of humankind.[18]

In considering African Americans, Jefferson recognized only one method for moving up in the "rank in the scale of beings [mandated by] their Creator": the body itself had to be transformed. When a young correspondent challenged Jefferson to explain how blacks might advance in society – assuming environmental change would not alter their position – Jefferson turned to mathematics. Following several pages of calculations, he concluded that when a "quarteroon" and a Caucasian produced children, "their offspring ... having less than ¼ pure negro blood, to wit ⅛ only, is no longer a mulatto." This "third" introduction of white genes "clears the blood." Octoroons, being seven-eighths Caucasian, were effectively purged of African blood and would improve their biological ranking. Should this child "be emancipated," Jefferson reasoned, "he becomes a free *white* man, and a citizen of the United States to all intents and purposes."[19]

Those more disposed than Jefferson to eradicate slavery thought little of this doctrine. St. George Tucker politely dissented from the theory, "as Mr. Jefferson seems to suppose, that the Africans are really an inferior race of mankind." Even more telling was the fact that, despite Jefferson's long membership in the American Philosophical Society, few if any members north of the Potomac accepted his extraordinary theory. Northern thinkers, whose science did not have to be twisted to fit their labor needs, were far more likely to adopt environmental explanations of human nature. Speaking to the Pennsylvania Abolition Society in early 1795, Jefferson's correspondent Benjamin Rush argued that slavery alone kept African Americans from producing a black Euclid. "By educating [blacks] in the higher branches of science, and in all the useful parts of learning," he insisted, "we shall ... confound the enemies of truth by evincing that the unhappy sons of Africa, in spite of the degrading influence of slavery, are in no wise inferior to the more fortunate inhabitants of Europe and America."[20]

To that, Jefferson would never agree. Although typically regarded as a disciple of the Enlightenment, not only was Jefferson out of step with prevailing scientific trends of the late eighteenth century, he also foreshadowed what would become the scientific racism of the late nineteenth century. While Charles Darwin's *Origin of the Species* (1859) undermined polygenist assumptions that Africans were a separate and inferior species, it also allowed for the possibility that, over time, blacks had evolved, or devolved, into a variety of humankind far below whites in intellectual ability. Although a staunch defender of polygenesis, Jefferson certainly would have agreed with an 1860s essay by Thomas H. Huxley, Darwin's leading British advocate. "[N]o rational man, cognizant of the facts, could deny that the Negro was inherently inferior," Huxley insisted. Wishful thinking alone led abolitionists to suggest that blacks could "compete successfully with [their] bigger-brained and smaller-jawed rival, in a contest which is to be carried on by thoughts and not by bites."[21]

Charitable scholars are inclined to dismiss Jefferson's objectionable racial views on the grounds that they were mere speculation. But Jefferson's scientific notions were more than abstract theory; the pattern suggests that he applied his unusual blood test to his mixed-race kinsmen, the Hemings family, six of whom were the quadroon offspring of his father-in-law, John Wayles, and Betty Hemings, a "bright" enslaved mulatto. Only two of Betty's quadroon children were freed by their brother-in-law; the 1801 suicide of one of them, James, evidently convinced Jefferson that they were as yet too low on the human scale to make their way as free citizens.[22] Altogether different was the treatment accorded to the six octoroon children born to Betty's daughter Sally, Jefferson's sister-in-law and almost certainly his "plantation wife" following the death of his white wife Martha Wayles Skelton. Of Sally's four children who lived to maturity, all were freed and three passed into the white community, thereby demonstrating the absurdity of their father's scientific categories; one of them, Eston Hemings, later adopted the surname of Jefferson. Unfortunately, Eston's mother retained too much of her African heritage to merit autonomy under Jefferson's precise racialist distinctions. Although Sally was a "handsome," light-skinned "quarteroon" with "long straight hair," she retained at least some "negro blood" and so, lover or not, in her master's eyes remained an inferior being, far below him on God's scale. Sally Hemings remained a bondwoman until after her master's death, and it fell to her new owner, Jefferson's daughter Martha Randolph, to free her enslaved aunt. The 1830 census indicated that the household of her son Eston Hemings included a free "white female" between the ages of "50 & 60"; this was almost certainly Sally. Madison Hemings later recalled that he and Eston "rented a house and took mother to live with us, until her death" in 1835.[23]

By stubbornly insisting that the problem of slavery in Virginia defied solution, Jefferson was able to then deny any personal responsibility in the quandary, despite his personal involvement in the institution on his hilltop. "[W]e have the wolf by the ear," he wrote in 1820, "and we can neither hold him, nor safely let him go." By 1804, however, every state north of Maryland either had freed its bond population outright, or had set out on a course of gradual emancipation. Virginia had a far larger slave population than did New York, but statesmen like St. George Tucker thought wise leadership could resolve this dilemma, whereas Jefferson stubbornly avoided every possible action or public statement on the issue. Nor was his private behavior any more pronounced. George Washington freed his slaves in his will, and Jefferson's distant cousin John Randolph of Roanoke not only did likewise, he set aside money for the purchase of land for them. Jefferson's enormous debts may have precluded him from doing the same, but the paltry number of slaves he manumitted during his lifetime suggests he had no intentions of doing so under any circumstances.[24]

NOTES

1. Jefferson, *Autobiography*, in *Thomas Jefferson: Writings*, ed. Merrill D. Peterson (New York: Library of America, 1984), 22.
2. TJ to Edward Coles, August 25, 1814, in *Thomas Jefferson: Writings*, 1343–6.
3. Ibid.
4. Noble E. Cunningham, *In Pursuit of Reason; The Life of Thomas Jefferson* (Baton Rouge: Louisiana State University Press, 1987), 12–13.
5. Lucia Stanton, "Jefferson and His Slaves," in *Jeffersonian Legacies*, ed. Peter S. Onuf (Charlottesville: University Press of Virginia, 2003), 174.
6. Jefferson, *Notes on the State of Virginia*, in *Thomas Jefferson: Writings*, 264.
7. St. George Tucker, *A Dissertation on Slavery with a Proposal for the Gradual Abolition of It in the State of Virginia* (Philadelphia: Mathew Carey, 1796), 93–103.
8. Robert McColley, *Slavery and Jeffersonian Virginia* (Urbana: University of Illinois Press, 1964), 125.
9. Douglas R. Egerton, *Gabriel's Rebellion: The Virginia Slave Conspiracies of 1800 and 1802* (Chapel Hill: University of North Carolina Press, 1993), 170–1.
10. Robert L. Paquette, "Revolutionary Saint Domingue," in *A Turbulent Time: The French Revolution and the Greater Caribbean*, ed. David Barry Gaspar and David Patrick Geggus (Bloomington: Indiana University Press, 1997), 220.
11. John C. Miller, *The Wolf By the Ears: Thomas Jefferson and Slavery* (New York: Free Press, 1977), 234–42, 273.
12. Jefferson, Will, March 17, 1826, in *Jefferson at Monticello*, ed. James A. Bear, Jr. (Charlottesville: University of Virginia Press, 1967), 122.
13. Jefferson, *Notes*, 266.
14. Michael Zuckerman, "The Color of Counter-Revolution," in *The Languages of Revolution*, ed. Loretta Valtz Mannucci (Milan: University of Milan Press, 1989), 83.
15. Donald R. Wright, *African Americans in the Colonial Era: From African Origins Through the American Revolution*, 2nd edn. (Arlington Heights: Harlan Davidson, 2000), 144–5; Jefferson, *Notes*, 269–70.
16. Jefferson, *Notes*, 171.
17. Ibid., 189; TJ to François Jean de Beauvoir, June 7, 1785, in *Papers of Thomas Jefferson*, ed. Julian P. Boyd *et al.* (Princeton: Princeton University Press, 1950–), VIII: 185–6.
18. TJ to Marie Jean Antoine Condorcet, August 30, 1791, in *Papers*, XXII: 98–9; Jefferson, *Notes*, 269–70.
19. TJ to Francis C. Grey, March 4, 1815, in *The Writings of Thomas Jefferson*, ed. Andrew A. Lipscomb and Albert Ellery Bergh, 20 vols. (Washington, DC: Thomas Jefferson Memorial Association, 1903), VI: 436–9.

20. Tucker, *Dissertation on Slavery*, 87; Benjamin Rush to the Pennsylvania Abolition Society, January 14, 1795, in *Letters of Benjamin Rush*, ed. L. H. Butterfield, vol. II (Princeton: Princeton University Press, 1951): 758.

21. George M. Fredrickson, *The Black Image in the White Mind: The Debate on Afro-American Character and Destiny, 1817–1914* (New York: Harper and Row, 1971), 232–5.

22. Isaac Jefferson, "Memoirs of a Monticello Slave," in *Jefferson at Monticello*, 4; Edwin Morris Betts (ed.), *Thomas Jefferson's Farm Book Commentary and Relevant Extracts from Other Writings* (Princeton: Princeton University Press for the American Philosophical Society, 1953), 15–16.

23. "Reminiscences of Madison Hemings," in Fawn M. Brodie, *Thomas Jefferson: An Intimate History* (New York: Norton, 1974), 475.

24. TJ to John Holmes, April 22, 1820, in *Thomas Jefferson: Writings*, 1434.

6

LUCIA STANTON

Jefferson's people: slavery at Monticello

Thomas Jefferson became a slaveholder by inheritance. From the summer of 1757, when his father wrote "I Give & Bequeath to my son Thomas my mulattoe Fellow Sawney," he was entangled in an unjust legal and economic system that he was unable to escape or abolish. When he turned 21, in 1764, he gained legal title to about 30 human beings from his father's estate. Ten years later he received 135 more after the death of his father-in-law, John Wayles. From 1770 Jefferson lived on the top of an 867-foot mountain in Albemarle County, directing the operations of a tract that grew from almost 3,000 to over 5,000 acres. John Wayles's death transformed Monticello from an ordinary tobacco plantation to the central nerve center of a far-flung economic enterprise. After the division of Wayles's estate in January 1774, Jefferson had tripled his real property, to 14,000 acres of land and 187 human beings. He now owned four major plantations in Virginia's Piedmont: Monticello, Elk Hill and Willis Creek 40 miles to the east, and Poplar Forest 90 miles to the southwest. A rather well-to-do planter had instantly become one of the wealthiest men in the colony.[1] Over his long life, during which he purchased fewer than 20 slaves, Jefferson considered himself the owner of more than 600 people – "those whom fortune has thrown on our hands."[2]

1774–1794

In April, 1782, a party of Frenchmen rode up to Monticello for a three-day visit. The Chevalier de Chastellux recorded his impressions of his host, a fellow philosophe who had "placed his mind, like his house, on a lofty height, whence he might contemplate the whole universe." Their conversation ranged widely, over literary and scientific topics, and particularly American natural history, which Jefferson was then pondering as he wrote what became his *Notes on the State of Virginia*. The epithets Chastellux used to describe Jefferson – "Musician, Draftsman, Surveyor, Astronomer, Natural Philosopher,

83

Jurist, and Statesman" – did not include the word "Farmer."[3] Chastellux was shown Jefferson's herd of tame deer, but there is nothing in his account about corn or tobacco or enslaved laborers at work in the fields. From his eminence, Jefferson kept his eyes focused on the universe rather than on the "slovenly business of tobacco making" taking place at his feet. In these early years, he was in the midst of re-creating the ideal world he saw in the paeans to country life of Horace and Virgil. He designed his house and its surroundings with the villas of the Romans in mind. He looked down on a landscape of literary allusions, its features bearing names he had given them to evoke ancient landscapes. Unlike many Virginia plantation owners who prided themselves on being clever "crop-masters," Jefferson was so little involved in the tobacco-making process itself that he could write, after more than thirty years in the business, that "I never saw a leaf of my tob[acc]o. packed in my life."[4]

In January, 1774, however, the Wayles inheritance had compelled Jefferson to pay attention to plantation management. In order to organize a transition he began what he called his "Farm-book," making three lists of men, women, and children and their locations: his 52 "proper slaves"; the 135 individuals inherited from Wayles; and the combined total of 187 people, many now in new locations.[5] After these arrangements were complete, Jefferson put the Farm Book away for the next twenty years, opening it very occasionally to note the births and deaths of slaves and the pedigrees of horses. Above the fray, he left the running of his plantations to a team of managers, including overseers at each place and intermediate functionaries – stewards and superintendents – to further protect him from the daily necessity of making enslaved workers raise a staple crop.

In this period Jefferson struggled, along with his more enlightened southern peers, to make ownership of humans compatible with new ideas and institutions, preserving conscience and principle by increasing the social distance between master and slave. He invariably used diminutives when referring to individuals: Edward became Ned, and Frances became Fanny. His views on racial inferiority pushed the blacks around him down the "scale of beings." Slaves were functionally children, as he implied in a letter of 1789: "To give liberty to, or rather, to abandon persons whose habits have been formed in slavery is like abandoning children."[6] He could thus see himself as the benevolent steward of the African Americans to whom he was bound in a relationship of mutual dependency and obligation, the "father" of those who needed his care as well as control. In 1776, he made a census of the "Number of souls in my family," totaling 117, including his wife and daughter, his overseers, hired workmen, and their families, and 83 enslaved African Americans.[7] Here Jefferson fit the traditional patriarchal pattern, using "family" in its most ancient usage, meaning the dependents of the head of a household.

In the hands-off plantation management of the 1770s, when he exercised less direct authority over his slaves, fealty was a particular concern. His 1771 plan for a burial ground includes a pyramid of rough stone on the grave of "a favorite and faithful servant," inscribed with stanzas from English poet William Shenstone's "Inscription for an African Slave." Might Jefferson have had in mind Jupiter, still very much alive, his personal servant and constant shadow on journeys throughout Virginia – a man exactly his own age who had grown up with him at Shadwell? On one occasion when this "trusty servant" abandoned his deferential conduct, Jefferson erupted in a display of anger his family had never seen before.[8] Jefferson even devised tests for the faithfulness of his slaves. In 1774 he determined to keep a tally of his bottles of Jamaica rum in order to "try the fidelity of Martin," his new butler. This was Martin Hemings, part of a family often described as "faithful" or "trusty." Hemings's mother, Elizabeth (Betty) Hemings, and her children had been an important element of Martha Wayles Jefferson's domestic household as she grew up. After the death of John Wayles, said to be the father of at least six of her children, Elizabeth Hemings and her family came to Monticello and filled virtually all the serving positions in the house. Over the next half-century, more than eighty of her descendants would live in slavery at Monticello. The favored status of this family is illustrated by the unusual freedom of movement Jefferson granted to her sons in this period. When not required at Monticello, Robert, James, and Martin Hemings were "at liberty" to hire themselves out to other masters and keep their wages for themselves.[9]

The Wayles inheritance marked the beginning of Jefferson's practice of shifting individuals and families among his different plantations, according to his operational needs. In the 1770s he concentrated tradesmen at Monticello, transferring almost fifty Wayles slaves there, including carpenters, blacksmiths, watermen, and a shoemaker. He then established his first blacksmith shop, hiring a free man to operate it, share its profits, and teach Barnaby, a 14-year-old smith brought from a Wayles plantation in Cumberland County. Over the next fifty years, Jefferson often engaged skilled craftsmen to stay at Monticello long enough to train enslaved men and women in their trades, making the mountaintop the site of skills in metal- and woodworking that were exceptional for its time and place.

Despite his aversion to selling human beings, Jefferson was forced to put both land and slaves up for sale in an effort to pay his enormous debts to several British mercantile firms. (By the time of the Revolution, these debts totaled more than £5,000 – three-quarters of it derived from the Wayles inheritance.) Because of revolutionary war inflation, Jefferson's sale of

10,000 acres of inherited lands netted him, as his daughter recalled, only enough money to buy a great coat. Consequently, at auctions in 1785, 1792, and 1793, he sold over seventy men, women, and children – none of them from Monticello.[10] Spouses were not separated in these sales, nor were children 12 or under sold away from their parents. Jefferson additionally "alienated" almost eighty more people by gifts to family members. There were a few individual sales as well. Jefferson sold several young men with a propensity for running away, in accordance with his policy of ridding his domain of disruptive elements. He sold Robin soon after he returned to Monticello, one of the few survivors among more than twenty enslaved people who sought freedom with the British army in 1781. Nineteen men, women, and children – several whole families – left Jefferson's Elk Hill and Willis Creek plantations, while Robin, Barnaby the blacksmith, and two other young men escaped from Monticello. Most of these bids for freedom ended tragically, in death from disease contracted in the British camps.

The Revolution left an indelible mark on Monticello's residents, and its events provided stories that descended through generations of families, both free and enslaved. In light of the war's outcome, it is not surprising that in African American families all the attempts to escape slavery were forgotten. Their principal stories focus instead on the symbiotic relationship between their ancestors and the master of Monticello, with varying tales of enslaved people helping Jefferson escape from British dragoons or saving his silver. Jefferson's descendants told the same stories as evidence of a benevolent master and loyal slaves, but for the descendants of the blacksmiths, grooms, and household servants who played the major roles in the revolutionary drama, the stories honored the ingenuity and indispensability of their ancestors.

After the death of his wife in 1782, Jefferson found solace in a return to public service, turning over all his plantation operations to the management of his neighbor Nicholas Lewis. Far from his mountaintop in France, New York, and Philadelphia, Jefferson considered the fate of his slaves. While slavery continued to be the law in Virginia, he did not intend to free them, but his financial problems compelled him to consider selling or leasing them. Although they would be subject to "ill usage" in both cases, he preferred hiring them out, which would at least be temporary and would, in his view, "end in their happiness."[11] He also explored a kind of share-cropping scheme by which he would bring industrious German farmers to Virginia and establish them on 50-acre plots "intermingled" with his slaves, whose children would thus be brought up "in habits of property and foresight."[12] Jefferson never pursued this chimerical project farther than some personal interviews on his travels in Germany in 1788. Instead, he directed his thoughts to reforming rather than ending the institution of slavery, and explored ways to improve the condition of the enslaved members of his own "family," by placing them "on an easier footing."[13] As he wrote in late 1793, when he was about to be "liberated from the hated occupations of politics," "I have my house to build, my feilds to form, and to watch for the happiness of those who labor for mine."[14]

1794–1809

In the last days of June, 1796, the Duc de La Rochefoucauld-Liancourt arrived at Monticello in the midst of the wheat harvest, noting that even "the scorching heat of the sun" did not prevent Jefferson's daily presence. This was a new Jefferson and a new era on the Monticello plantation. For the first time, he was personally involved in its day-to-day operations, constantly in the fields, realigning their boundaries, weighing the grain they produced, or testing new machinery (including his own improved plow). This is the period – three years of retirement from 1794 to 1797 – in which he called himself "the most ardent and active farmer in the state."[15]

As one who lived the Enlightenment every day of his life, Jefferson pursued the improvement of the human condition as a passionate Baconian, gathering information with the aid of his watch, ruler, and scales. He applied his measuring mind to plantation projects in a search for economy and efficiency. He enveloped his unwieldy operations in the consoling security of mathematical truths, driving a further psychological wedge between himself and the enslaved people living so close to him. His many monumental earth-moving projects, in particular, led to a lifetime of time-and-motion calculations: how many cubical yards could Phill dig and carry in a twelve-hour day or what was the daily progress of "3. hands" carving a road through the woods of Monticello?[16] At the same time that Jefferson applied a geometric grid of field boundaries to the irregular features of his mountain, he imposed Enlightenment ideals of economy and order on the people who lived there. He acquired a Chinese gong to broadcast the measurement of time across the whole plantation. His plan for a more efficient harvest in 1796 literally turned his slaves into parts of a machine. It called for assembling the necessary equipment, assigned people of all ages to a variety of tasks, and devised a means for having ever-sharp scythe blades so the mowers could cut the wheat "constantly." "In this way," he wrote of this combination of tools, carts and wagons, mules and oxen, and almost sixty human beings, "the whole machine would move in exact equilibrio, no part of the force could be lessened without retarding the whole, nor increased without a waste of force."[17]

While Jefferson's mathematical calculations and mechanistic planning reduced enslaved men, women, and children to cogs in the many wheels of a plantation machine, he remained conscious of their humanity, not forgetting to watch for their "happiness." At this time he held 155 slaves, one-third of them living on his Poplar Forest plantation. What did he actually do to improve their lives and place them "on the comfortable footing of the laborers of other countries?"[18] The food and clothing allotments he began to record in December 1794 were not notably different from those on other plantations in the upper South; his meat allowance was even rather stingy. Everyone, regardless of age, received a weekly peck of cornmeal. Adults were given four salt herring and half a pound of salt pork or pickled beef each week; children received smaller amounts of meat and fish according to age. The clothing allowance was a summer and winter outfit each year, with shoes for all over the age of 10 and, every three years, a blanket.

Anxious to minimize "hard driving" and the use of the whip, Jefferson focused most of his attention on the conditions of labor. "My first wish is that the labourers may be well treated," he wrote in 1792, and he soon began to look outside Virginia for overseers who would be less severe than local men without sacrificing productivity. He fixed on Cecil County, Maryland, where the farmers used both free and enslaved labor and thus, in Jefferson's opinion, would "understand the management of negroes on a rational and humane plan."[19] For reasons that can no longer be recovered, this experiment with overseers from farther north failed and was never repeated. In 1796, when a newly appointed overseer did not appear, Jefferson promoted the best farmer at Monticello, his 66-year-old head man, George Granger (Great George), to the highest position, the only enslaved man among almost fifty overseers hired over the years. Clearly struggling to achieve Jefferson's dual goals, Granger, "steady and industrious," made outstanding tobacco crops but was reportedly unable to "command his force" and "needs to be supported."[20]

Jefferson returned to free Virginia overseers, trying to avoid those with reputations for severity.[21] But despite his instructions to minimize corporal punishment, the whip was never banished from his fields, and some overseers gained reputations for cruelty. Disillusioned with his efforts to find managers who could unite both productivity and humanity, he declared in 1799, "I find I am not fit to be a farmer with the kind of labour we have."[22] By then he had leased out his cultivated lands and the laborers who worked them and did not take them back into his control for ten years. He gave long leases for the fields but leased the field hands and their families only from year to year, "so that I may take them away if ill treated."[23] The men and women who plowed and hoed his land would never be the "chosen people of God" of Jefferson's agrarian ideal.[24]

Jefferson was both more comfortable and more successful with another segment of the enslaved labor force. He could personally superintend the work of his tradesmen, testing methods of management on humanitarian principles that were being applied in reformed institutions of discipline and control, such as schools, factories, and prisons, on both sides of the Atlantic. In Philadelphia, Jefferson had seen the transforming effects of a new regime at the Walnut Street Prison, where corporal punishment was dispensed with and prisoners were treated as potentially useful members of society – as moral and rational human beings, capable of reformation. Jefferson applied these same principles in a new enterprise at Monticello, a nail-making factory, in which young enslaved boys aged 10 to 16 made hand-forged nails of all sizes. In the first years of its existence, he supervised its operations, visiting it daily to weigh the iron nailrod supplied to each nailer as well as the nails he produced. In this way he could monitor the efficiency as well as the productivity of the workers, by calculating how many pounds of iron they "wasted" in the nail-making process.

A dozen teenaged boys, cooped up in a smoky shop, carrying out a boring and repetitive task for ten to fourteen hours a day, were a management challenge. "He animates them by rewards and distinctions," the Duc de Liancourt noted.[25] Jefferson built esprit de corps through special food and clothing rations and improved performance by stimulating competition in a race for efficiency. He cautioned his overseer to refrain from using the whip in the nailery except "in extremities," describing the key to his mode of "government" as "the stimulus of character" rather than "the degrading motive of fear." When urging restraint in disciplining the nailers, he wrote that "it would destroy their value in my estimation to degrade them in their own eyes by the whip."[26] The youth of the nailers was an important factor. When Jefferson expanded the operation in its third year, instead of bringing older boys from the fields to the shop, he purchased two 11-year-old boys and moved four others to Monticello from Poplar Forest.

Jefferson used character-building management techniques with his older tradesmen as well, encouraging a consciousness of measurable achievement and offering financial incentives for the first time. He paid Frank, the charcoalburner, according to how efficiently he burned his coal kiln and suggested to his son-in-law John Wayles Eppes that he have the wood for his own charcoalburner corded, "in order to excite him to an emulation in burning it well."[27] Jefferson inaugurated an actual profit-sharing arrangement with the enslaved managers in the nailery and he allowed his carpenters, smiths, and charcoalburners an unusual freedom from supervision.[28] This worried his son-in-law Thomas Mann Randolph, who expressed surprise at the results: "The thorough confidence you place in the companies of tradesmen is less abused than I expected but I am still convinced that being under no command whatever they will become idle and dissipated tho' I am clear that it confirms them in honesty."[29] (He and Jefferson usually used "honesty" in its broad meaning encompassing virtue, integrity, and morality.) Randolph soon adopted the same rational management as his father-in-law, dismissing the whip from his plantation and never physically punishing slaves who showed signs of "a manly and moral character." Most overseers, in Randolph's view, "could not understand the value of character in a slave, and concluded that fear would be safer security for good conduct than any determination to do right."[30]

The character traits Jefferson wanted to instill were not so very different from those he sought in his free workmen or recommended to youthful free Virginians: honesty, industry, and sobriety in the former, and "honesty, knowledge, and industry" for the latter.[31] Since the enslaved workmen were denied access to both alcohol and education, Jefferson's main goals for them were industry and honesty, the core virtue in his system of morality. These qualities, combined with the absolute subordination that his plantation law required, contributed to his own profit and tranquillity. Many of the nailers and tradesmen fulfilled his objectives, became "trusty servants," and were placed in charge of his house, stables, garden, and shops.

Jefferson's innovative management methods, with unaccustomed autonomy for some men, coincided with a new agricultural regime that led to decreased superintendence. On his retirement to Monticello in 1794, he launched a reforming crusade against the ravages of soil exhaustion. Tobacco was temporarily banished, replaced by wheat as the cash crop. The continuous monotonous labor of tobacco culture was superseded by the varied routine of a mixed grain and livestock operation, requiring more vehicles, draft animals, and complicated machinery. This more diversified operation called for a wide range of tasks spread widely across the plantation at different sites of activity. A single overseer could no longer closely monitor all the laborers in his charge.

The transition from tobacco to wheat culture, which demanded more land for cultivation, affected the lives of the enslaved as well as their work. Archaeological excavations at Monticello have revealed that, in the 1790s, housing patterns were transformed, as slave cabins were moved from clustered quarters near the overseer's house to scattered sites on the fringes of cultivated lands. By this time the dwellings themselves were also different. The large multi-family cabins of the 1770s had been replaced by smaller single-family dwellings. The desire of Monticello's African Americans to live independently – not just agricultural reform – undoubtedly contributed to the changes. Jefferson's policy of having houses built for enslaved women once they had children was probably active well before his statement to an overseer in 1818: "Maria having now a child, I promised her a house to be built this winter."[32]

The top of Monticello mountain was also transformed in the 1790s, becoming a construction site – as the main house was enlarged and remodeled – and a bustling village with an international flavor. Housejoiners from northern Ireland, a German plasterer, a gardener from Scotland, a blacksmith from Philadelphia, and other craftsmen from beyond Virginia lived and worked on Mulberry Row. Enslaved men John Hemmings,[33] son of Elizabeth Hemings, and Lewis assisted and learned from the joiners, carrying on the notable work of the joinery after their departure. Three other members of the Hemings family – Wormley Hughes, Joseph Fossett, and Burwell Colbert – received training in gardening, blacksmithing, and painting and glazing. With a near-monopoly on the household and most important trades positions, the members of this family were a kind of caste apart. Their occupations gave them the greatest access to money – through tips and work incentives – and their social separateness was reflected in their marriage choices. None of Elizabeth Hemings's twelve children, and only two of her grandchildren, found spouses at Monticello. Her grandsons Joseph Fossett and Wormley Hughes married into Monticello families, but other family members found wives in the household staffs of neighboring plantations and husbands in the local community, both free black and white.

The Duc de Liancourt and other Monticello visitors saw enslaved people on the mountaintop who "neither in point of colour nor featurs, shewed the least trace of their original descent."[34] Elizabeth Hemings's daughters Mary, Betty, and Sally entered into long-term relationships with white men, similar to the probable one between their mother and John Wayles. In September, 1802, in an article in a Richmond newspaper, James Thomson Callender blew the lid off a simmering story that spread across the country and down through decades of controversy. President Jefferson "keeps, and for many years past has kept, as his concubine, one of his own slaves. Her name is SALLY."[35] Jefferson and his family members were publicly silent on the issue, while Sally Hemings's son Madison, in 1873, stated that Jefferson was his father and had promised his mother that her children would all become free at the age of 21. Privately, Jefferson's grandson Thomas Jefferson Randolph admitted that the light-skinned children of Sally Hemings and her sister Betty Brown resembled his grandfather, but he insisted that Jefferson's Carr nephews were their fathers.[36] While the father of Betty Brown's children is not certainly known, genetic testing in 1998 ruled out the Carr brothers in the case of the paternity of Sally Hemings's youngest son, Eston, indicating that a male Jefferson was his father. Science shifted opinion from doubt to qualified belief, and most historians of the period now acknowledge that Thomas Jefferson was the father of Hemings's known children, born from 1795 to 1807. While Jefferson's paternity is not proven, the preponderance of evidence – drawn from a combination of scientific and statistical evidence, the documentary record, and Hemings family oral history – strongly favors the existence of a long-term connection that produced at least six children. Whoever the fathers, black–white sexual encounters seem to have been quite common at Monticello. Skin tone allowed at least four slaves to vanish into free society unpursued. As Jefferson's granddaughter recalled, "their whereabouts was perfectly known but they were left to themselves – for they were white enough to pass for white."[37]

The comings and goings of Jefferson, the Hemings men, and the free and enslaved men hired for Jefferson's major plantation and building projects had a destabilizing effect on the Monticello community. Five children of Elizabeth Hemings left the mountain between 1792 and 1796. When Jefferson left for France in the 1780s, her oldest daughter, Mary, had been leased out to local white merchant Thomas Bell, who became her common-law husband, purchased her freedom, and acknowledged paternity of their children. Martin Hemings had a falling-out with Jefferson and left Monticello, his fate unknown. After accompanying Jefferson to Paris to train as a chef, James Hemings used his skills and knowledge of a wider world to achieve freedom soon after his return to Virginia. Jefferson reluctantly emancipated him after he passed his knowledge on to his brother Peter. Jefferson sold Thenia Hemings to James Monroe, possibly at her wish and to unite her with her husband. In the course of his own travels, Robert Hemings found a wife, Dolly, and persuaded her owner to help him purchase his own freedom. Both Jefferson's and Hemings's responses to this transaction reveal the striking distortions slavery produced in the feelings of the humans locked in its grip. Jefferson was angry at Hemings for behavior he considered disloyal and ungrateful, while Hemings was, according to Jefferson's daughter, "so deeply impressed with a sense of his ingratitude as to be rendered quite unhappy by it but he could not prevail upon himself to give up his wife and child."[38] Jefferson expected loyalty in exchange for the "indulgences" he had granted Hemings, and could not understand that a slave might choose freedom and family over fidelity to the master.

The dynamics of the African American community shifted because of the need for extra manpower for Jefferson's most substantial undertakings, pursued while he was absent in Philadelphia and Washington as vice president and president: completion of the main house, construction of a canal and two grain mills, the leveling of an immense terraced vegetable garden, and continued road-building. From 1795 to 1809 he hired up to sixteen enslaved men a year, some from as far away as Caroline and Spotsylvania counties. This not only accentuated the imbalance of the ratio of males to females but led to unrest and frequent runaways. Even among the tradesmen, all was not tranquil with Jefferson rarely present to supervise them personally. The nail boys, growing older and more unruly, were too ungovernable for a blacksmith from Philadelphia. In 1803 the nailery erupted in violence, when Cary brought his hammer down on the head of Brown Colbert and nearly killed him. Violation of plantation rule, or "delinquency," inevitably led to separation. In this extreme case, Jefferson ordered not mere removal from Monticello but sale so far away that it would be "as if [Cary] were put out of the way by death." "So distant an exile" for the offender would be an exemplary punishment "in terrorem to others, in order to maintain the police so rigorously necessary among the nailboys."[39]

Since the time of the Revolution, there had been few recorded attempts to escape from slavery at Monticello, although there were no doubt cases of temporary absences not intended as flights to permanent freedom. During Jefferson's presidency, however, besides the hired men who tried to run back to their homes and families, two nailers and a blacksmith left the mountain without permission. The 18-year-old Kit was quickly apprehended and, as quickly, sold. The 22-year-old James Hubbard headed north in 1805, almost reaching Washington, DC. After several months in Fairfax County jail, he was taken back to Monticello and given a second chance. Joseph Fossett's concern was family, not freedom. He made his way to Washington because of an urgent need to see his wife, Edith, who had been transferred there to learn the art of French cookery in the presidential kitchen. Easily captured, he was brought back to Monticello, where he resumed his work in the blacksmith shop and was eventually reunited with his wife.

1809–1826

In the middle of November, 1813, Edward Ross rode over the Monticello plantation with Jefferson, who showed him "all his Mills, farms, Machineries, Curiosities &c. &c."[40] It was the mills and "Machineries" that dominated Jefferson's daily horseback rides of plantation superintendence. He had left the presidency in the hands of James Madison in 1809 and returned to Monticello, at last "free to follow the pursuits of my choice."[41] He took the farms back into his control, but, except for a few short spells of redesigning fields and drawing up rotation plans, again lost interest in the production of his crops and increasingly turned agricultural matters over to his grandson Thomas Jefferson Randolph. Madison Hemings recalled the man he knew as his father as having "but little taste or care for agricultural pursuits" in this period: "It was his mechanics he seemed mostly to direct, and in their operations he took great interest." An apprentice carpenter, Hemings would have experienced this interest directly, as would his sister Harriet Hemings, who worked in the textile shop that Jefferson had begun to enlarge and mechanize in 1811. In the "factory" were spinning jennies with up to forty-eight spindles, looms with fly shuttles, and carding machines. Jefferson drew up complex charts of the daily tasks of his spinners and weavers, calibrating the ounces of cotton or yards of shirting they had to spin or weave according to the length of the working day, which grew from nine hours in midwinter to fourteen hours in high summer.[42]

In 1811, Jefferson designed a mill complex with a single waterwheel to drive a sawmill, gristmill and grain elevators, threshing machine and winnowers, and a hemp beater. Although he had leased out his mill at Shadwell, he retained control of the coopers' shops there. Seeking to increase the number of flour barrels to sell to the tenants of his larger grain mill, he encouraged his coopers, Barnaby Gillette and Nace, by allowing them to keep one barrel out of every thirty-one they made, to sell for their own profit. Jefferson's interest in stimulating efficiency was reflected in a new term – "premium" – he gave to the payments to his current charcoalburner, David Hern.

Designing a mechanical method of beating hemp solved a problem that had caused Jefferson to stop cultivating this staple in cloth production, because the laborious process was "so much complained of by our laborers."[43] There is plenty of evidence that Monticello's African Americans made effective use of the strategies of complaint, persistent petitioning, and artful negotiation, especially in appeals for the preservation of family integrity. Philip Hubbard ran away from Poplar Forest to Monticello to complain that the overseer was preventing him from being with his wife. Jefferson interceded to unite the spouses, at the same time granting Hubbard another favor for which he had been "long petitioning" – moving from one quarter to another, where the rest of his family lived.[44] Moses Hern, a blacksmith, persisted for years in asking Jefferson to buy his wife, Mary, a slave on another plantation. Finally, in 1807, when Mary's owner was about to remove to Kentucky, Jefferson reluctantly agreed to buy her and her sons, mentioning his strong desire "to make all practicable sacrifices to keep man and wife together who have imprudently married out of their respective families" – if the purchase could be made "with convenience."[45] In several other cases, Jefferson had to make inconvenient purchases or sales because workmen, overseers, or neighbors were about to leave the area with their enslaved property, who had "imprudently" married men and women at Monticello.

Of the almost thirty married couples that can be followed in Jefferson's Monticello records, all but one remained together until the death of one partner or the end of recordkeeping at Jefferson's death. Enduring unions were the rule at Monticello, a situation Jefferson fostered for the sake of the smooth and profitable running of his operation, as well as an eye to the bottom line. As he wrote on more than one occasion, "a child raised every 2. years is of more profit than the crop of the best laboring man." He offered material incentives – pots and mattress covers – to women who found husbands "at home," considering his slaves "worth a great deal more in that case than when they have husbands and wives abroad."[46] Despite his wishes, the number of "abroad" marriages was continually on the rise, from about one-third of adults under 45 in the 1780s to almost two-thirds by the 1820s.

The work of enslaved family members was not over after their long days in the shops and the fields. They supplemented their rations and gained further access to money through work they did "in their own time." Virtually all had poultry yards, selling eggs and chickens to Jefferson's household and probably in the neighborhood. At night or on Sundays, many worked in their gardens, producing a wide variety of vegetables for Jefferson's table as well as their own. Bagwell Granger, a farm laborer, was particularly enterprising, fishing in the Rivanna River, trapping animals, growing a crop of hay as well as vegetables, and – when Jefferson inaugurated a brewing operation – cultivating a hop garden.

When they could return to their own world of nights, Sundays, and occasional holidays, Monticello's African Americans participated in a flourishing cultural and spiritual life far removed from Jefferson's observation or interference. There is evidence of both thriving Christian and African religious beliefs. John Hemmings, who was literate, and his wife, Priscilla, held prayer meetings in their cabin on Mulberry Row, while the Granger family consulted a black conjurer about their worries and ailments. A number of African Americans aspired to literacy. Two former Monticello slaves recalled learning their letters from Jefferson's grandchildren. Unlike many slaveholders, Jefferson did not try to prevent his slaves from learning to read (although there is evidence he frowned on the second stage of the learning process, writing), but he apparently took no active part in providing them with an education. As he wrote in 1808, "letters are not the first, but the last step in the progression from barbarism to civilisation."[47]

In these final years Jefferson held more slaves than at any time since the 1780s, with a high of 230 in 1817, 140 of them living at Monticello. His most articulated thoughts on his role as a slaveholder are found in this period, when he was a magnet for letters, books, and personal appeals from authors and antislavery crusaders. In 1811 he wrote of "the moral duties which [the master] owes to the slave, in return for the benefits of his service, that is to say, of food, cloathing, care in sickness, & maintenance under age & disability, so as to make him in fact as comfortable, & more secure than the laboring man in most parts of the world."[48] A slave, as both property and human being, embodied a harsh duality in which Jefferson was able to find a kind of consolation. Steeped in the moral sense philosophy of Francis Hutcheson and other Enlightenment writers, he was certain that the "soundly calculated" self-interest of individuals (and nations) was entirely compatible with moral duties. "So invariably do the laws of nature create our duties and interests," he wrote in 1804, "that when they seem to be at variance, we ought to suspect some fallacy in our reasonings."[49] Jefferson's constant recourse to the interest–duty principle, then being applied to various institutions on both sides of the Atlantic, is revealed in letters like that to his Poplar Forest steward in 1819. He wrote that "moral as well as interested considerations" dictated mild treatment of pregnant enslaved women: "In this, as in all other cases, providence has made our interests & our duties coincide perfectly."[50]

Keeping the delicate mechanism of interest and duty in perfect equilibrium was an impossible task. Jefferson was on an inexorable collision course with both the bottom line and the demands of an institution founded on and maintained by force. Further financial reverses led him again to consider sales and leases, but when someone offered to lease Poplar Forest, Jefferson wrote that "nothing could induce me to put my negroes out of my protection." In the same year, he expressed his "scruples against selling negroes but for delinquency, or on their own request," but gratefully accepted his son-in-law John Wayles Eppes's offer of a loan of $4,000, to be "paid for" two years later in slaves in Bedford County. Since Eppes's son Francis was to inherit Poplar Forest, Jefferson was relieved that "in this way they will continue undisturbed where they always have been, without separation from their families."[51] In cases of "delinquency," however, Jefferson did not relax his severity. Moral duties were waived and malfunctioning parts of the plantation machine had to be removed. Four men who attacked and stabbed the Poplar Forest overseer in 1822 were sent to New Orleans for sale. James Hubbard's second chance ended in exile, after he ran away a second time in 1811. When he was brought back to Monticello in irons after more than a year on the run, Jefferson "had him severely flogged in the presence of his old companions, and committed to jail."[52] He had already sold him *in absentia*.

Men who grew up under Jefferson's supervision, exemplified his expectations, and earned his trust – all Hemingses – found a surer path to freedom. Even if he thought the cultivation of character was preparing some of his slaves for lives as free men, instilling in them the "habits of property and foresight" as in the German immigrant scheme, he did little to change their status. He freed only five men in his will: John Hemmings, Joseph Fossett, Burwell Colbert, and the brothers Madison and Eston Hemings, according to a promise made to their mother. By all accounts, the humane modifications Jefferson made to slavery at Monticello made the lot of his slaves comparatively lighter than elsewhere in Virginia. Some of them told a French visitor in 1824 that they were "perfectly happy, that they were subject to no ill-treatment, that their tasks were very easy, and that they cultivated the lands of Monticello with the greater pleasure, because they were almost sure of not being torn away from them, to be transported elsewhere, so long as Mr. Jefferson lived."[53] But his death changed everything. Jefferson's fantasy of "protection" was shattered by the magnitude of his debt, and the entire Monticello "family" was dispersed. His white relations were forced to move away, and nearly 200 black men, women, and children mounted the auction block. Over sixty years, Jefferson "alienated" by gift or sale more than 400 of the 600 people that "fortune" had thrown on his hands.

After 1826

Jefferson's death was, as Israel Gillette Jefferson remembered, "an affair of great moment and uncertainty to us slaves." He and all but five of the other Monticello slaves knew they were not to be freed and feared the sales that inevitably followed.[54] Even Joseph Fossett, who was to be free a few months later, had to watch his wife and children sold to several different bidders at the estate sale in January 1827. Fossett, whom Jefferson had described as "strong and resolute," had plenty of foresight, the characteristic Jefferson always claimed was absent in a slave.[55] The Monticello blacksmith found surrogate purchasers for some of his family members before the sale and saved the money he made by working after-hours. By pursuing his trade in freedom, he was able to buy back some of his children and become a property owner. Fossett clearly had the highest expectations and ambitions for his children as can be seen in his gifts of a silver watch and a writing book to his still-enslaved son Peter.[56] The Fossett family moved to Cincinnati, Ohio, in the early 1840s, where they were successful blacksmiths and caterers as well as dynamic political, religious, and educational leaders. Joseph and Edith Fossett's great-grandson was William Monroe Trotter, famous in his time as an uncompromising enemy of discrimination and racial injustice, just one of many descendants of Monticello's enslaved families who strove to make the nation live up to the ideals of freedom and equality expressed in Jefferson's Declaration of Independence.

NOTES

1. Peter Jefferson will, July 13, 1757, Albemarle County Deed Book, 2.33. In the first Albemarle County tax list, in 1782, Thomas Jefferson owned the second-largest number of slaves. Lester J. Cappon (ed.), "Personal Property Tax List of Albemarle County, 1782," *Papers of the Albemarle County Historical Society*, 5 (1944–5): 47–73.

2. TJ to Edward Coles, August 25, 1814, in *Thomas Jefferson: Writings*, ed. Merrill D. Peterson (New York: Library of America, 1984), 1346.

3. François Jean, Marquis de Chastellux, *Travels in North America in the Years 1780, 1781 and 1782 by the Marquis de Chastellux*, ed. and trans. Howard C. Rice, Jr. (Chapel Hill: University of North Carolina Press, 1963), 391–2.

4. TJ to Francis Willis, July 15, 1796, in *Papers of Thomas Jefferson*, ed. Julian P. Boyd *et al.* (Princeton: Princeton University Press, 1950–), XXIX: 153; TJ to Thomas Leiper, February 23, 1801, in *Papers*, XXXIII: 50.

5. Edwin Morris Betts (ed.), *Thomas Jefferson's Farm Book: Commentary and Relevant Extracts from Other Writings* (Princeton: Princeton University Press, 1953), facsimile pp. 5–18.

6. TJ to Edward Bancroft, January 26, 1789, in *Papers*, XIV: 492.

7. *Farm Book*, facsimile pp., 27.

8. *Jefferson's Memorandum Books: Accounts, with Legal Records and Miscellany, 1767–1826*, ed. James A. Bear, Jr., and Lucia C. Stanton (Princeton: Princeton University Press, 1997), 246–7; Lucia Stanton, *Free Some Day: The African-American Families of Monticello* (Charlottesville: Thomas Jefferson Foundation, 2000), 21, 26.

9. *Memorandum Books*, 371; Stanton, *Free Some Day*, 104.

10. *Memorandum Books*, 380; "Negroes Alienated from 1784–1794 Inclusive," in Lucia Stanton, *Slavery at Monticello* (Charlottesville: Thomas Jefferson Memorial Foundation, 1996), 16.

11. TJ to Nicholas Lewis, July 29, 1787, in *Papers*, XI: 640.

12. TJ to Edward Bancroft, January 26, 1789, in *Papers*, XIV: 492.

13. TJ to Nicholas Lewis, July 29, 1787, in *Papers*, XI: 641.

14. TJ to Angelica Church, November 27, 1793, in *Papers*, XXVII: 449.

15. Merrill D. Peterson (ed.), *Visitors to Monticello* (Charlottesville: University Press of Virginia, 1989), 28. TJ to Philip Mazzei, May 30, 1795, in *Papers*, XX: 270.

16. *Memorandum Books*, 282; *Farm Book*, facsimile pp., 69.

17. *Farm Book*, facsimile pp., 46.

18. TJ to Samuel Biddle, December 12, 1792, in *Papers*, XXIV: 725.

19. TJ to Thomas Mann Randolph, April 19, 1792, in *Papers*, XXIII: 436; to Thomas Mann Randolph, February 18, 1793, in *Papers*, XXV: 230.

20. TJ to Thomas Mann Randolph, January 25, 1798, in *Papers*, XXX: 56; Randolph to TJ, January 13, February 3 and 26, 1798, in *Papers*, XXX: 28, 79, 145.

21. One prospect was "a very good manager; but his severity puts him out of the question" (TJ to Thomas Mann Randolph, August 26, 1811, in *Papers: Retirement Series*, IV: 101).

22. TJ to Stevens T. Mason, October 27, 1799, in *Papers*, XXXI: 222.

23. TJ to Thomas Mann Randolph, February 18, 1793, in *Papers*, XXV: 230.

24. Jefferson, *Notes on the State of Virginia*, ed. Frank Shuffelton (New York: Penguin Putnam, 1999), 170.

25. Peterson (ed.), *Visitors to Monticello*, 28.

26. TJ to Thomas Mann Randolph, January 23, 1801, in *Papers*, XXXII: 499–500.

27. *Memorandum Books*, 1001; TJ to John Wayles Eppes, December 21, 1797, *Papers*, XXIX: 586.

28. "Statement of Nailery Profits," in *Papers*, XXIX: 540–1.

29. Thomas Mann Randolph to TJ, February 3, 1798, in *Papers*, XXX: 79.

30. Thomas Mann Randolph to Nicholas P. Trist, November 22, 1818, ViU [University of Virginia Library]: 10487.

31. TJ, statement of recommendation for Richard Richardson, June 1, 1801, Massachusetts Historical Society (MHi); TJ to Thomas Mann Randolph, November 25, 1785, in *Papers*, IX: 60.

32. TJ to Joel Yancey, November 15, 1818, in *Farm Book*, 41.

33. John Hemmings spelled his surname differently from other members of his family.

34. Peterson (ed.), *Visitors to Monticello*, 30.

35. Richmond *Recorder*, September 1, 1802.

36. Henry S. Randall to James Parton, June 1, 1868, Harvard University Library.

37. Ellen Coolidge to Joseph Coolidge, October 24, 1858, copy in Coolidge Letterbook, ViU: 9090, 98–9.

38. Martha J. Randolph to TJ, January 15, 1795, in *Papers*, XXVIII: 247.

39. TJ to Thomas Mann Randolph, June 8, 1803, in *Farm Book*, 19.

40. Edward Ross to David Parish, November 23, 1813, St. Lawrence University Library.

41. TJ to Martha J. Randolph, February 27, 1809, in *The Family Letters of Thomas Jefferson*, ed. Edwin Morris Betts and James A. Bear, Jr. (Charlottesville: University Press of Virginia, 1986), 385.

42. Madison Hemings recollections, *Pike County* [Ohio] *Republican*, March 13, 1873; reprinted in Annette Gordon-Reed, *Thomas Jefferson and Sally Hemings: An American Controversy* (Charlottesville: University Press of Virginia, 1997), 245–48; *Farm Book*, facsimile pp., 116, 152.

43. *Memorandum Books*, 1287, 1354, 1361, 1395; TJ to George Fleming, December 29, 1815, in *Farm Book*, 252–3.

44. TJ to Jeremiah Goodman, January 6, 1815, in *Thomas Jefferson's Garden Book, 1766–1824*, ed. Edwin Morris Betts (Philadelphia: American Philosophical Society, 1944), 540; Stanton, *Free Some Day*, 78–9.

45. TJ to Randolph Lewis, April 23, 1807, in *Farm Book*, 26.

46. TJ to Joel Yancey, January 17, 1819, in *Farm Book*, 43; TJ to Jeremiah Goodman, January 6, 1815, in *Garden Book*, 540.

47. TJ to James Pemberton, June 21, 1808, Library of Congress.

48. TJ to Clement Caines, September 16, 1811, in *Papers: Retirement Series*, IV: 157.

49. TJ to Jean Baptiste Say, February 1, 1804, in *Thomas Jefferson: Writings*, 1144.

50. TJ to Joel Yancey, January 17, 1819, in *Farm Book*, 43.

51. TJ to Henry Clark, October 18, 1820, in *Farm Book*, 46; TJ to John Wayles Eppes, June 30, and July 29, 1820, ViU.

52. TJ to Reuben Perry, April 16, 1812, in *Farm Book*, 35.
53. Auguste Levasseur, *Lafayette in America, in 1824 and 1825* (New York, 1829), 218.
54. Israel Gillette Jefferson recollections, *Pike County Republican*, December 25, 1873; Gordon-Reed, *Thomas Jefferson and Sally Hemings*, 250.
55. TJ to Joseph Dougherty, July 31, 1806, in *Farm Book*, 23.
56. Peter Fossett recollections, *New York World*, January 30, 1898.

7

TIMOTHY SWEET

Jefferson, science, and the Enlightenment

A visitor to the White House in the summer of 1808 might have found the president in the East Room, studying a large collection of fossil bones spread out on the floor. Jefferson, president at that time of the American Philosophical Society as well as the United States, had long been interested in bones of the American "mammoth" and other fossil remains, for he was an avid student of all aspects of natural history. The evidence of natural history was, for example, the basis of Jefferson's famous dispute with one of the most prominent scientists of his day, Georges-Louis Leclerc, Comte de Buffon. Buffon claimed that American nature was inferior – specifically, that the New World produced fewer kinds of large quadrupeds than did the Old World, that these were less robust than their Old World analogues, and that Old World animals imported to the New World degenerated. Such claims about the supposed inferiority of American nature, Jefferson felt, had important implications for American culture and the future of the republican project.

Jefferson opened the dispute with Buffon with a discussion of fossil remains of the mammoth in *Notes on the State of Virginia* and continued it in a scientific paper on fossils published in 1799 in the American Philosophical Society's *Transactions*. This paper, an account of bones discovered in a cave in Greenbrier County (now West Virginia), attempted the preliminary reconstruction of an animal, apparently previously undescribed, that Jefferson named the Megalonyx ("Great Claw"). Jefferson continued to pursue his study of fossils and, in 1807, he employed William Clark (of Lewis and Clark fame) to excavate Big Bone Lick (a mineral spring in Kentucky rich in late Pleistocene fossils) and to ship the bones to Washington. Jefferson enlisted Caspar Wistar, professor of anatomy at the University of Pennsylvania and the nation's preeminent expert on vertebrate fossils, to describe and catalog the bones, before sorting them into three groups destined for the American Philosophical Society's collection in Philadelphia, Jefferson's own collection at Monticello, and the Muséum National d'Histoire Naturelle in Paris. At the

Muséum and its associated Institut, the intellectual center of natural history in the early nineteenth century, the fossils were examined by Georges Cuvier, who was working on what would become the founding text of modern paleontology, the *Recherches sur les ossemens fossiles*.[1]

Jefferson was not a very good paleontologist by modern standards, although his efforts did contribute to the advancement of that science.[2] His strengths and weaknesses here indicate some larger tendencies. Jefferson saw himself as a member of the transnational "fraternity" of science, which he likened to the "republic of letters."[3] However, in the paper on the Megalonyx, the disinterested cosmopolitanism of the scientific method gave way to an interested nationalism or hemispheric chauvinism. Jefferson wanted the Megalonyx to have been a large carnivore, preferably a lion (which Buffon had observed was altogether absent from the New World), so as to provide additional, dramatic evidence against the claim of the inferiority of American nature. He held out this hope against Wistar's alternative (and ultimately correct) identification of the remains as belonging to a large herbivore, a ground sloth, and against an article by Cuvier describing a similar species.[4] By 1808, however, he was quite willing to defer to Wistar's expertise, content to play the role of patron and promoter of science, as he did so often throughout his career.

Jefferson would only reluctantly have admitted paleontology as a distinct field of study, premised as it is on the investigation of extinct organisms, for the idea of extinction challenged his faith in a rational order of nature.[5] The extent of that challenge – and the ultimately theological effort he found necessary to meet it – are evident in an 1823 letter to John Adams. Here Jefferson reflects on a lifetime of scientific study:

> It is impossible, I say, for the human mind not to believe, that there is ... design, cause and effect, up to an ultimate cause, a Fabricator of all things from matter and motion, their preserver and regulator while permitted to exist in their present forms, and their regenerator into new and other forms. We see, too, evident proofs of the necessity of a superintending power, to maintain the universe in its course and order. Stars, well known, have disappeared, new ones have come into view; comets, in their incalculable courses, may run foul of suns and planets, and require renovation under other laws; certain races of animals are become extinct; and were there no restoring power, all existences might extinguish successively, one by one, until all should be reduced to a shapeless chaos.[6]

Jefferson gives us the standard Newtonian-deist picture of the universe running down like a clock, requiring periodic adjustments, perhaps in the form of comets, by the divine clockmaker. Yet his concerns extend well beyond the mechanics of inert matter to the organic world, the question of the persistence of life.

At the time he composed the *Notes*, Jefferson found the idea of extinction abhorrent: "Such is the oeconomy of nature, that no instance can be produced of her having permitted any one race of her animals to become extinct; of her having formed any link in her great work so weak as to be broken."[7] However, the letter to Adams indicates a clear acceptance of extinction as geohistorical fact and suggests some awareness of Cuvier's theory of periodic mass extinctions, first advanced in the 1812 edition of the *Recherches*. Cuvier solved the problem of the variation in the fossil record among different geologic strata by concluding that the original plenitude of creation was subsequently decimated by periodic extinctions.[8] Such a sequence, continued long enough, could result in a descent into "shapeless chaos," as Jefferson puts it, with the extinction of all life. As Jefferson came to grapple with the concept of deep time through his readings in geology (even as he sometimes dismissed theoretical geology as an "idle" pursuit[9]), his acceptance of the idea of extinction was accompanied (and here seems mitigated) by a proto-evolutionary imagination of the transformation of species. That is, in contrast to Cuvier's theory of the increasing decimation of life on earth, Jefferson names a "power" that can evidently maintain a relatively constant volume of life, a "preserver and regulator" of "all things" and "their regenerator into new and other forms." The nature of that "restoring power" as a capacity for self-organization (rather than as an external, divine agency) could not be understood before the work of Charles Darwin or James Watson and Francis Crick – it is fair to say that it is not yet fully understood.

During the fifty years spanning Jefferson's composition of the *Notes* and the letter to Adams, the sciences underwent great transformations and increasing specialization. While Jefferson generally saw these developments as continuing to reveal the rational order of the world, in some cases greater knowledge produced greater uncertainty. In his best moments, Jefferson recognized the limitations of scientific understanding. In some other, more politically charged moments, he failed of this recognition.

Influences

In the parlor at Monticello, Jefferson prominently displayed portraits of Francis Bacon, Isaac Newton, and John Locke. These were his "trinity of the three greatest men the world ha[s] ever produced," because they had "laid the foundation of those superstructures which have been raised in the Physical and Moral sciences."[10] Of this Enlightenment "trinity," we probably associate Locke most closely with Jefferson. It is generally agreed that Jefferson's political thought was influenced by Locke's *Two Treatises of Government* (1690). Relevant to the physical sciences, Locke also provided an epistemology in the *Essay Concerning Human Understanding* (1690), according to which sensory experience, operated on by the mental faculty of reflection, is the only source of knowledge. This sensationist epistemology was consistent with the Baconian empiricist tradition. As to the vulnerability of a sensationist epistemology to the charge of solipsism (how can we be certain that our senses do not deceive us?), Jefferson held to Locke's own answer, as we have seen in the letter to Adams: probabilism. When that failed, he had recourse to faith.

The history of Enlightenment science can be thought of in the broadest terms as the history of conflict and creative cross-fertilization between the Newtonian and Baconian traditions: between deduction and induction; between demonstration and observation; between the impulse to reduce nature to a few fundamental laws and the impulse to trace out nature in all its infinite variety. As the traditions sorted themselves out in the wake of the conceptual revolution occasioned by Newton's publication of the *Philosophiae naturalis principia mathematica* (1687), as, for example, in debates over the importance of mathematics in the scientific endeavor, "natural philosophy" came generally to indicate what we would now call the physical sciences, and "natural history" to indicate what we would now call the earth and life sciences.[11] We must bear in mind, however, that all these labels merely provide convenient ways to refer to methodological tendencies or objects of study.

As a Newtonian, Jefferson studied and promoted natural philosophy, from his reading of the *Principia* as an undergraduate at William and Mary College through his plans for an astronomical observatory at the University of Virginia.[12] Yet as an empiricist, Jefferson resisted premature theorizing (though he did indulge himself on occasion) and this meant that he was sometimes reluctant to entertain new ideas.[13] He remarked in the *Notes* that "Ignorance is preferable to error; and he is less remote from the truth who believes nothing, then [*sic*] he who believes what is wrong." However, in a more expansive moment, he wrote that he was "pleased ... to see the efforts of hypothetical speculation because by the collisions of different hypotheses, truth may be elicited and science advanced in the end."[14]

One historian of science has suggested that Jefferson's career indicates a third model of doing science, distinct from the Baconian or Newtonian traditions. The "Jeffersonian research program" – "basic scientific study which had no certain payoff in the short term but was targeted at an area of national importance" or at "an area of basic scientific ignorance that lies at the heart of a social problem" – is exemplified by the Lewis and Clark expedition.[15] Another example would be Jefferson's ongoing research in meteorology and climatology, including a proposal for the establishment of a national weather bureau.[16] The question of climate is of paramount importance for an agrarian nation and is the only topic addressed in Query VII of the *Notes*, "A Notice of All What Can Increase the Progress of Human Knowledge?" Here Jefferson suggested that the clearing of forest had altered the Virginia climate. Elsewhere he modeled this process of climate change, working from elementary fluid mechanics and thermodynamics and assuming different solar reflection rates of forest and cleared land.[17]

Natural philosophy

Although he made no original contributions, Jefferson kept up with the latest developments in physics and mathematics. For example, he read Joseph Lagrange's *Mécanique analytique* soon after its publication in 1788 and provided a correspondent with an in-depth summary. His reading of Pierre Laplace's *Exposition du système du monde* (1796) prompted speculations on the beginning and end of the universe. He commented favorably on the adoption of the "French" (Leibnizian) over the Newtonian notation for the teaching of calculus.[18] This fluency in the language of Newtonian science lent itself to numerous practical applications.

As secretary of state in the Washington administration, Jefferson was charged with developing a system of standard measures, weights, and currency to facilitate interstate commerce. Recognizing that any such system was necessarily arbitrary, he nevertheless set out to derive one entirely from natural phenomena and substances, for such a system would be reproducible anywhere without recourse to a unique object. Jefferson proposed that the standard unit of length be defined as the length of an ideal pendulum whose period is one second: the equation is familiar to anyone versed in Newtonian mechanics. Standard volumes would be defined in terms of the cube of that length, standard weights defined as the weight of rainwater occupying a given volume, and standard coinage as given volumes of gold and silver. Jefferson dealt skillfully with the translation of the ideal pendulum into real terms, including weight, friction, variation of length with temperature, and variation of gravitation with latitude, producing an exhaustively detailed report. Congress may have found the report too complicated, for it failed to pass the proposal.[19]

A better-known engineering project is Jefferson's design of a plow with a "mold board of least resistance." Existing plows were both inefficient and unique, as individual craftsmen wrought (in wood) by tradition and trial and error. Jefferson wanted a design that was both maximally efficient and easily reproducible. He began with a wedge of flat plane surfaces, but recognized the need for a curved surface. Through correspondence with Robert Patterson, professor of mathematics at the University of Pennsylvania, he recalled that the "doctrine of fluxions" (i.e., Newtonian calculus) would enable him to calculate "the best form of a body for removing an obstacle in a single direction." Jefferson transferred the calculation of the three-dimensional curve to wood through a series of measured cuts in successive increments, which were then smoothed by a rasp to produce the final surface of the mold board – as in the calculus, where the slope of a curve is conceptualized as the limit of a set of increasingly close tangent lines. The plow gained the approbation of numerous agricultural societies until an iron plow devised by a Vermont blacksmith named John Deere became popular.[20]

In the context of the Newtonian revolution, it is interesting to imagine Jefferson as engaged in another sort of application of science to a real-world problem, the engineering of the Declaration of Independence. We usually trace the genealogy of the phrase "Laws of Nature and Nature's God" (from the first paragraph of the Declaration) to the tradition of natural law: Hugo Grotius, Samuel von Pufendorf, and so on through Locke.[21] However, Jefferson's particular choice of phrasing, "laws of nature" rather than "natural law", may indicate a specifically Newtonian conceptualization; and the postulation of certain "truths" as being "self-evident" may attribute to these truths the status of scientific axiom, something that is simply stated and cannot be made more plain through demonstration.[22] The question of influence here opens onto the dual valence of "law" in jurisprudence (prescriptive) and in science (descriptive – predictive): in the latter context, a "law" is inviolable.

Natural history

In the wake of the Newtonian revolution, natural historians too began to conceptualize the world in terms of fundamental laws. In some cases, this meant quantitative experimentation, such as Stephen Hales's work on the pressure of sap in plants or blood in animals (*Vegetable Staticks*, 1727; *Statical Essays*, 1733). In other cases, nature's regularity proved less susceptible of mathematization, as in, for example, Mark Catesby's work on climate, which posited that the New World was more disorderly than the Old. Such work raised the question of what counted as a fundamental law. In the case of Catesby, subsequent natural historians, including Jefferson, generally ignored the theoretical dimension of the work and read it as empirical data-gathering.[23] Buffon, the most important natural historian of Jefferson's generation, began his career as a student of mathematics and physics. He found in the principle of universal gravitation a conceptual model for the origins of life in the coming together of organic particles; he later adopted Newton's account of the formation of the solar system in his own account of geological history.[24]

Buffon's theory of American inferiority was thus born of a desire to describe the natural world, as Newton had done, in terms of fundamental laws. Opposing what he saw as the arbitrariness of Linnaean taxonomy, he organized his catalogs of species by geographical region. This attempt to theorize the relation between organism and environment in effect founded the study of biogeography and provided Darwin with significant evidence towards his identification of the mechanism of evolution.[25] Buffon came to his conclusions deductively, working from geological theory and organizing data from natural history to fit the patterns. In the first volume of the 1749 *Histoire naturelle*, he presented a model of continual but directionless climate change, land masses being variously eroded and built up, so that a given locale might have been submerged or dry, cold or hot, at different times. However, since this model could not easily accommodate the Newtonian account of planetary formation, Buffon developed a directional model, published in the *Epoques de la nature* (1778), according to which the earth had originated as a fragment of the sun and was subsequently continually cooling; this model better accorded with new fossil evidence, such as the remains of elephant-like animals in Siberia.[26]

In the *Histoire naturelle*, Buffon claimed that the New World was "new" not just to Europe, but absolutely new, that is, more recently emerged from a period of submersion and not yet dried out, thus, as Jefferson translated, "nature is less active, less energetic." By this, Buffon meant that such a wet climate, less receptive to the sun's warmth, was unfavorable to large, warm-blooded animals and favorable to cold-blooded animals (insects, amphibians, reptiles), which Buffon considered inferior. He claimed that the New World naturally produced fewer kinds of large, warm-blooded animals than did the Old World; that those kinds it did produce were smaller than their Old World analogues; and that domestic animals imported to the New World decreased in size and vigor over subsequent generations. Moreover, this claim extended to the indigenous human beings of America, who, consistent with the "shrinking of living nature in all of that continent," were supposed to be physically, emotionally, and socially "cold" and "feeble."[27]

By the time Jefferson responded to Buffon's theory of American inferiority, it was the subject of considerable debate. While Jefferson was aware of this debate, he cited little of it explicitly in the *Notes*, preferring to engage with Buffon as the superior interlocutor.[28] In Query VI, Jefferson refutes Buffon's claims by marshaling a great deal of empirical counter-evidence, for example the tables of kinds and weights of American versus European animals, as well as other data concerning animals indigenous and imported. If domestic animals transported to a new climate were theoretically subject to "degeneracy," as Jefferson admitted elsewhere, observation showed that this was not the case for European animals imported to North America.[29] Fossil remains play an important role in the refutation, as Jefferson weighs the evidence of the remains of the mammoth. Following a complex discussion concerning the identification of species (was the mammoth an elephant?) and their suitability to cold or warm climates – some of it at cross-purposes and further complicated by Buffon's ongoing revision of his own theories – Jefferson rests on what he says is "easier to believe," given the fossil evidence.[30] In the *Epoques*, Buffon concludes that the mammoth was adapted to a warm climate (for warm climates favor large quadrupeds, and this was one of the largest) and so had retreated or died as the continent cooled. Jefferson assumes that the climate of North America has remained constant over time and that the mammoth was adapted to a cool climate but has been driven north or west (where it may still exist) by the encroachment of civilization.[31] Jefferson continued this aspect of the debate beyond the pages of the *Notes* when the two met in Paris; he also sent Buffon a panther skin and a moose hide and antlers. Later he claimed that, on the basis of this physical evidence, Buffon "acknowledged his mistake, & said he would correct it in his next volume," but died before he was able to do so.[32]

A second strand of the inferiority debate concerned human beings. Buffon theorized that climate was among the most important causes of human variation.[33] Jefferson himself had entertained a causal correlation of climate to character, comparing inhabitants of the northern and southern states, but did not include it in the *Notes*.[34] While the passage Jefferson chooses to represent Buffon's characterization of indigenous Americans is among the most negative in the *Histoire naturelle*, it does not directly address the question of cause as Buffon does elsewhere. Jefferson's refutation proceeds as in the debate about animals, with the marshaling of empirical counter-evidence. Here, however, Jefferson is more willing to gesture towards conclusions. Perhaps the political context – the war to substantiate a document grounding a government in the "Laws of Nature" – made generalizations a matter of greater urgency than in the case of moose or mammoth. Apparent differences between Native Americans and Europeans, Jefferson says, concern manner and customs but do not go to "nature." Deploying the authority of the Linnaean system against the anti-taxonomist Buffon, Jefferson suggests that Native Americans "are formed in mind as well as in body, on the same module with the 'Homo sapiens Europaeus.'"[35] Linnaeus had identified six varieties of *Homo sapiens*, some geographically specific, some not: feral, American, European, Asiatic, African, and *monstrosus*.[36] Jefferson suggests that two of these categories should be collapsed: American and European could be treated as one "module." His logic concerning civilization and proof of "genius" is the same in the case of indigenous Americans and European colonists: time will produce population and progress (and in this, he implicitly agrees with Buffon's claim that America is still young).[37] Nothing in American nature, Jefferson argued, caused the degeneration of human beings.

Jefferson brought the method of natural history to bear on what he recognized was the largest problem of American civilization: slavery. In examining Native Americans as objects of natural history, Jefferson had seen difference as culture. Subjecting Africans to similar analysis, however, he tends to see difference as nature. The analyses are inflected by two distinct contexts: Native Americans are mainly discussed in Query VI, on natural productions; Africans mainly in Query XIV, on laws.[38] In terms of the law of nations, Native Americans were historically free members of sovereign polities and thus potentially republican citizens (although we must recognize that European concepts such as sovereignty distorted pre-contact worldviews, and that treaties were generally violated in practice). Africans were subject to the slave codes, which worked to deny the potential of citizenship.

In his account of Africans, Jefferson fails to reflect on the ways in which the narrowness of his range of observation limits empirical validity.[39] It is obvious to us that a claim such as "they secrete less by the kidnies [sic], and more by the glands of the skin," might be observationally true of anyone working hard on a hot day, but Jefferson reports this point as evidence of difference rather than sameness. The paradigm of taxonomic natural history organizes the proliferation of such observations under the primacy of some visible structure. For Linnaean botany, this structure was stamens and pistils. For Jefferson's natural history of *Homo sapiens*, "the first difference ... is that of colour." This difference, "fixed in nature," held cultural implications, as, for example, the failure of the African's skin to register emotions, such as blushing.[40] Buffon would have disagreed that the "first difference ... is that of colour," arguing that climate was a prior cause. If climate could be altered through human labor on the natural environment – as Jefferson agreed[41] – then perhaps the "first difference" was, in the end, that of culture. Jefferson attempts to accommodate both the Linnaean and Buffonian approaches to some degree, while calling for more data:

[T]hough for a century and a half we have had under our eyes the races of black and red men, they have never yet been viewed by us as subjects of natural history. I advance it therefore as a suspicion only, that the blacks, whether originally a distinct race, or made distinct by time and circumstances, are inferior to the whites in the endowments both of body and mind. It is not against experience to suppose, that different species of the same genus, or varieties of the same species, may possess different qualifications.[42]

In the last sentence, the operation of taxonomy is brought in to forestall any causal question. Yet the redundant profusion of taxonomic terms ("races," "species," "varieties") and the possibility of supposition against experience (even if denied) suggest that the paradigm of natural history itself lacked clarity in regard to the question of "man": what kind of object was being identified here?

New paradigms

In the complications and confusions involved in Linnaeus's, Buffon's, and Jefferson's attempts to extend the methods of natural history to the question of human variation, we see the context for the emergence of the human sciences. New disciplines such as anthropology, sociology, and philology began to understand human beings primarily as producers of culture. Michel Foucault has argued that the human sciences emerged from the recognition of a gap in the Enlightenment scientific paradigm. The model of observing subject / observed object could not produce a self-reflective understanding of the production of knowledge itself.[43] This gap is illustrated rather bluntly in Jefferson's observation that "the races of black and red men … have never yet been viewed by us as subjects of natural history." Jefferson does not imagine viewing himself as an object of natural history. Nor does he reflect critically on his own process of data-gathering and inference, nor on the larger implications of the paradigm in which he works. Certainly, he was aware that taxonomies such as Linnaeus's included Europeans or some such "racial" category into which he would fit. Yet his removal of himself from the gaze of natural history indicates the larger sequestering of the operation of taxonomizing from the reflective scrutiny of science.

The era of natural history was, however, waning. "Philosophy" would soon cease to include the physical sciences and would take its place at the intellectual center of the self-reflective disciplines constituting the new human sciences. With the emergence of disciplinary specialization – biology moving inward, from structure to function; geology moving outward, to the conceptualization of deep time – there was less opportunity for amateurs such as Jefferson to engage meaningfully with the producers of scientific knowledge.

In this context, Jefferson worried about a consequent loss of science's capacity to provide a "universal language." Assessing the innovations in taxonomic systems that marked these transformations in science, he observed (ironically echoing Buffon) that "Classes, orders, genera, species, are not of [Nature's] work. Her creation is of individuals." Thus all such systems are arbitrary. He continued to prefer the Linnaean taxonomy, which was based on "such exterior and visible characteristics as every traveller is competent to observe, to ascertain, and to relate," over functional taxonomies recently introduced by Cuvier and others, which required dissection, the study of embryos, and other techniques beyond the reach of amateurs.[44] If Jefferson considered the orderly totality of the Linnaean system as a model for an orderly society, his tone of loss takes on additional resonance.[45] Yet Jefferson is not so concerned here with an allegory of government: if anything, these new taxonomies claimed to be more "natural" than Linnaeus's, perhaps a better model for a social structure founded on natural law. Jefferson does not prefer the Linnaean system on the basis of closeness of fit to nature, but rather on the basis of shared discursive convention. He is primarily concerned with the communicability of reason, the heart of the Enlightenment project. Without a "universal language" of reason, Jefferson feared, "we shall become unintelligible to one another."[46]

NOTES

I would like to thank John Ernest and Laura Brady for their helpful comments.
1. Howard C. Rice, Jr., "Jefferson's Gift of Fossils to the Museum of Natural History in Paris," *Proceedings of the American Philosophical Society*, 95.6 (December 1951): 597–627.
2. On Jefferson as a paleontologist, see George Gaylord Simpson, "The Beginnings of Vertebrate Paleontology in North America," *Proceedings of the American Philosophical Society*, 86.1 (September 1942): 130–88, esp. 151–7; Martin J. S. Rudwick, *Bursting the Limits of Time: The Reconstruction of Geohistory in the Age of Revolution* (Chicago: University of Chicago Press, 2005), 269–70, 373–6.
3. TJ to John Hollins, February 19, 1809, in *The Writings of Thomas Jefferson*, ed. Andrew A. Lipscomb and Albert Ellery Bergh, 20 vols. (Washington, DC: Thomas Jefferson Memorial Association, 1903), XII: 253.
4. Jefferson, "Memoir on the Megalonyx," in *Papers of Thomas Jefferson*, ed. Julian P. Boyd *et al.*, (Princeton, Princeton University Press, 1950–), XXIX: 291–304; Jefferson, "A Memoir on the Discovery of certain Bones of a Quadruped of the Clawed Kind in the Western Parts of Virginia," *Transactions of the American Philosophical Society*, 4 (1799): 246–60; Caspar Wistar, "A Description of the Bones deposited, by the President, in the Museum of the Society," *Transactions of the American Philosophical Society*, 4 (1799): 526–31.
5. In Jefferson's day, paleontology was not recognized as a discipline distinct from zoology and botany; the *Oxford English Dictionary* dates the use of the term to Charles Lyell's *Elements of Geology* (1838).
6. TJ to John Adams, April 11, 1823, in *Thomas Jefferson: Writings*, ed. Merill D. Peterson (New York: Library of America, 1984), 1467.
7. TJ, *Notes on the State of Virginia*, ed. Frank Shuffelton (New York: Penguin, 1999), 55. See Arthur O. Lovejoy, *The Great Chain of Being: A Study of the History of an Idea* (Cambridge, MA: Harvard University Press, 1936).
8. Rudwick, *Bursting the Limits of Time*, 502–12.
9. See Jefferson's commentary on the Neptunist vs. Vulcanist controversy, TJ to John Emmett, May 26, 1826, in *Thomas Jefferson: Writings*, XV: 168–72.

10. TJ to Benjamin Rush, January 16, 1811, in *Thomas Jefferson: Writings*, XIII: 4; TJ to John Trumbull, February 15, 1789, in *Papers*, XIV: 561.
11. See, e.g., Mordechai Feingold, "Mathematicians and Naturalists: Sir Isaac Newton and the Royal Society," in *Isaac Newton's Natural Philosophy*, ed. Jed Buchwald and I. Bernard Cohen (Cambridge, MA: MIT Press, 2001), 77–102.
12. Silvio Bedini, *Thomas Jefferson: Statesman of Science* (New York: Macmillan, 1990), 28, 454–8.
13. The resistance to theory is a standard critique of Lockean sensationism. See Charles A. Miller, *Jefferson and Nature: An Interpretation* (Baltimore: Johns Hopkins University Press, 1988), 27–31.
14. *Notes*, 35; TJ to George F. Hopkins, September 5, 1822, in *Thomas Jefferson: Writings*, XV: 394–5.
15. Gerald Holton, *The Advancement of Science, and Its Burdens* (Cambridge: Cambridge University Press, 1986), 281; Holton, *Science and Anti-Science* (Cambridge, MA: Harvard University Press, 1993), 115.
16. Bedini, *Thomas Jefferson*, 492.
17. *Notes*, 83–4, 87; TJ to Jean Baptiste Le Roy, November 13, 1786, in *Papers*, X: 524–30.
18. Bedini, *Thomas Jefferson*, 322; I. Bernard Cohen, *Science and the Founding Fathers: Science in the Political Thought of Thomas Jefferson, Benjamin Franklin, John Adams, and James Madison* (New York: Norton, 1995), 100–1.
19. Bedini, *Thomas Jefferson*, 203–6; Cohen, *Science and the Founding Fathers*, 102–8.
20. All correspondence and illustrative figures are provided in Edwin Morris Betts (ed.), *Thomas Jefferson's Farm Book* (Princeton: Princeton University Press for the American Philosophical Society, 1953), 47–64; quotations taken from 50, 51, 52. See also Bedini, *Thomas Jefferson*, 260–2; Cohen, *Science and the Founding Fathers*, 101–2, 293–5.
21. Miller, *Jefferson and Nature*, 155–216.
22. Cohen, *Science and the Founding Fathers*, 108–34.
23. Joyce Chaplin, "Mark Catesby, a Skeptical Newtonian in America," in *Empire's Nature: Mark Catesby's New World Vision*, ed. Amy R. W. Meyers and Margaret Beck Pritchard (Chapel Hill: University of North Carolina Press, 1998), 34–90.
24. John Lyon and Philip R. Sloan (eds. and trans.), *From Natural History to the History of Nature: Readings from Buffon and His Critics* (Notre Dame: University of Notre Dame Press, 1981), see esp. 41–9, 177–9, 151–63. See also Ernst Mayr, *The Growth of Biological Thought: Diversity, Evolution, and Inheritance* (Cambridge, MA: Harvard University Press – Belknap Press, 1982), 330–1.
25. Mayr, *The Growth of Biological Thought*, 336, 440–1.
26. Rudwick, *Bursting the Limits of Time*, 139–50. On Siberian elephant fossils, see TJ, *Notes*, 44–5, 302 n. 58.
27. *Notes*, 48, 305–6 n. 91.
28. For an exhaustive history of the reception of Buffon's theory, see Antonello Gerbi, *The Dispute of the New World: The History of a Polemic, 1750–1900*, trans. Jeremy Moyle (Pittsburgh: University of Pittsburgh Press, 1973). On Jefferson's awareness of the larger context, see, for example, his letter to the Marquis de Chastellux, June 7, 1785, in *Papers*, VIII: 184–6.
29. *Notes*, 51–4, 174.
30. Ibid., 47.

31. Neither is consistent with current theories of extinction due to over-hunting and/or climate change at the end of the last ice age. On the former theory, see Shepard Krech III, *The Ecological Indian: Myth and History* (New York: Norton, 1999), 29–43.

32. Bedini, *Thomas Jefferson*, 148–51; Daniel Webster, *Papers: Correspondence*, ed. Charles Wiltse, 2 vols. (Hanover: University Press of New England, 1974), I: 376.

33. See the selection from Buffon in Emmanuel Chukwudi Eze, *Race and the Enlightenment: A Reader* (Oxford, Blackwell, 1997), 15–28. Eze's selection is from volume III of the *Histoire naturelle* of 1749 (William Smellie's 1781 translation), on the varieties of the human species. The passage quoted at length by Jefferson in the *Notes* is from volume IX of the *Histoire naturelle* of 1761, on animals common to both Europe and America.

34. TJ to the Marquis de Chastellux, September 2, 1785, in *Papers*, VIII: 467–9.

35. *Notes*, 66.

36. See the selection in Eze, *Race and the Enlightenment*, 10–14 (trans., London, 1802–6).

37. *Notes*, 68.

38. Shuffelton, Introduction to *Notes*, xxviii.

39. On Jefferson's claims to empiricism in the *Notes*, see Bruce Dain, *A Hideous Monster of the Mind: American Race Theory in the Early Republic* (Cambridge, MA: Harvard University Press, 2002), 1–39.

40. *Notes*, 146, 145.

41. Ibid., 87.

42. Ibid., 150–1.

43. Michel Foucault, *The Order of Things: An Archaeology of the Human Sciences* (New York: Vintage, 1973). Foucault's scheme of epistemological breaks has drawn criticism from historians of science; see, e.g., Mayr, *The Growth of Biological Thought*, 113. At stake here is not the internal history of a science such as biology, however, but rather the constitution of cultural categories such as "race" by means of different paradigms of knowledge production.

44. TJ to John Manners, February 22, 1814, in *Thomas Jefferson: Writings*, xiv: 97, 98, 103. On Cuvier's innovations, see Mayr, *The Growth of Biological Thought*, 182–4, 188.

45. Christopher Looby, "The Constitution of Nature: Taxonomy as Politics in Jefferson, Peale, and Bartram," *Early American Literature*, 22 (1987): 252–73.

46. TJ to John Manneus, February 22, 1814, in *Thomas Jefferson: Writings*, xiv: 103.

8

RICHARD GUY WILSON

Thomas Jefferson and the creation of the American architectural image

The importance for Thomas Jefferson of a building's design and appearance is revealed in his observation: "Architecture is my delight, and putting up and pulling down one of my favorite amusements."[1] As a plantation owner, he needed functional structures and he designed them along with his dwellings, whether in Virginia, Philadelphia, or Paris. His main house, Monticello, became a life-long experiment in new ideas and forms. He took obvious pride in the praise it engendered, as with the Duc de la Rochefoucauld-Liancourt's observation that Monticello "was infinitely superior to all other houses in America." During the Frenchman's visit in 1796, Jefferson showed him a scheme for a major rebuilding and Rochefoucauld-Liancourt claimed that the new Monticello: "will certainly deserve to be ranked with the most pleasant mansions in France and England."[2]

Jefferson also saw architecture as existing with a public purpose. He explained that he drew upon the first-century BC, Roman, Maison Carrée in Nîmes, France, for the new Virginia State Capitol in Richmond because "How is a taste for a chaste & good style of building to be formed in our countrymen unless we seize all occasions which the erection of public buildings offers, of presenting to them models for their imitation?"[3] He advised Americans who might travel in Europe to look at the paintings and sculpture; however, architecture was "among the most important arts," and, along with gardens, the only one worthy of real study.[4]

Buildings, as Jefferson knew, had a purely functional element: they provided shelter, but also they should inspire and convey identity. He wrote to James Madison that the classical Virginia state house would "improve the taste of my countrymen, to increase their reputation, to reconcile them to the rest of the world, and procure them its praise."[5] Jefferson's architectural accomplishments were many, but perhaps his most important lies with the establishment of an American architectural identity rooted in the classical architecture of Europe.

Jefferson's architectural involvement began in the 1760s with Monticello and, at his death, his final great design, the University of Virginia, was just reaching completion. Some of his work was personal, such as Monticello and its gardens and grounds or his retreat at Poplar Forest (1806–12). He also advised friends living in the Piedmont, such as James and Dolly Madison at Montpelier (c. 1797, c. 1810), near Orange, and Governor James Barbour at nearby Barboursville (c. 1817–22). He designed a huge temple-fronted façade and entertainment rooms for Farmington (1802), a plantation house near Charlottesville. The exact number of Jefferson's house designs remains uncertain but he advised or contributed to at least seven houses. How to count some of Jefferson's personal work is difficult; for example Monticello was initially designed in the late 1760s to early 1770s, then revised, and then totally redesigned in the 1790s and rebuilt, and then tinkered with until his death. He also designed its interiors, some furnishings, and gardens, along with more practical structures such as a saw mill, slave quarters, and farm buildings. Jefferson also designed – in conjunction with Charles-Louis Clérisseau – the Virginia State Capitol (design 1785, construction finished 1798). For the new national capitol, Washington, DC, Jefferson, as George Washington's secretary of state (1790–3), suggested a layout with squares set aside for the President's House and the Capitol and linked by a public garden. This provided the genesis for Major Pierre Charles L'Enfant's plan of 1791. Additionally, Jefferson made designs for the Capitol and Executive Mansion that were not executed. He was involved in the competitions and selection of architects for both buildings in 1792. Later as president (1801–9), Jefferson commissioned major additions to the Executive Mansion, appointed a new architect for the Capitol, and freely offered his advice – which was not always well received. Back in Virginia after 1809, Jefferson, in addition to his own personal work, designed several county court houses, sundry other structures such as a jail, and the University of Virginia (1814–26), one of the largest projects in the country at the time.[6]

Given the amount of Jefferson's architecture, a synthetic approach that examines certain themes and results is necessary. Certainly there is a "Jefferson look" or "style," which might be characterized as red brick, white trim, classical details, and frequently a full temple-fronted portico of large columns. Jefferson's architecture does change and he develops as a designer, as can be seen in a comparison of the relatively crude first Monticello with the much more refined later version. At the basis of all of his work, certain themes can be distinguished that allow a synthetic examination. They can be characterized as: agenda, precedent, training, vernacular, and site–landscape, and finally a consideration of his achievement.

Agenda

Jefferson's architectural agenda contained several elements that included appropriate models for houses and public buildings, along with the development of a trained cadre of architects and workers who could design and build them. Both of these themes were spelled out in his *Notes on the State of Virginia*, written *c.* 1781 and published a few years later. In a long and much-quoted passage, Jefferson complained: "The genius of architecture seems to have shed its maledictions over this land, ... the first principles of the art are unknown, and there exists scarcely a model among us sufficiently chaste to give an idea of them." He bemoaned the American tendency to build in wood since such structures lack permanence, and in another passage he called several of the major public buildings of the colonial capital of Williamsburg: "rude, misshapen piles" and "brick-kilns." Jefferson excoriated most Virginia (and by extension the other states') public buildings, houses, churches, and other structures as lacking in taste, symmetry, and decorated with "barbarous ornaments." The only structure that escaped his wrath was the Williamsburg Capitol which he praised as light and airy, but condemned its portico, columns, and proportions. "Yet," he writes, "on the whole, it is the most pleasing piece of architecture we have."[7]

The reason for such low-grade architecture lay with the lack of appropriate models on which one could draw, and, also, a "workman could scarcely be found capable of drawing an order."[8] The problem of "workmen not very expert in their art" upset him with the Virginia State Capitol.[9] Sufficiently skilled individuals did not exist and Jefferson hypothesized: "Architecture being one of the fine arts, and as such within the department of a professor of the college, ... perhaps a spark may fall on some young subjects of natural taste, kindle up their genius, and produce a reformation in this elegant and useful art."[10] Over thirty years later, Jefferson returned to this theme when he suggested that the different façades of the pavilions at the University of Virginia might serve as "specimens of orders for the architectural lectures."[11] The proposal for the teaching of architecture at the collegiate level came to naught, and not until the 1860s did the Massachusetts Institute of Technology create the first American school of architecture.

Precedent

In common with most architects and builders of the period – whether in America or Europe – Jefferson looked at prior buildings as models for the present day. But, differing from many of his American contemporaries who drew upon the existing vernacular, he also turned to the authority of books and the great classical monuments of Europe, both the ancient and the recent. In this he was very much a part of the European architectural community of his day – the age of Enlightenment – that saw classicism as the ruling element in all composition. During his lifetime, a small group of architects and others began to reassess the medieval period and Gothic architecture, but for Jefferson this always remained on the periphery. For Jefferson, architecture was controlled by rules of proportion, size, and composition which were originally derived from the Greeks by the Romans, and then modified and codified in the so-called "modern" period (i.e., 1400 to the present) by architects and authors in Italy, France, and England. The orders – Tuscan, Doric, Ionic, Corinthian, and Composite – provided the key. "Ancient" to Jefferson meant Greece (which was closed to most westerners and hence unknown) and Rome, while "modern" meant the legacy of what has come to be called (since 1840) "the Renaissance."

For Jefferson, important buildings should be based upon the timeless monuments of the past. He explained: "The Capitol in the city of Richmond … is on the model of the temples of Erectheus at Athens and of Balbec, and of the Maison quarree of Nismes [sic] all of which are nearly of the same form & proportions and are considered as the most perfect examples of Cubic architecture, as the Pantheon of Rome is of the Spherical."[12] The implication is clear: certain ancient buildings exhibited a perfection that should be followed.

Precedent included not just entire buildings but the details, such as the proportions of the different orders and the composition of the entablature. For Jefferson this was essential and he gloried in the minuteness of detail and the figuring-out of the different proportional systems. Regarding the orders at the Virginia Capitol, he wrote to a correspondent: "They are simple and sublime. More cannot be said. They are not the brat of whimsical conception never before brought to light, but copied from the most precious, the most perfect model of ancient architecture remaining on earth."[13]

Jefferson's explanation above included the Pantheon, a temple from the time of Emperor Hadrian, as an example of the spherical. One of the best-preserved of the Roman buildings, the Pantheon with its circular plan contained a sphere. Jefferson never actually visited the Pantheon but it appeared in many architectural books he owned. Its perfect form became an icon for Jefferson and he initially adopted it for his US Capitol scheme of c. 1790, and then ultimately for the Rotunda at the University of Virginia.[14]

Jefferson's usage of precedent included not just the ancient past but the more recent. For the president's house in Washington, DC, Jefferson wrote to L'Enfant: "I should prefer the celebrated fronts of modern buildings which have already received the approbation of all good judges. Such are the Galerie du Louvre, the Garde Meubles; and two fronts of the Hotel de Salm."[15] These were French classical buildings that dated from the seventeenth and eighteenth centuries, which Jefferson admired while in Paris. The division between modern and ancient is made apparent at the University of Virginia in the pavilion fronts that line the central lawn. Each of the façades was to be different and Jefferson employed two architectural treatises in their design. One was *The Architecture of A. Palladio* (London, 1715, 1721, 1742), an English translation of the Venetian Renaissance master whom Jefferson considered a modern. The other book used, Charles Errand and Roland Freart de Chambray's *Parallèle de l'architecture antique avec la moderne* (Paris, 1766), delineated the ancient sources. Hence, Pavilion I, located on the west side, is derived from the Doric of Diocletian's Baths in Rome, as shown in Chambray, while across from it stands Pavilion II, which displays the Ionic of the Temple of Fortuna Virilis in Rome, as published in Palladio. A similar confrontation continues down the lawn, a modern across from an ancient. On the lawn at the University, the ancients and moderns are in dialogue, symbolic of the educational mission.

Training

As a self-trained architect, and because he never received reimbursement for his designs, Jefferson falls into the "gentleman," or "amateur," architect category. However, architecture schools did not exist and the profession of architecture was very rare in the colonies and young republic. Most architects emerged from the ranks of builders, and training came through apprenticeship. A few apprentice-trained architects immigrated, such as Benjamin Henry Latrobe who arrived in 1795 and became a friend of Jefferson. Architects designed buildings but an integral part of their job was supervising construction.[16]

Jefferson superintended the building of many of his own personal projects and much later the University of Virginia (he did not supervise the Virginia Capitol or many of the houses). As the architect, Jefferson had to know construction: he would determine how many bricks were needed, how much timber, how and where to order the glass and hardware, and how to lay out the ground plan. Notes and drawings from the university illuminate his deep involvement with every aspect of construction. He worked with tools. While in London he purchased a tool chest from one Thomas Robinson on April 4 1786 for £11, which he later shipped back to Virginia.[17] A visitor to the Executive Mansion in Washington during his tenure recalled one of his rooms dominated by "a carpenter's work-bench with a vast assortment of tools ... a favorite amusement."[18] Jefferson's slave Isaac recalled his tools and his facility with keys and locks, while in 1822 a visitor from Vermont saw the 79-year-old Jefferson take a chisel from the hand of a stonecutter and demonstrate how to turn the volute of a capital.[19]

Books were another source of Jefferson's architectural knowledge and he assembled one of the largest libraries of treatises and handbooks in the colonies and young republic.[20] He both used the books and loaned them to other individuals. In 1815 he sold most of his library to the federal government in Washington, where it formed the nucleus of the Library of Congress. Without his architecture books Jefferson needed help, and that is one of the reasons that, in May 1817, he contacted Dr. William Thornton, the original architect of the United States Capitol, and then in June 1817 Latrobe, requesting: "will you set your imagination to work & sketch some designs for us."[21] Their suggestions were valuable and led to some changes in the design, such as Latrobe's for a Pantheon type of structure as the central building. Still Jefferson needed the books and he purchased another copy of his beloved Leoni edition of Palladio, along with Errand and Freart de Chambray's *Parallèle de l'architecture*. Some books could not be purchased, and hence he borrowed a copy of Philbert Delorme's *Nouvelles inventions* (1561), which he had owned and used for the dome at Monticello, as the basis for the laminated wood construction of the Rotunda's dome.[22]

Another major source of Jefferson's architectural knowledge came from travel and observation both in the United States and abroad.[23] He knew the cities of Baltimore, Boston, Philadelphia, New York, and smaller places such as Newport, Rhode Island, which possessed the first full temple-fronted building in the British colonies, the Redwood Library (1748–50) by Peter Harrison. Between 1784 and 1789, Jefferson resided in Paris as the American minister to France and observed architecture (along with purchasing books, sampling wine, and other amusements). He observed closely new buildings going up in Paris, such as the Hotel de Salm, and traveled to see the older ones such as the Maison Carrée. His five years included trips to the south of France, northern Italy (but not Venice or Rome), the Low Countries, and Britain. With John Adams he visited notable English gardens such as Stowe, and on his own Jefferson saw Lord Burlington's Palladian masterpiece, Chiswick. The impact of these trips was considerable, as an examination of his redesigned Monticello in comparison to the Hotel de Salm in Paris and to Chiswick will reveal. He drew upon both for the exterior of Monticello, while on the interior his rows of statues of "worthies" came from the Temple of Worthies he saw in the garden at Stowe.

Vernacular

Although Jefferson was a worldly, well-traveled individual, still he was rooted to a particular time and place, which was Virginia, and the Piedmont in particular. His designs attempted to escape the local and aspired to be international, but in many ways they remained Virginian.

Materials are one example, for, although Jefferson despised the common wooden buildings, still the permanent material he selected, brick, was very Virginian. Possibly he would have preferred to use stone and build masonry structures, however the technical ability did not exist in Virginia during his lifetime and hence he turned to brick, and, in some cases, such as with the Virginia State House, covered it with stucco and scored it to resemble stone. Jefferson was fortunate that in Virginia a high degree of technical ability with brick making and laying had developed, and he was able to employ some of the masters, such as William B. Phillips, for his various projects, including the university. The university brickwork displays a hierarchy, and typically the more important façades such as the fronts of the pavilions have smooth-faced brick with very tight incised joints, whereas the sides, or lesser faces, have rougher brick and not so fine joints. Jefferson's brick designs – as fine as they may be – give his work a certain tentativeness and lack of substantiality, or as Fiske Kimball, the first major scholar of Jefferson's architecture, summed up years ago, Jefferson never entirely broke with the "colonial manner" and progressed to an international refinement.[24]

Jefferson's house floor plans became more sophisticated over the course of his career, but always a Virginia element remained. Jefferson's earliest built structure, the so-called "honeymoon cabin," or east pavilion, at Monticello had a two-room plan based upon vernacular Virginia houses. Many of his early schemes for the main house at Monticello show him wrestling with a formal symmetrical façade derived from English pattern books such as those by Kent, Morris, Gibbs, and others, but the plan is irregular with different-sized rooms on the interior, similar to the Virginian spatial planning he knew.

Jefferson's transfiguration of the extended wing villa, as shown in Palladio's Veneto farmhouses, to a sub-terrain basement has been extensively praised by scholars as an example of his architectural ingenuity, but it served a very Virginian purpose. The scheme of burying all services was to remove the servant and slave population from sight. The dining room employs a variety of techniques, such as a revolving service door for food and dumb waiter for the wine cellar, that kept the slaves hidden and not in view.[25] Jefferson was ingenious in these designs but most large Virginia houses also kept slaves at a distance through interior barriers. Finally to be noted, Jefferson does not emphasize his staircases, and, while the large Virginia house frequently had major stairs, smaller ones compressed them, as did Jefferson.

Although the exterior of the Richmond Capitol referenced ancient sources, the interior as designed by Jefferson drew on the layout of the colonial Capitol in Williamsburg, which he knew well. His scheme had a large central hall with a statue of George Washington by Jean-Antoine Houdon – that Jefferson had commissioned – and it mimicked the Williamsburg Capitol's central hall, which contained a statue of Lord Botetourt. Both buildings had the lower house across the rear and the upper house on the second floor at the opposite end over the general court.[26]

Site and landscape

Many of Jefferson's designs show a preference for a dominant placement of the structure and also for integrating it into the landscape through gardens. Monticello (meaning "little mountain") was placed on top of a prominent hill that gave it a prospect and asserted its importance. However, the site was impractical since, during the summer, the high well dried up and water had to be hauled up. Initially Jefferson drew up a scheme for leveling part of the hill so as to create a broad terrace for the house and other structures, but only part of it was carried out. The site gave Monticello a presence on the horizon: he liked to have a large expanse of sky with the building rising up. A similar approach can be observed at the State Capitol where he sited the structure on top of Shocko Hill, and for years it dominated the town of Richmond and the James River below. The ground plan of the university follows the same format, the Rotunda is placed at the highest point, and faces south so that it is silhouetted against the sky, and extensive leveling operations – by slaves and freedmen, horses and mules – created a series of flat terraces on which the pavilions and dormitories could be placed. Jefferson liked his buildings to be dominant elements, but they also created space and enclosed activities.

Jefferson's interest in gardening has been mentioned; in 1805 he wrote to a granddaughter:

> I must observe that neither the number of the fine arts nor the particular arts entitled to that appellation have been fixed by general consent. many reckon but five Painting, sculpture, architecture, music & poetry. to these some have added Oratory ... others again add Gardening as a 7th fine art. not horticulture, but the art of embellishing grounds by fancy.[27]

While in Europe he not only toured English gardens with Adams but, on the Continent, visited many of the famous landscapes, admiring some and deploring others. His library contained a number of books on landscape design. The initial schemes at Monticello followed the formal geometrical patterns dominant on the Continent; however, after his European sojourn, he changed the style of Monticello's garden into a curvilinear path similar to the picturesque gardens observed in England. At Poplar Forest his plan remained more formal but at a large scale.

Although some of Jefferson's garden design imitated foreign models, he recognized fundamental differences between the European and American situations. In a letter he noted: "Their [England's] sun light has permitted them to adopt what is certainly a beauty of the very first order ... Their canvas is of open ground vanquished with clumps of trees distributed with taste." In contrast, the "beaming almost vertical sun of Virginia" meant a different response, and he claimed: "shade is our Elysium." Jefferson recommended – and carried out at Monticello – a design in which trees were trimmed of lower branches but their tops remained united; hence, they would "yield a dense shade."[28]

In his design for the University of Virginia, Jefferson intended that the central lawn would be "grass & trees."[29] Behind the pavilions, he placed gardens enclosed with serpentine walls. The exact plans for these gardens remain unknown, but clearly the intention was to provide a contrasting and more intimate space against the public nature of the lawn. Near Jefferson's death, the university purchased 100 locust and 116 poplar trees to be planted on the grounds, to provide the needed shade.[30]

Achievement

On a personal level, Jefferson created, with Monticello and Poplar Forest, houses that stood out from their contemporaries in their form, plan, landscape, and style. With these houses and others, Jefferson helped to create certain features, such as the full temple portico, that became exceedingly popular in succeeding years.

Jefferson (with the assistance of Clérisseau) inaugurated a style of public building that became the national norm for many years, and still typifies what many think of as a national architecture. It is his most important single design. The Capitol was the first major public building after the Revolution and, if compared with earlier structures such as Independence Hall in Philadelphia, the Williamsburg Colonial Capitol, Colony House in Newport, or the old State House, Boston, the revolutionary nature of Jefferson's design becomes apparent. The classical agenda of drawing upon European models, set with the Virginia Capitol, carried forth in an even more grand way in Washington, DC.

Jefferson did not create this American architecture alone, many of the other founding fathers – Washington, Adams, Madison, and Monroe – had architectural interests. Also, during the federal period, a few architects emerged such as Charles Bulfinch, Asher Benjamin, Robert Mills, William Thornton, along with the *émigrés* B. H. Latrobe, Maximilian Godefroy, and Joseph Jacques Ramée. They and the many patrons, both public and private, contributed to making classicism the American national style.

The question of what meanings were implied by Jefferson in the selection of ancient sources must be approached with care. Since Jefferson was a founding father and a politician, does his architecture contain political messages and symbols? However, in this area Jefferson is frequently opaque and elliptic, and the writings that tie architectural style and political symbols together are fragmented. It has been suggested that Jefferson chose the Maison Carrée as the source for the Virginia State Capitol because he thought it a symbol of Roman republicanism and hence a fitting symbol for the young republic; but this is questionable. The Palladio edition that Jefferson read noted that the inhabitants of Nîmes claimed it had been a basilica, or a court of justice; however, the text went on to assert that "it had been a Temple."[31] Jefferson admired and utilized many forms and details from the Roman Empire, not the least of which was the Pantheon, which he drew on for the United States Capitol in *c.* 1790, and later reconstructed at the University of Virginia. Jefferson did see some political symbolism, as when he wrote to Latrobe concerning the US Capitol as "the first temple dedicated to the sovereignty of the people, embellishing with Athenian taste the course of a nation looking far beyond the range of Athenian destinies."[32] This type of associative identification became more common during the 1820s and onwards with the Greek Revival.

Jefferson's choice of buildings lay with their perfection; they had received approval or, as he explained, "the suffrage of the whole world."[33] The buildings he admired were perfect examples of cubic or spherical architecture, irrespective of their political origins. Jefferson's choice of words indicates that he viewed the Maison Carrée and the Pantheon from a Burkeian sense; they had the approbation of the ages, and were models of natural law.[34] Or, as Jefferson had read in Lord Shaftesbury: "What is beautiful is harmonious and proportionable; what is harmonious and proportionable is true, and what is at once both beautiful and true is of consequence agreeable and good."[35] Jefferson provided the architectural models upon which Americans could draw.

Finally, Jefferson set about both promoting the few architects existing in the young United States, such as Benjamin Henry Latrobe, and providing training to young aspiring designers, such as Robert Mills who spent a number of months working with Jefferson's books and drawings. Equally important was the creation of a cadre of workmen who could design and draw an order. The initial workmen's group contained only a few, such as John Neilson and James Dinsmore, both Irish immigrants who worked for him at Monticello and Poplar Forest. They became involved in other projects such as Madison's Montpelier, John Hartwell Cocke's Bremo in Fluvanna County, and the university. The enormous construction project for the University of Virginia offered a much larger opportunity for training for the several hundred workmen employed there, such as Dabney Crosby, John Blackburn, William Philips, and Malcolm Crawford, who carried Jeffersonian classicism throughout Virginia and the South.[36]

Jefferson helped create an American architectural identity based upon classical models of France, England, Italy, Rome, and Greece. This was an architectural language traditionally associated with monarchy, the church, and imperial power, now transformed into emblems of the new American experiment with democracy. Jefferson's role in this new emblem for America was central.

NOTES

This chapter builds on the work of numerous colleagues and I would like to acknowledge Calder Loth, Charles Brownell, and Bryan Clark Green.

1. Jefferson quoted in Margaret Bayard Smith, *A Winter in Washington* (New York: E. Bliss & E. White, 1824), II: 261.
2. Quoted in Sarah N. Randolph, *The Domestic Life of Jefferson* (New York: Harpers & Brothers, 1871), 236.
3. TJ to Edmund Randolph, September 20, 1785, in *Papers of Thomas Jefferson*, ed. Julian P. Boyd *et al.* (Princeton: Princeton University Press, 1950–), VIII: 538.
4. Jefferson, "Objects of Attention for an American," June 19, 1788, in *Papers*, XIII: 269.
5. TJ to James Madison, September 20, 1785, in *Papers*, VIII: 535.
6. Delos Hughes, "The Courthouses of Buckingham County: Jefferson and Beyond," *Arris*, 15 (2004): 1–25, and John O. Peters and Margaret T. Peters, *Virginia's Historic Courthouses* (Charlottesville: University Press of Virginia, 1995).
7. Thomas Jefferson, *Notes on the State of Virginia*, ed. William Peden (Chapel Hill: University of North Carolina Press, 1954), 152–3.
8. Ibid.
9. TJ to James Buchanan and William Hay, January 26, 1786, in *Papers*, IX: 221.
10. Jefferson, *Notes*, 153.
11. TJ to Benjamin H. Latrobe, June 12, 1817, in *The Correspondence and Miscellaneous Papers of Benjamin Henry Latrobe*, ed. John C. Van Horne *et al.* (New Haven: Yale University Press, for the Maryland Historical Society, 1984–8), III: 902.
12. Jefferson, "An Account of the Capitol in Virginia" (1785), in Fiske Kimball, *The Capitol of Virginia*, ed. Jon Kukla with Martha C. Vick and Sarah Shields Driggs (Richmond: Library of Virginia, 2002), 7.
13. TJ to James Currie, January 28, 1786, in *Papers*, IX: 240.

14. Charles Brownell in Brownell, Calder Loth, William M.S. Rasmussen, and Richard Guy Wilson, *The Making of Virginia Architecture* (Richmond: Virginia Museum of Fine Arts, 1992), 218–19.

15. TJ to L'Enfant, April 10, 1791, in *Thomas Jefferson and the National Capitol*, ed. S.K. Padover (Washington, DC: US Government Printing Office, 1946), 59.

16. Carl Lounsbury, *An Illustrated Glossary of Early Southern Architecture and Landscape* (Oxford: Oxford University Press, 1994), 9, notes that architect meant: "An individual engaged in the design and the supervision of construction of buildings and structures."

17. Ross Watson, "Thomas Jefferson's Visit to England, 1786," *History Today*, 27 (January, 1977): 9.

18. Smith, *A Winter*, 265.

19. Isaac Jefferson, "Memoirs of a Monticello Slave," in *Jefferson at Monticello*, ed. James A. Bear, Jr. (Charlottesville: University of Virginia Press, 1967), 18; Daniel Pierce Thompson, an editor from Vermont, in H.M. Kallen, "The Arts and Thomas Jefferson," *Ethics*, 53:4 (July 1943): 274, originally published in *Harper's Magazine*, 26 (1863): 833–5; republished as *Green Mountain Boy at Monticello: A Talk with Jefferson in 1822* (Brattleboro: Book Cellar, 1962), 20.

20. William Bainter O'Neal, *Jefferson's Fine Arts Library: His Selections for the University of Virginia Together with His Own Architectural Books* (Charlottesville: University Press of Virginia, 1976).

21. TJ to Dr. William Thornton, May 9, 1817, University of Virginia Library, Special Collections; TJ to William Henry Latrobe, June 12, 1817, Library of Congress.

22. TJ to General Joseph Smith, June 21, 1825, University of Virginia Library, Special Collections.

23. Edward Dumbauld, *Thomas Jefferson, American Tourist* (Norman: University of Oklahoma Press, 1946); Howard C. Rice, Jr., *Thomas Jefferson's Paris* (Princeton: Princeton University Press, 1991); George Green Shackelford, *Thomas Jefferson's Travels in Europe, 1784–1789* (Baltimore: Johns Hopkins University Press, 1995); William Howard Adams, *The Paris Years of Thomas Jefferson* (New Haven: Yale University Press, 1997).

24. S. Fiske Kimball, *Thomas Jefferson, Architect, Original Designs in the Coolidge Collection of the Massachusetts Historical Society* (Boston: Privately Printed, 1916), 82.

25. Dell Upton, *Architecture in the United States* (New York: Oxford University Press, 1998), 26–9.

26. Mark R. Wenger, "Thomas Jefferson and the Virginia State Capitol," *Virginia Magazine of History and Biography*, 101 (January 1993): 77–102.

27. TJ to Ellen Randolph, July 10, 1805, in Eleanor D. Berman, *Thomas Jefferson Among the Arts* (New York: Philosophical Library, 1947), 40; and in Edwin M. Betts, *Thomas Jefferson's Flower Garden at Monticello* (Richmond: Dietz Press, 1941), 303–4.

28. TJ to William Hamilton, July, 1806, Library of Congress.

29. TJ to Thornton, May 9, 1817, University of Virginia Library, Special Collections.

30. Information drawn from Proctor's Journal, 1819–28 (April 5, 1823), 206; Proctor's Daybook, 1821–8 (April 5, 1823), 151, and (April 15, 1823), 154; University of Virginia Library, Special Collections.

31. *The Architecture of A. Palladio*, trans. G. Leoni (London: John Watts, 1715–20), IV, Ch. 28 [11].

32. TJ to B.H. Latrobe, July 12, 1812, in *The Writings of Thomas Jefferson*, ed. Andrew A. Lipscomb and Albert Ellery Bergh, 20 vols. (Washington, DC: Thomas Jefferson Memorial Association, 1903), XIII: 179.

33. TJ to James Buchanan and William Hay, January 26, 1786, in *Papers*, IX, 220–2.

34. Berman, *Thomas Jefferson Among the Arts*, 124.

35. Anthony Earl of Shaftesbury, *Characteristics of Men, Manners, Opinions, Times, Etc*, ed. J. M. Robertson (London: Grant Richards, 1900 [1711]), II: 268–9.

36. Bryan Clark Green, *In Jefferson's Shadow: The Architecture of Thomas R. Blackburn* (New York: Princeton Architectural Press, 2006); Richard C. Cote, "The Architectural Workmen of Thomas Jefferson in Virginia," Ph.D. dissertation, Boston University, 1986; K. Edward Lay, *The Architecture of Jefferson Country: Charlottesville and Albemarle County, Virginia* (Charlottesville: University Press of Virginia, 2000); William Bainter O'Neal, "The Workmen at the University of Virginia 1817–1826," *Magazine of Albemarle County History*, 17 (1958–9): 5–48.

9

DARREN STALOFF

The politics of pedagogy:
Thomas Jefferson and the education
of a democratic citizenry

Like any disciple of the Enlightenment, Thomas Jefferson believed that knowledge was power. Indeed, freedom itself was, as he informed François D'Ivernois, "the first born daughter of science." It is therefore hardly surprising that historians have seen education as central to Jefferson's political thought. Education for Jefferson was "one of the primary functions of republican government," according to Norman K. Risjord. The distinguished scholar of American education Lawrence Cremin saw it as "a crucial element in the Jeffersonian program," while Paul A. Rahe has concluded that it was "a central, lifelong concern" of the Virginian. As Ralph Lerner has noted, Jefferson believed that public education was critical to his entire political project; "if self-governance were not to become a hollow or a bitter joke, a people had to be prepared, qualified to rule itself." Richard K. Matthews has put the point even more forcefully, claiming that public education was an essential precondition of Jefferson's "faith in the people" and their ability "to govern themselves." Perhaps Merrill D. Peterson expressed the scholarly consensus most succinctly: public education was "the backbone of Jefferson's republic."[1]

Education was then, understandably, a lifelong concern of Jefferson's. In the 1790s he unsuccessfully sought to transfer the College of Geneva, one of the premier institutions of higher learning in Europe, to the United States. During his presidency, he urged Congress to amend the Constitution so that funds could be appropriated for public education and a national university. In his retirement, he tried to establish a public lending library in his native state, offered an architectural plan for East Tennessee College, and designed a curriculum for Albemarle Academy as part of a larger educational scheme. His most sustained and significant efforts, however, came at the beginning of his political career and at the end of his life. During the struggle for independence he outlined what he later called "a systematical plan of general education" that would serve as the basic outline for his subsequent educational initiatives.[2] Perhaps most famously, in his final years he served as "father of the University of Virginia," one of the three accomplishments he wanted listed on his epitaph "as testimonials that I have lived" and by which "I wish most to be remembered."[3] These two moments, separated by roughly thirty years, constitute the alpha and omega of Jefferson's thoughts on education. It is there that Jefferson disclosed his pedagogical politics.

Most scholars have argued for a fundamental continuity in these two great efforts. The main reason is that both are seen in the light of Jefferson's stated principles, whether of a democratic or liberal nature. The problem with such an interpretation is that it ignores the changes in the nature of Jefferson's political thought and rhetoric. When Jefferson wrote his "systematical plan," he had yet to embrace the radical and ideological politics of principle that he articulated almost a decade later.[4] Such an interpretation also ignores the vastly different challenges Jefferson responded to. In the 1770s he sought to secure the liberties of a newly established and potentially fragile republican order in his state. His last campaign was against a perceived sectional threat. In fact, Jefferson's educational reforms comprised two distinct missions in their emphases. The first was to "illuminate, as far as practicable, the minds of the people at large." Only his second effort, the creation of the University of Virginia, served to protect and "carry hence the correct principles of the day."[5] But these principles had less to do with liberalism and democracy than with a perceived sectional threat to the slave-owning South.

Jefferson's first foray into educational reform came in the form of three separate bills submitted in 1778. The first, entitled A Bill for the More General Diffusion of Knowledge, mandated a system of public elementary and grammar schools throughout the state. The second reconstituted the College of William and Mary as a purely secular institution of higher learning, and the third called for the establishment of a research library in Richmond. Of the three, Jefferson considered the first the most critical. In fact, he subsequently pronounced it "by far the most important bill in our whole code" of 126 laws he and his fellow revisers submitted, including the abolition of primogeniture and entail, and the establishment of religious freedom. What made this "the most important bill" were two striking provisions, both profound innovations in a state lacking any public education. The first provided for three years of primary schooling in basic literacy and mathematics for all free children, with reading lessons drawn from classical and Anglo-American history rather than scripture. The second mandated a system of scholarships to both the grammar schools and the university for boys of "the best and most promising genius" whose parents were "too poor to give them further education." Jefferson summarized his rationale for these provisions in *Notes on the State of Virginia*. Elementary education ensured the enlightenment of the people at large and thus made them "the safe, as they are the ultimate, guardians of their own liberty." Scholarships for the indigent worthy would promote the Enlightenment ideal of the career open to talents "which nature has sown as liberally among the poor as the rich, but which perish without use, if not sought for and cultivated."[6]

Scholars have depicted Jefferson's bill as remarkably egalitarian in its political import. Primary education would teach people to "think for themselves" and thus allow them "to participate as equals in political democracy." The cultivation of genius among poor boys would replace the elite gentry rulers of Virginia with an officialdom drawn from a learned "natural aristocracy" of talent.[7] Scholars have offered this interpretation because they have read the bill in light of democratic-sounding principles Jefferson expressed, albeit after he drafted the legislation, as well as claims he made in the bill itself. Thus Jefferson sought to enlighten the people in elementary schools because of his principled belief that they were the only "safe depository of the ultimate powers of the society," as well as the "source of all authority," and therefore comprised the entire "sovereign legislative, judiciary and executive power." And as Jefferson states in the preamble to his bill, scholarships for the indigent were the only way to ensure "that those persons, whom nature hath endowed with genius and virtue, should be rendered by liberal education worthy to receive, and able to guard the sacred deposit of the rights and liberties of their fellow citizens, and that they should be called to that charge without regard to wealth, birth or other accidental condition or circumstance."[8]

The problem with this "egalitarian" reading is that it is contradicted both by some of Jefferson's more private musings and by the actual details of the bill itself. Primary education would not provide for democratic self-government because Jefferson's proposed curriculum was, in his own mind at least, inadequate for that end. Similarly, scholars have vastly exaggerated the extent of educational mobility the bill contained, an exaggeration begun by Jefferson himself in later years. Nor did Jefferson privately believe that those indigent geniuses who would be trained in higher learning would use their high cultural expertise in the realm of politics. What Jefferson really intended with his Bill for the More General Diffusion of Knowledge had little to do with his subsequent democratic principles and everything to do with the politics of Enlightenment he had not yet dispensed with.

For the vast bulk of Virginians, Jefferson proposed a political education based on readings in "Graecian, Roman, English and American history." Decades later, he claimed that such reading would "instruct the mass of our citizens" in "their rights, interest and duties, as men and citizens."[9] At no point, however, did he argue that it would enable them to fully assume the reins of government and make informed decisions regarding substantive policy, much less constitutional design. That is because historical understanding had a very limited, if important, role in Jefferson's political theory. As Jefferson explained to John Norvell in a long letter on political education written during his second term as president, "history, in general, only informs us what bad government is." History was important because it disclosed the patterns of usurpation by which regimes had undermined the liberties of the people. Such knowledge had its political uses, as we shall soon see, but they did not include delineating "good government," the pattern which must inform enlightened policy as well as the very structure of the state. That higher knowledge required a systematic understanding of political society, one which he told Norvell "presents in one full & comprehensive view the system of principles on which such an organization should be founded, according to the right of nature." In contrast to the historical and inductive "political science" of his friend and rival John Adams, Jefferson believed knowledge of 'what good government is' was acquired through abstract and deductive reasoning which theorized natural rights in an overarching "system of principles." That is why he told Norvell that the best works on government were those based on reasoning from natural rights, such as Locke's *Second Treatise*, Priestley's *Essay on the First Principles of Government*, and even Beccaria's *On Crimes and Punishments*, "because of the demonstrative manner in which he has treated that branch of the subject."[10] And that is also why he later championed the famed ideologist Destutt de Tracy's *A Commentary and Review of Montesquieu's Spirit of Laws* – "the best elementary book on the principles of government," he informed one political associate – as well as his *A Treatise on Political Economy*.[11] For Jefferson, what made Tracy such a brilliant political theorist, not to mention "the ablest writer living on intellectual subjects," was precisely his deductive "analytic" mode of reasoning, one "in which all its principles are demonstrated with the severity of Euclid."[12] Indeed, Jefferson was so enamored of De Tracy's deductive manner of demonstration, as well is its findings, that he had both the aforementioned books translated and published in the United States.[13]

Obviously, the higher deductive science of political theory could not be garnered by the mass of the people from three years of basic reading in history. Nor could it be acquired by those rare geniuses among them granted six years of instruction at Jefferson's "grammar schools." Essentially college preparatory institutions, these schools were devoted to the study of classical languages, "English grammar, geography, and the higher part of numerical arithmetick."[14] Thus, aside from perhaps some additional reading in history, grammar school instruction was largely devoid of political content. The only place future statesmen could learn the truths of politics and government was at the university level, as Jefferson himself made clear in his bill reforming the

College of William and Mary. It was in "that seminary," he insisted, where "those who are to be the future guardians of the rights and liberties of their country may be endowed with science and virtue, to watch and preserve the sacred deposit." Nor would it be inculcated there from study in history, for, in Jefferson's revised curriculum, politics and commerce would be the provenance of the law professor, while the instructor in "the laws of nature and nations" would also have to cover fine arts and moral philosophy, rather than history.[15] Perhaps the small fraction of indigent geniuses educated at the university could aspire to truly participate fully in the political life of Virginia, but the mass of their fellow commoners simply lacked the knowledge to responsibly exercise that power. Jefferson's educational scheme, combined with his equation of knowledge and power, precluded any meaningful devolution of political authority. Jefferson's prescribed primary education was simply not a pedagogical stepping stone to participatory democracy.

Nor were Jefferson's meritocratic scholarships likely to produce a natural aristocracy. To begin with, the program was not particularly generous. In fact, Jefferson occasionally exaggerated the number of opportunities his plan provided. Thus, in *Notes on the State of Virginia*, he claimed that one student would be selected annually from each primary school to attend the nearest of twenty grammar schools to be established throughout the state, while the bill actually conferred one scholarship for every ten schools.[16] Of this small number (Merrill Peterson estimated it at "perhaps sixty or seventy"), one-third would be dismissed after one year, and all but one per grammar school after the second, leaving, as Jefferson famously put it, "twenty of the best geniuses" in the state to be "raked from the rubbish annually." In the very next sentence in *Notes*, Jefferson went on to claim that, after six years of college preparation, one half, or ten, of these students would be "chosen for the superiority of their parts" and sent to William and Mary at public expense.[17] Notwithstanding that almost every study of Jefferson has repeated this claim, the language of the bill is so ambiguous that, as Richard Brown has concluded, Jefferson might have inflated the number of scholarships tenfold. The bill divided the twenty grammar school districts into two zones divided by the James River, and the visitors in the grammar school districts in each zone would, in alternate years, "chuse one among the said seniors" who were then authorized "to proceed to William and Mary College."[18] If, as Brown has concluded, the visitors were to choose one student from their zone rather than their district, then only one indigent scholar would be sent to the college each year. On the face of it, one poor graduate per year sounds more like a natural monarchy than an aristocracy.[19]

Even if Jefferson's bill had provided for ten university scholarships rather than one (its final clause is sufficiently opaque for either to be possible), there are compelling reasons to conclude that he would have neither expected nor desired that they enter the political realm as natural aristocrats. First of all, the strict winnowing of intellectual talent in Jefferson's plan would have resulted in a residue of genius so pure that it would simply have been wasted on politics. That Jefferson would have thought this is suggested by a letter he wrote to David Rittenhouse at roughly the same time he was completing the draft of his educational plan. Jefferson urged the celebrated scientist to stop wasting his talents on government: "there is an order of geniuses above that obligation," he insisted, pointedly adding that "nobody can conceive that nature ever intended to throw away a Newton upon the occupations of a crown."[20] Second, and more important, was Jefferson's private belief that political office could only be held by those of independent means. Jefferson shared this conviction with his nephew Peter Carr in a long letter he wrote on his system of public education for Virginia. Making Carr "the depository of my ideas on the subject," Jefferson frankly distinguished two strata of the "learned class." On the one hand were those "who are destined for the learned professions, as means of livelihood," and, on the other, "the wealthy, who, possessing independent fortunes, may aspire to share in conducting the affairs of the nation."[21] "Raked from the rubbish," Jefferson's merit scholars clearly fell within the former strata. For them, high cultural training was an avenue to higher income in a "learned profession," not political office.

Jefferson's educational reforms failed to support the egalitarian principles of Jeffersonian democracy precisely because he had yet to articulate or embrace those principles. When he devised his plan, Jefferson was still immersed in the politics of Enlightenment, and his educational reforms were part of that more focused, if moderate, program.[22] Specifically, Jefferson had two tangible goals. He sought to "illuminate, as far as practicable, the minds of the people at large" through primary education as a means to safeguard the liberties of the newly established republican order in Virginia. He tried to reform both college preparatory and university education to cultivate rather than replace the existing aristocracy of gentry planters.

Like most enlightened republicans, Jefferson recognized that even the "best forms" of government were liable to "degeneracy." The greatest danger to popular government was from the usurpation of ambitious statesmen who "by slow operations, perverted it into tyranny."[23] Jefferson's fear of ambition was shared by most enlightened writers. Even David Hume, whom Jefferson considered a rank Tory, acknowledged that in matters of politics "every man ought to be supposed a *knave*" and animated solely by "insatiable avarice and ambition."[24] Instruction in history might not provide the people with an adequate understanding of good government to undertake democratic self-rule, but it would "qualify them as judges of the actions and designs" of their representatives. It would do this by disclosing examples of "ambition under every disguise it may assume." Once acquired, this knowledge of ambition would allow the people "to defeat its views."[25] Primary reading in history was thus a prophylactic against the rise of "tyranny," replacing or supplementing the deference of the many to the few with a politics of republican suspicion. Obviously, such historical education would have to be of the "Whig" variety if it was to produce a healthy jealousy of ambition, and it was for this reason that Jefferson in later years became so concerned with the baleful effects of Hume's popular "revisionist" history of England.[26]

Ambition was not the only source of tyranny. Equally dangerous, at least for Jefferson, was the specter of superstition which could blind the minds of the people. Jefferson's educational scheme eliminated this danger by replacing, rather than supplementing, scripture as a source of primary instruction in reading. Jefferson objected to "putting the Bible and Testament into the hands of the children, at an age when their judgments are not sufficiently matured for religious enquiries" and were thus likely to adhere to scriptural dogma.[27] In fact, the establishment of public schools throughout the state entailed eliminating clerics as potential purveyors of primary education. Forestalling the possibility of such an educational "alliance between church and state" was critical for Jefferson to curtail the tyrannical urges of the established clergy, who "oppose all advances which might unmask their usurpations, and monopolies of honors, wealth and power." Enlightening the people against the dangers of ambition and superstition would be a costly endeavor, indeed too costly for the legislature of Virginia, but Jefferson considered it a trifle compared to "what will be paid to kings, priests & nobles who will rise up among us if we leave the people in ignorance."[28]

The common people were not the only ones subject to the dangers of ignorance and superstition. All too often the gentry fell under the pedagogical sway of the clergy, as did Jefferson himself during his college preparation. Jefferson sought to obviate this danger by one of the provisions of his bill which receives the least attention, namely the establishment of public grammar schools for "the furnishing to the wealthier part of the people convenient schools, at which their children may be educated." The political value of this second tier of public education for Jefferson can be seen in the fact that, while wealthy parents would have to pay their children's tuition, his bill provided that the schools themselves would be built at public expense. Indeed, the importance of these schools helps to explain why Jefferson was so eager to nurture the talents of poor geniuses at the grammar schools. It was from among those "best geniuses" annually "raked from the rubbish" who were not sent on to William and Mary that he predicted "the grammar schools will probably be supplied with future masters," just as primary school teachers would likely be culled from those worthy few dismissed after one or two years of college preparation.[29] While not the only end of Jefferson's support of poor geniuses, the separation of church and school may well have been the primary one. It was the only way to ensure that the future leaders of the state were not blinded by religious dogma and superstition.

If secularizing grammar school education was important for Jefferson, it was even more vital at the university level for it was there that the future statesmen would "be rendered by liberal education worthy to receive, and able to guard the sacred deposit of the rights and liberties of their fellow citizens." So that "the future guardians of the rights and liberties of their country may be endowed with science and virtue," Jefferson called for severing all links between William and Mary and the still-established "English Church."[30] In place of theology and divinity, Jefferson proposed a fully secular curriculum in the modern arts and sciences. Oversight would be taken from the church and placed in the hands of the political authorities. In fact, he may well have hoped that a future purely secular faculty could be culled from those few poor scholars endowed with a university education. Jefferson's own college education had come at the hands of just such a scholar. The only non-cleric on the faculty at the time, William Small, certainly lacked an "independent fortune," yet it was from this recent graduate of the University of Aberdeen that Jefferson "got my first views of the expansion of science & of the system of things in which we are placed." Indeed, he later claimed that it was his studies with Small that "probably fixed the destinies of my life."[31] Jefferson was truly fortunate in this regard, because he considered the educational offerings of the clerical instructors available to most Virginians woefully inadequate. At least that is how he justified to François Marbois the advanced education he gave his daughter. "The chance that in marriage she will draw a blockhead I calculate at about fourteen to one," he explained, and therefore "the education of her family will probably rest on her own ideas and direction."[32] Given that his daughter was unlikely to marry out of the upper echelons of the ruling gentry elite, Jefferson clearly had a dim view of the cultural attainments of his peers. These were aristocrats who desperately needed the cultivation and "naturalizing" influence of a thoroughly modern, secular education.

As important as higher education was for the ruling elite, it took second place in Jefferson's mind to primary education for the masses, at least until the founding of the University of Virginia in the final years of his life. Every form of government contained "some trace of human weakness, some germ of corruption and degeneracy, which cunning will discover, and wickedness insensibly open, cultivate and improve." That is why even in republics like Virginia's, power could never be "trusted to the rulers of the people alone."

In order to check this danger, the people must be trained "to choose with discretion the fiduciary" of their rights among the ruling elite "and to notice their conduct with diligence."[33] In some sense then, the people were the ultimate "depositories" of political authority. Jefferson did not believe that the people could actually govern themselves because, as he insisted, "they were unqualified for the management of affairs requiring intelligence beyond the common level." But they were "competent judges of human character" and could thus monitor their rulers and replace them when they betrayed their trust.[34] In order for them to fulfill this vital monitoring role, "their minds must be improved to a certain degree."[35] For the vast bulk of his life, providing this "certain degree" of education remained Jefferson's primary pedagogical project.

Jefferson's commitment to primary education for the common folk remained a central part of his labors well into his retirement. Elements of it underwent modification, most notably his transformation of primary school districts into self-governing "wards," a provision he rather characteristically misremembered as part of his original plan, in a letter to John Adams.[36] Nonetheless, as late as January 1818 he announced that "a system of general education" would be "the latest of all the public concerns in which I shall permit myself to take an interest." Before that year was over, however, Jefferson had shifted his priorities and placed his still considerable energies behind the establishment of the University of Virginia.

Some scholars have seen Jefferson's labors on behalf of his university as the culmination of his prior educational efforts. Richard K. Matthews has described them as the "capstone" of his lifelong efforts towards "establishing a public school system for Virginia."[37] In fact, however, Jefferson's "fathering" of the university at Charlottesville ran at cross-purposes to his previous commitment to primary education. To begin with, the public financing for his college was drawn from the state's previously created "Literary Fund," whose express purpose was to provide primary education for the indigent. Thus, the creation of the University of Virginia came directly at the expense of elementary education for the masses, a fiscal turn of events that, once he was informed of it, "Jefferson rejoiced in."[38]

The real mark of Jefferson's transformed educational agenda was the expanded mission he outlined for his projected institution of higher learning. To be sure, Jefferson still sought "to form the statesmen, legislators, and judges, on whom public prosperity and individual happiness are so much to depend." Now, however, he added an additional desideratum. The new university would "expound the principles and structure of government" and "a sound spirit of legislation." These principles were not those broad generalities that underlay enlightened politics but rather the narrow strictures of the Jeffersonian Republican party he helped form. In classic Jeffersonian fashion, the sage of Monticello announced in advance that these principles would "leave us free to do whatever does not violate the equal rights of another," as well as "harmonize the interest of agriculture, manufactures, and commerce."[39] Jefferson himself acknowledged that among the most striking "novelties" in his plan for the University of Virginia was its inclusion "of a professorship in the principles of government," rightly conceived. Certainly nothing like it was in his previous proposed reform of William and Mary. Part of this change reflects Jefferson's immersion in the proto-Romantic politics of principle, an immersion that began after his "enlightened" educational proposals of the 1770s.[40] But even more important was his growing concern that those principles which had come to define the party he had created, and the political movement it represented, were under assault.

Long before Jefferson began to contemplate founding a university in Charlottesville, he had been concerned by the rise of dangerous political heresies. Despite the apparent demise of Federalism after the "revolution of 1800," he was troubled by "the change of political principles which has taken place" among many within his own state as well as others, and in particular by "the general political disposition of those to whom is confided the education of the rising generation." Even the "academies" of his native Virginia did not leave him "free from grounds of uneasiness" at the spread of dangerous political principles.[41] In the years following his election to the presidency, Jefferson came to see one source of this danger in David Hume's *History of England*, a work which "makes an English Tory, from whence it is an easy step to American Toryism" or Federalism. It was also at this time that Jefferson found a solution to this danger in John Baxter's bowdlerized version of Hume's masterwork, an "editic expurgation" which Jefferson thought should be read first by students, rather than risk poisoning their minds with the Tory principles of the Scottish scholar.[42] Even more troubling was the revival of the tenets of Federalism in the decisions of the Marshall court and the "consolidationist" projects of internal improvements bandied about during Monroe's administration. These heresies threatened the state's rights principles of strict construction which delegated all domestic concerns to the states and limited the federal government to external affairs; "the one is the domestic, the other the foreign branch of the same government."[43] Yet, despite these concerns, Jefferson was still content to leave these problems to the rising generation.

That changed with the eruption of the controversy over Missouri. The "firebell in the night" that "awakened and filled me with terror," Jefferson considered the "Missouri question" without exception "the most portentous one which ever yet threatened our Union."[44] In his eyes, the issue had less to do with slavery than with power. At bottom, it was an attempt by northern crypto-Federalists to regain their lost public sway by embracing a position with "just enough of the semblance of morality to throw dust in the eyes of the people and fanaticise them." Despite being "a mere party trick," the danger to the republic was nonetheless genuine. "A geographic line, coinciding with a marked principle" would not only permanently divide the nation but "every new irritation will make it deeper and deeper."[45] As grave as the threat was to the union, however, it paled in comparison to what the Missouri question portended for the southern states. The presumption that the federal government could interfere in the "private" relations of southern slaveholders in violation of state's rights and a strict construction of the constitution raised the prospect of forced emancipation followed by race war or, worse, slave insurrection itself. "The real question" raised by the controversy, he insisted, was "are our slaves to be presented with freedom and a dagger?" This was not merely a matter of different political priorities for Jefferson, "it is a question of existence."[46] Understandably, it became imperative for Jefferson to restore the authentic principles of republican government to their rightful place in the public mind. The vehicle Jefferson chose for this restoration was the University of Virginia.

In the aftermath of the Missouri controversy, the principles Jefferson sought to uphold took on a distinctly southern hue. Inevitably the same coloring infused his projected university which, as Merrill Peterson acknowledged, Jefferson increasingly conceived "as a state or sectional bulwark of Old Republicanism against the advance of 'consolidation' and kindred political heresies in the North."[47] In fact, Jefferson saw the need for a thoroughly southern education as imperative. Sending southern youths to Harvard, for example, was an act of sectional suicide, for that institution "will return them to us fanatics and tories."[48] But Harvard was hardly unique, at least in Jefferson's mind. All "northern seminaries" were taught by "those who are against us in position and principle," and the 500 "of our sons" that Virginia annually dispatched to such institutions were "imbibing opinions and principles in discord with those of their own country." Jefferson described this state of affairs as a "canker" that was "eating on the vitals of our existence, and if not arrested at once, will be beyond remedy."[49] The only recourse was an orthodox southern education at his projected university. Only there could "that vestal flame" of true republicanism "be kept alive" and eventually "spread anew" across the land.[50] Once inculcated in the "correct principles" of state's rights, strict construction, and anti-consolidation, the university's graduates would "carry hence" these fundamental truths to the nation at large as well as bringing to Virginia's government "a degree of sound respectability it has never known."[51]

Education in the correct principles of politics at the University of Virginia would occur in the school of law and government, and it was there that Jefferson devoted most of his attention. In Jefferson's previous projected reform of William and Mary he had sought to modernize the institution by revising the subjects of study offered. Now he went further, not only setting the curriculum but actually prescribing the texts to be used. Jefferson recognized that this pedagogical micro-management was unusual and inappropriate "generally in our university." When it came to instruction in government, however, he considered it "a duty in us to lay down the principles which are to be taught." The best way to do this, he argued, was "by a previous prescription of the texts to be adopted."[52] The prescribed sources of "the general principles of liberty" were John Locke's *Second Treatise of Government* and Algernon Sidney's *Discourses Concerning Government.* The principles of American constitutionalism were to be limned in *The Federalist* and "The Declaration of Independence as the fundamental act of Union of these States." Further light could be found in Madison's Virginia resolutions "on the subject of the alien and sedition laws," whose state's rights doctrines "appeared to accord with the predominant sense of the people of the United States." Although the extensive writings of John Adams, James Wilson, and Alexander Hamilton did not make the list that "shall be used as the text and documents of the school" of law and government, Jefferson acquiesced to Madison's urging and begrudgingly included "the valedictory address of President Washington, as conveying political lessons of peculiar value."[53]

Not content with setting the texts for the school of law, Jefferson also demanded strict political orthodoxy from its instructor. "In the selection of our law Professor," he insisted to Madison, "we must be rigorously attentive to his political principles."[54] Those principles should include state's rights, strict construction, opposition to consolidation and judicial "supremacy" (i.e. judicial review), as well as a clear understanding that any "compromise" on the Missouri issue was an abrogation of constitutional rights. Acquiring such a scholar was no mean feat. Certainly he could not be found among the "Richmond lawyers" whose obeisance to the Marshall Court rendered them "rank Federalists as formerly denominated, and now consolidationists."[55] Nor was it easy to find a candidate willing to submit to such narrow ideological constraints; six candidates refused before John Taylor Lomax finally relented.[56]

Jefferson's University of Virginia thus radically departed from his prior educational efforts in two important ways. First, Jefferson shifted priorities from educating the masses through primary education to training statesmen at the university level. Second, the education of these statesmen no longer consisted in a broad exposure to modern learning but instead took on the forms of a narrow political indoctrination, one meant to inculcate a southern version of what some might now call political correctness. Part of this disjuncture was the result of the changing circumstances Jefferson confronted. When Jefferson outlined his "general system of education" in the 1770s, he was responding to the challenge of establishing a republican regime within the highly stratified and deferential society of his native Virginia. The University of Virginia, by contrast, was a response to an external, sectional threat that became palpable to Jefferson in the aftermath of the Missouri controversy. Yet part of this disjuncture also lay in the changed nature of Jefferson's political thought. The Thomas Jefferson of the 1770s was an enlightened statesman whose republicanism was tempered by a strong tincture of political "optimacy." It is this that explains the fundamentally moderate rather than egalitarian nature of his educational reforms. Beginning in the mid-1780s, Jefferson abandoned the politics of Enlightenment and began articulating a radically transformative proto-Romantic politics of principle. That politics of principle is reflected in his establishment of the University of Virginia, an institution whose primary political purpose was to safeguard and propagate "the correct principles of the day."[57] To that extent, scholars are right to see this last great educational effort of Jefferson's as a reflection of his political principles. But the principles at issue were different from those we associate with both Jefferson the democrat and with Jefferson the liberal. They were the principles of Jefferson the Virginian and southern slave-owner, the champion of state's rights and diffusion.

NOTES

1. TJ to François D'Ivernois, February 6, 1795, in *Papers of Thomas Jefferson*, ed. Julian P. Boyd *et al.* (Princeton: Princeton University Press, 1950–), XXVIII: 262; Norman K. Risjord, *Thomas Jefferson* (Madison, WI: Harper & Row, 1994), 38; Lawrence A. Cremin, *American Education: The Colonial Experience, 1607–1783* (New York, 1970), 439; Paul A. Rahe, *Republics Ancient and Modern*, vol. III, *Inventions of Prudence: Constituting the American Regime* (Chapel Hill: University of North Carolina Press, 1994): 159; Ralph Lerner, *The Thinking Revolutionary: Principle and Practice in the New Republic* (Ithaca: Cornell University Press, 1979), 61; Richard K. Matthews, *The Radical Politics of Thomas Jefferson* (Lawrence: University of Kansas Press, 1984), 88; Merrill D. Peterson, *Thomas Jefferson and the New Nation* (New York: Oxford University Press, 1970), 145.
2. See *The Autobiography of Thomas Jefferson*, in *Thomas Jefferson: Writings*, ed. Merrill D. Peterson (New York: Library of America, 1984), 42.
3. Quoted in Peterson, *New Nation*, 988.
4. On Jefferson's turning from an enlightened optimate to a proto-Romantic champion of the politics of principle, see Darren Staloff, *Hamilton, Adams, Jefferson* (New York: Hill and Wang, 2005), 248–309.

5. A Bill for the More General Diffusion of Knowledge, in *Papers*, II: 526.

6. TJ to William B. Giles, December 16, 1825, in *Writings of Thomas Jefferson*, ed. Paul Leicester Ford, 10 vols. (New York: G. P. Putnam, 1892–9), X: 354–7; TJ to George Wythe, August 13, 1786, in *Papers*, X: 244; A Bill for the More General Diffusion of Knowledge, in *Papers*, II: 532; *Notes on the State of Virginia*, ed. William Peden (Chapel Hill: University of North Carolina Press, 1954), 148.

7. Holly Brewer, "Beyond Education: Thomas Jefferson's 'Republican' Revision of the Laws Regarding Children," in *Thomas Jefferson and the Education of a Citizen*, ed. James Gilreath (Washington: Library of Congress, 1998), 54, and James Oakes, "Why Slaves Can't Read: The Political Significance of Jefferson's Racism," in *Education of a Citizen*, 188; Rahe, *Inventions of Prudence*, 159–63; and Lerner, *Thinking Revolutionary*, 79–81.

8. TJ to William Charles Jarvis, September 28, 1820, in *Writings of Thomas Jefferson*, ed. Ford, X: 160–1; "Opinion on the Treaties with France," April 18, 1793, in *Papers*, XXV: 608–9; TJ to Edmund Randolph, August 18, 1799, in *Writings of Thomas Jefferson*, ed. Ford, IX: 74; General Diffusion, 527.

9. General Diffusion, 528; "Excerpts from the Report to the Legislature of Virginia Relative to the University of Virginia, August 1818," in *The Basic Writings of Thomas Jefferson*, ed. Philip S. Foner (New York: Wiley Beak Co., 1944), 401. Jefferson used almost identical language in *Autobiography*, 44.

10. TJ to John Norvell, June 14, 1807, in *Writings of Thomas Jefferson*, ed. Ford, IX: 71–4.

11. TJ to Joseph C. Cabell, February 2, 1816, in *Thomas Jefferson: Writings*, 1378.

12. TJ to John Adams, October 14, 1816, in *The Adams–Jefferson Letters*, ed. Lester J. Cappon (Chapel Hill: University of North Carolina Press, 1959), 491.

13. On Jefferson's relations with De Tracy, see Emmet Kennedy, *A Philosophe in the Age of Revolution: Destutt de Tracy and the Origins of "Ideology"* (Philadelphia: American Philosophical Society, 1978), 208–50.

14. General Diffusion, 531.

15. A Bill for Amending the Constitution of the College of William and Mary, and Substituting More Certain Revenues for Its Support, in *Papers*, II: 539–42.

16. *Notes*, 146. Jefferson's bill required each "overseer" to select "some one of the best and most promising genius" from among the poor boys in the ten schools "under his superintendance." General Diffusion, 528, 532.

17. Peterson, *New Nation*, 148; and *Notes*, 146.

18. General Diffusion, 533.

19. The author would like to thank Stanley Brubaker for this suggestion.

20. TJ to David Rittenhouse, July 19, 1778, in *Papers*, II: 202–3.

21. TJ to Peter Carr, September 7, 1814, in *Writings of Jefferson*, ed. Bergh and Ellis, XIX: 212, 214.

22. See Staloff, *Hamilton, Adams, Jefferson*, 249–61.

23. General Diffusion, 526.

24. David Hume, "Of the Independency of Parliament," in Hume, *Essays Moral, Political and Literary*, ed. Eugene F. Miller (Indianapolis: Hill and Wang, 1985), 42.

25. *Notes*, 148. Jefferson used almost identical language in General Diffusion, 526–7.

26. Jean M. Yarbrough, *American Virtues* (Lawrence: University of Kansas Press, 1998), 104. See Douglas L. Wilson, "Jefferson vs. Hume," *William and Mary Quarterly*, 3rd ser., 46 (1989): 49–70.
27. *Notes*, 146–7.
28. "Report Relative to the University of Virginia," 403; TJ to George Wythe, August 13, 1786, in *Papers*, X: 245.
29. *Notes*, 146–7.
30. General Diffusion, 527; Bill for Amending William and Mary, 539.
31. *Autobiography*, 4.
32. TJ to François Marbois, December 5, 1783, in *Papers*, VI: 374.
33. *Notes*, 148; "Report Relative to the University of Virginia," 148.
34. TJ to P. S. DuPont de Nemours, April 24, 1816, in *Works of Jefferson*, ed. Ford, XI: 520.
35. *Notes*, 148.
36. TJ to John Adams, October 28, 1813, in *Adams–Jefferson Letters*, 390.
37. Matthews, *Radical Politics*, 88.
38. Peterson, *New Nation*, 996–7.
39. "Report Relative to the University of Virginia," 401.
40. On Jefferson's articulation of the "politics of principle," see Staloff, *Hamilton, Adams, Jefferson*, 280–309.
41. TJ to Jeremiah Moor, August 14, 1800, in *Papers*, XXXII: 103.
42. Wilson, "Jefferson vs. Hume," 63–5; TJ to George Washington Lewis, October 25, 1825, in *Writings of Jefferson*, XVI: 128.
43. TJ to Major John Cartwright, June 5, 1824, in *Writings of Thomas Jefferson*, ed. Ford, XVI: 47.
44. TJ to John Holmes, April 22, 1820, in *Writings of Thomas Jefferson*, ed. Ford, X: 158; TJ to Hugh Nelson, February 7, 1820, in *Writings of Thomas Jefferson*, ed. Ford, X: 157.
45. TJ to David Bailey Warden, December 26, 1820, in *Writings of Thomas Jefferson*, ed. Ford, X: 71–3; TJ to Charles Pinckney, September 30, 1820, in *Writings of Thomas Jefferson*, ed. Ford, X: 161–3; TJ to John Holmes, April 22, 1820, XII.158.
46. TJ to John Adams, January 22, 1821, in *Adams–Jefferson Letters*, 570; TJ to Albert Gallatin, December 26, 1820, in *Writings of Thomas Jefferson*, ed. Ford, X: 75–8.
47. Peterson, *New Nation*, 981.
48. TJ to Joseph Cabell, January 22, 1820, in *Writings of Thomas Jefferson*, ed. Ford, X: 154–5.
49. TJ to James Breckenridge, February 15, 1821, in *Thomas Jefferson: Writings*, 1452.
50. TJ to James Madison, February 17, 1826, in *The Republic of Letters*, ed. James Morton Smith, 3 vols. (New York: W. W. Norton, 1995), 1967.
51. TJ to William B. Giles, December 26, 1825, in *Writings of Thomas Jefferson*, ed. Ford, X: 354–7.
52. TJ to James Madison, February 1, 1825, in *Republic of Letters*, 1923–4.
53. "From the Minutes of the Board of Visitors, University of Virginia," March 4, 1825, in *Thomas Jefferson: Writings*, 479–80. Madison had also requested the

inclusion of Washington's inaugural address, but Jefferson refused. See James Madison to TJ, February 8, 1825, in *Republic of Letters*, 1925.

54. TJ to James Madison, February 17, 1826, in *Republic of Letters*, 1967.
55. TJ to James Madison, February 1, 1826, in *Republic of Letters*, 1923–4.
56. Peterson, *New Nation*, 985–6.
57. TJ to William B. Giles, December 26, 1825, in *Writings of Thomas Jefferson*, ed. Ford, x: 354–7.

10

RICHARD SAMUELSON

Jefferson and religion: private belief, public policy

Jefferson was of two minds on the subject of religion, which has sometimes confused both his critics and his champions. He wrote John Adams in 1817:

> If by religion we are to understand sectarian dogmas, in which no two of them agree, then your exclamation on that hypothesis is just, "that this would be the best of all possible worlds, if there were no religion in it." But if the moral precepts, innate in man, and made a part of his physical constitution, as necessary for a social being, if the sublime doctrines of philanthropism and deism taught us by Jesus of Nazareth, in which all agree, constitute true religion, then, without it, this would be, as you again say, "something not fit to be named" even, indeed, a hell.[1]

Jefferson had little use for the "sectarian dogmas" which were commonly called "religion," yet he believed that "the moral precepts, innate in man," were essential. The latter constituted "true religion." There are two sides to the story of Jefferson's religious ideas – private and public. What were Jefferson's personal religious beliefs? And what did Jefferson mean when he said in his famous letter to the Danbury Baptists that there ought to be a "wall of separation between church and state."[2]

Jefferson's religious journey

Jefferson's religious opinions changed as he aged. Jefferson's family raised him in the Anglican church. Either before or during his college years, he drifted away from whatever Christian faith he had, and remained rather skeptical through much of his adulthood. In the mid-1790s, or perhaps a bit before then, he started to study the life, works, and philosophy of Jesus quite closely. In time he would edit his own, personal edition of the Gospels and would think that Jesus was one of history's greatest moral teachers.[3]

Because we have few papers from Jefferson's youth, our understanding of young Jefferson's religion must remain speculative. What we can say is that he was raised in the fashion of the son of a frontier planter in eighteenth-century Virginia. When he was born, his father, a vestryman in the local parish, almost certainly had him baptized. As he grew up, Anglican clergymen served as his principal tutors. At the College of William and Mary, where he went in 1760, six of its seven faculty members were Anglican clerics. His earliest extant letters show an easy familiarity with scripture, which he playfully exploits to literary effect. Writing on Christmas Day in 1762, Jefferson compares his trials as a young lover to those of Job:

> this very day, to others a day of greatest mirth and jollity, sees me overwhelmed with more and greater misfortunes than have befallen a descendant of Adam for these thousand years past, I am sure; and perhaps, after excepting Job, since the creation of the world. I think his misfortunes were somewhat greater than mine; for, although we may be pretty nearly on a level in other respects, yet, I thank my God, I have the advantage of brother Job in this, that Satan has not as yet put forth his hand to load me with bodily afflictions.[4]

Young Jefferson learned to observe the formalities of Virgina's official communion even as his mind drifted away from its theological core. Years later, Jefferson called Reverend Maury, one of his tutors, "a correct classical scholar," which says something about what he found most valuable in his early education, and of his college years he reflected that "it was the great good fortune, and what probably fixed the destinies of my life that Dr. Wm. Small of Scotland was then professor of Mathematics, a man profound in most of the useful branches of science."[5] Small, the one non-cleric on the faculty of the college at the time, introduced Jefferson to the concatenation of ideas that we now call the "Enlightenment."

Whatever Jefferson believed, he remained conventionally observant. He attended church services with some regularity, and he probably had his children baptized into the Anglican church. Jefferson refused to serve as godfather to the children of a friend, however. To do that job, one had to believe rather more than Jefferson could: "The person who becomes sponsor for a child … makes a solemn profession before God and the world, of faith in the articles, which I had never sense enough to comprehend, and it has always appeared to me that comprehension must precede assent."[6]

Young Jefferson read a good deal of ancient and modern philosophy. He became particularly enamored of epicurean thought, though he also had great respect for stoicism. He also read such modern authors as the Enlightened eighteenth-century Tory, Lord Bolingbroke. His literary commonplace book of the 1760s is littered with passages taken from Bolingbroke, often his notoriously scathing criticisms of biblical religion. We can get some insight into Jefferson's thoughts on religion in these years by looking at his advice to others about religious study. In 1771, a friend asked Jefferson to recommend books for a gentleman's library. Jefferson responded in detail. Under the heading of "religion" he included Locke, Xenophon, Epictetus, Antoninus, Seneca, Cicero, Bolingbroke, Hume, Kames, Sterne, and one or two other like authors.[7] This is roughly the same list he recommended under the heading "morality" in 1785 to Peter Carr, his nephew and ward, when advising the young man what he ought to read.[8] Two years later, he wrote Carr again. Turning to the subject of "religion," Jefferson advised that "your reason is now mature enough to examine this object." Carr should "fix reason firmly in her seat, and call to her tribunal every fact, every opinion. Question with boldness even the existence of a god; because, if there be one, he must more approve of the homage of reason, than that of blindfolded faith." Carr should read the Bible, "as you would read Livy or Tacitus. The facts which are within the ordinary course of nature you will believe on the authority of the writer … but those facts in the bible which contradict the laws of nature, must be examined with more care."[9] Revelation must vindicate itself before the bar of empirical science.

Jefferson's disposition towards Jesus changed, probably in the 1790s, but perhaps a bit earlier. While visiting London in 1786, Jefferson met the Unitarian minister, Richard Price, and, as well, Joseph Priestley, the scientist and Unitarian theologian. Jefferson soon read Priestley's theological works with care – with particularly great interest his *History of the Corruptions of Christianity* and *History of Early Opinions Concerning Jesus Christ.* Jefferson met Priestley again in Philadelphia in the late 1790s, and began attending his church. Jefferson became, and for the rest of his life remained, convinced of Jesus' greatness. Jesus "corrected the Deism of the Jews, confirming them in their belief of one only God, and giving them juster notions of his attributes and government";[10] "Jesus, taking for his type the best qualities of the human head and heart, wisdom, justice, goodness, and adding to them power, ascribed all of those, but in infinite perfection, to the Supreme Being, and formed him really worthy of admiration … [He] preached philanthropy and universal charity and benevolence."[11] Moreover, Jefferson held that "the doctrines of Jesus are simple, and tend all to the happiness of man."[12] In short, Jesus took the monotheism of the Jews and made it a truly ethical monotheism by connecting it with the notions that, before their creator, all men were equal, and that His will might be understood by all. The good life was not open only to one particular nation or class. He excoriated the original corrupters of Jesus' teaching, in addition to more recent ones, particularly Calvinists.[13]

Because he posed a threat to the religious and political powers of his day, Jesus was cut down when he was still young. A conspiracy of priests and kings then corrupted Jesus' teachings, perverting them to suit their own ends:

> a short time elapsed after the death of the great reformer of the Jewish religion, before his principles were departed from by those who professed to be his special servants, and perverted into an engine for enslaving mankind, and aggrandizing their oppressors in Church and State: that the purest system of morals ever before preached to man has been adulterated and sophisticated by artificial constructions, into a mere contrivance to filch wealth and power to themselves.[14]

Jesus' simple, clear teachings threatened the special status of priests and kings. They responded by warping his teachings, making them serve their own ends. The result was injustice to Jesus: "Rational men, not being able to swallow their impious heresies, in order to force them down their throats, they raise the hue and cry of infidelity, while themselves are the greatest obstacles to the advancement of the real doctrines of Jesus, and do, in fact, constitute the real Anti-Christ."[15]

During his presidency, Jefferson grew frustrated with the facile use of the Gospel to level charges of infidelity against himself and his political friends. He responded privately, with two products: a "Syllabus of an Estimate of the Merit of the Doctrines of Jesus, Compared with those of Others," and the "Jefferson Bible."[16] The former outlined the main tenets of the Philosophers, the Jews, and Jesus, comparing and contrasting them to the advantage of Jesus. The latter is Jefferson's redacted abstract of the Gospels. "In the New Testament," Jefferson wrote, "there is internal evidence that parts of it have proceeded from an extraordinary man; and that other parts are of the fabric of very inferior minds. It is as easy to separate those parts, as to pick out diamonds from dunghills."[17] Jefferson, who called Francis Bacon, Isaac Newton, and John Locke the three greatest men who had ever lived, subjected the Bible to the test of the modern scientific method.[18] That which was incredible was not creditable. Miracles were out; ethical teachings remained. Hence the Jefferson Bible began not with the word, but, like the American Revolution, with the tax: "and it came to pass in those days, that there went out a decree from Cesar Augustus, that all the world should be taxed."[19]

Jefferson's religious beliefs

Jefferson's changing understanding of Christianity turned in relation to his two definitions of religion. In his younger days, Jefferson regarded Christianity as superstition, associating all of Jesus' teachings together. He changed his mind as the years passed, separating the reasonable teachings of Jesus from the "sectarian dogmas" foisted upon him by religious-system builders. Against the "Platonizing Christians," Jefferson upheld what he called "Christianism," a rationalistic form of Unitarianism.[20] Once the wheat was separated from the chaff, there remained "the outlines of a system of the most sublime morality which has ever fallen from the lips of man."[21] According to Jefferson, Jesus taught three main things: "1. That there is only one God, and he all perfect. 2. That there is a future state of rewards and punishments. 3. That to love God with all thy heart and thy neighbor as thyself, is the sum of religion."[22]

However much reverence Jefferson had for Jesus, he did not think Jesus' teachings were without fault:

> But while this syllabus is meant to place the character of Jesus in it's true and high light, as no imposter himself, but a great Reformer of the Hebrew code of religion, it is not to be understood that I am with him in all his doctrines. I am a Materialist; he takes the side of spiritualism; he preaches the efficacy of repentance towards forgiveness of sin, I require a counterpoise of good works to redeem it, &c. &c.[23]

Jefferson blamed these defects on Jesus' enemies, who killed him before he could perfect his ideas. Jesus "fell an early victim to the jealousy and combination of the altar and the throne ... Hence the doctrines which he really delivered were defective as a whole."[24] In Jesus, rightly understood, Jefferson found a close approximation of his own beliefs, but not an exact match.

We probably will never attain an exact understanding of Jefferson's beliefs, for he was quite reluctant to express them. "I have ever thought religion a concern purely between our god and our consciences," Jefferson wrote, "for which we were accountable to him, and not to the priests. I never told my own religion, nor scrutinised that of another."[25] Even so, we might be able to discover some tenets that were particularly important to him. His central religious idea appears to be that the world was good, and that nature made sense. That is what he meant when he said "that heaven did not make man in it's wrath."[26]

Jefferson believed that there was a logic in creation. When discussing the moral sense, he noted that "the Creator would indeed have been a bungling artist, had he intended man for a social animal, without planting in him social dispositions."[27] He wrote similarly about natural aristocracy: "It would have been inconsistent in creation to have formed man for the social state, and not to have provided virtue and wisdom enough to manage the concerns of the society."[28] Jefferson believed that there was an order in nature that human reason might discern. God had made that order in such a way that men might flourish in it. Jefferson did not think one had to believe in God to believe that there was order in nature. After noting that, in Catholic countries, philosophes subscribed to a "system of atheism," but in Protestant countries "infidelity ... took generally the form of Theism," he noted that "both agreed in the order of the existing system, but the one supposed it from eternity, the other as having begun in time."[29]

Believing that nature was created under the benevolent eye of providence forced Jefferson to confront the problem of evil. If men were capable of self-government, why had republics always collapsed in the past?[30] Traditional religion's answer to this problem of evil was that most men were bad, and few were good. Hence governments had to work hard to keep men in line, and priests had to assert their authority to teach men the difference between righteousness and wickedness. By contrast, Jefferson held that most men were fundamentally good. He blamed past failures on bad men who had conspired to keep others down.

Another way to understand Jefferson's religious beliefs is to consider two of his favorite psalms. "In contemplation of a being so superlative, the hyperbolic flights of the Psalmist may often be followed with approbation, even with rapture," he wrote; "I have no hesitation in giving the psalm over all the Hymnists of every language, and of every time. Turn to the 148th. psalm in Brady and Tate's version. Have such conceptions been ever before expressed? Their version of the 15th psalm is more to be esteemed for its pithiness, than it's poetry."[31] Psalm 148 is a hymn of praise to the creator of heaven and earth. In the translation that Jefferson recommended, the third verse begins: "Let them adore the Lord / and praise his holy name, / By whose almighty word / They all from nothing came"; and the sixth reads: "Let all of royal birth, / with those of humbler frame, / And judges of the earth, / His matchless praise proclaim. / In this design / Let youth with maids, / And with hoary heads / With children join." Meanwhile, the fifteenth psalm turns to the duties of man. It begins, "Lord, who's the happy man that may / to thy blest courts repair? / Not, stranger-like, to visit them, / but to inhabit there? / 'Tis he, whose ev'ry thought and deed / by rules of virtue moves; / Whose gen'rous tongue disdains to speak / the thing his heart disproves."[32] Combining the two, we find that Jefferson praised the Almighty Author of creation, who made a world with a moral economy. All were equal before the Lord, and therefore all were equally enjoined to pursue happiness by practicing the virtues. The good life and the virtuous life were one and the same.

Jefferson was convinced that these beliefs were congruent with modern science. Although he allowed that many truths were beyond the reach of human reason, Jefferson did not think there were any such truths that were necessary to a good life on earth. When John Adams pushed him on philosophical fundamentals in 1820, Jefferson replied:

I was obliged to recur ultimately to my habitual anodyne, "I feel: therefore I exist." I feel bodies which are not myself: there are other existences then. I call them *matter*. I feel them changing place. This gives me *motion*. Where there is absence of matter, I call it *void*, or *nothing*, or *immaterial space*. On the basis of sensation, of matter and motion, we may erect the fabric of all the certainties we can have or need.[33]

Jefferson believed that "all the certainties we can have or need" could be had via the senses, combined with the method of modern empirical science. To believe otherwise was to open up nature to the possibility of chaos, and man to a future as full of tyranny and war as the past had been. It was this very same premise that made the Jefferson Bible possible. Literal reading was the only legitimate way to read a religious text. "If histories so unlike as those of Hercules and Jesus, can, by a fertile imagination and allegorical interpretations, be brought to the same tally," he wrote, "no line of distinction remains between fact and fancy."[34] One Jewish commentator, he complained, "takes passages of Scripture from their contexts ... strings them together, and makes them point towards what object he pleases; he interprets them figuratively, typically, analogically, hyperbolically; he calls in the aid of ... every other figure of rhetoric."[35] The paradox of revelation – how can a being with infinite intellect reveal Himself to beings with limited intellect – did not interest Jefferson. Jefferson preferred his truths to be clear and distinct. Were it the case that certain important truths could only be discovered by metaphor, analogy, or dialectic, then the priests may have had a point. Jefferson dismissed that argument. On the contrary, he wrote, "I consider belief to be the assent of the mind to an intelligible proposition."[36] Any truth that could not be discovered clearly and distinctly to the human mind via the empirical method was, by definition, not necessary to the good life. That was, Jefferson thought, the divine economy of nature.

Almighty God hath created the mind free

Jefferson's understanding of the divine order of nature is the proper context in which to understand his belief in "a wall of separation" between church and state. Inside the wall were those things which were amenable to reason; outside of it were speculative opinions and superstitious beliefs. This distinction explains an apparent contradiction in Jefferson's *Notes on the State of Virginia*. In Query XVII, he complained that:

the error seems not sufficiently eradicated, that the operations of the mind, as well as the acts of the body, are subject to the coercion of the laws. But our rulers can have authority over such natural rights only as we have submitted to them. The rights of conscience were never submitted, we could not submit. We are answerable for them to our God. The legitimate powers of government extend to such acts only as are injurious to others. But it does me no injury for my neighbor to say there are twenty gods, or no god. It neither picks my pocket nor breaks my leg.[37]

Having said that, in the very next Query, he wrote: "can the liberties of a nation be thought secure when we have removed their only firm basis, a conviction in the minds of the people that these liberties are the gift of God? That they are not to be violated but with his wrath?"[38] Jefferson thinks it neither picks my pocket nor breaks my leg for my neighbor to say there are twenty gods, or no god. And yet, he also suggests that, in a good regime, men believe that their "liberties are the gift of God." The wall of separation resolves the paradox. Citizens as a group must believe that they have rights because their creator endowed them with rights. In private conversation, however, they may be free to question everything, and maintain whatever opinions they choose – for such is their God-given liberty.

This understanding of religion and of liberty explains the language of the Virginia Statute for Religious Freedom, which Jefferson drafted in the 1770s and which, with a few modifications, became law in 1786. Jefferson's draft of the bill begins, "Well aware that the opinions and belief of men depend not on their own will, but follow involuntarily the evidence proposed to their minds; that Almighty God hath created the mind free; and manifested his supreme will that free it shall remain by making it altogether insusceptible of restraint."[39] When Jefferson "swore upon the altar of god, eternal hostility against every form of tyranny over the mind of man," he was affirming his belief that the Author of Nature so ordered things that the human mind was designed to be free.[40] Human reason discovered the order of nature – an order so designed that the mind could not be contained by tyranny. Liberate the human mind from tyranny, Jefferson thought, and men would flourish.

In the Virginia Statute, Jefferson seems to distinguish "belief" from "opinion." At the start, the bill mentions "opinions and belief," later on, it says that "our civil rights have no dependence upon our religious opinions, any more than our opinions in physics or geometry" and that "the opinions of men are not the object of civil government, nor under its jurisdiction." Belief has disappeared, only to return in the active part of the statute: "no man shall be compelled to frequent or support ... nor shall otherwise suffer, on account of his religious opinions or belief." This linguistic tergiversation might be inadvertent. It appears, however, to reflect something deeper. If belief was "the assent of the mind to an intelligible proposition," and if a belief in the rational order of creation was essential to good government, then belief in certain truths about God, man, and the universe were themselves necessary to the regime. There was a reason inherent in the constitutional order which, by definition, the constitutional order supported.[41] Opinion, on the other hand, was speculative. In the realm of opinion, no two religions agreed. That distinction might explain why Jefferson thought it was important to keep the name Jesus out of the Virginia Statute for Religious Liberty.

This reading of the Virginia Statute reminds us of the political purpose of disestablishment. To do away with religious establishments, Jefferson thought, was to dry the wellspring of false religion. In the Virginia Statute, Jefferson denounced "the impious presumption of legislators and rulers, civil as well as ecclesiastical, who, being themselves but fallible and uninspired men, have assumed dominion over the faith of others, setting up their own opinions and modes of thinking as the only true and infallible." These evil men "hath established and maintained false religions over the greatest part of the world and through all time." By contrast, Jefferson asserted "that truth is great and will prevail if left to herself; that she is the proper and sufficient antagonist to error, and has nothing to fear from conflict unless by human interposition disarmed of her natural weapons, free argument and debate." Absent religious establishments, truth would prevail. When Connecticut ended its establishment, he wrote: "I rejoice that in this blessed country of free inquiry and belief, which has surrendered its creed and conscience to neither kings nor priests, the genuine doctrine of one only God is reviving, and I trust that there is not a young man now living in the United States who will not die an Unitarian."[42] Liberate man from religious coercion, and true religion would rise.

In religion, as in so much else, Jefferson was rather more restrained in practice than he was in theory. The Virginia Statute was one of five bills regarding religion in the general revision of Virginia's code of laws that Jefferson undertook after July, 1776. The other four were: a "bill for saving the property of the church heretofore by law established," "a bill for punishing disturbers of religious worship and sabbath breakers," "a bill for appointing days of public fasting and thanksgiving," and "a bill annulling marriages prohibited by the levitical law, and appointing the mode of solemnizing lawful marriage."[43] These bills had more to do with regulating actions than belief. Even so, they did bring the state into matters religious. Perhaps Jefferson thought that the state had to take affirmative steps to guarantee religious liberty. Moreover, Jefferson understood that, in order to serve the very principle of liberty of conscience, he had to respect the conscientious wishes of Virginians – whatever those wishes were. To impose his own views on others was no less a violation of the rights of conscience than was any other form of religious establishment. This idea was behind his articulation of the powerful metaphor of the "wall of separation" in his famous letter to the Danbury Baptists of January, 1802.

The wall of separation, Jefferson thought, was part of God's plan. Once it was in place, Jefferson could be quite liberal towards various religions. "In our village of Charlottesville," he wrote late in his life:

> there is a good degree of religion, with a small degree of fanaticism. We have four sects, but without either church or meeting-house. The court-house is our common temple, one Sunday in the month each. Here, Episcopalian and Presbyterian, Methodist and Baptist, meet together, join in hymning their Maker, listen with attention and devotion to each others' preachers, and all mix in society in perfect harmony.[44]

That men could live in such harmony was one of the reasons why Jefferson believed "that it is a good world on the whole, ... it has been framed on a principle of benevolence."[45]

NOTES

1. TJ to John Adams, May 5, 1817, in *The Writings of Thomas Jefferson*, ed. Andrew A. Lipscomb and Albert Ellery Bergh (Washington, DC: Thomas Jefferson Memorial Foundation, 1903), XV: 109. I have used the CD-rom version sold by H-Bar Enterprises, 1996.
2. TJ to Nehemiah Dodge *et al.*, January 1, 1802, in *Thomas Jefferson: Writings*, ed. Merrill D. Peterson (New York: Library of America, 1984), 510.
3. On Jefferson's religious biography, I found particularly helpful Edwin S. Gaustad, *Sworn on the Altar of God* (Grand Rapids, MI: William B. Eerdmans, 1996); Charles B. Sanford, *The Religious Life of Thomas Jefferson* (Charlottesville: University Press of Virginia, 1984); the introduction to Dickinson W. Adams (ed.), *Jefferson's Extracts From the Gospels* (Princeton: Princeton University Press, 1983); and Paul K. Conkin, "The Religious Pilgrimage of Thomas Jefferson," in *Jeffersonian Legacies*, ed. Peter S. Onuf (Charlottesville: University Press of Virginia, 1993), 19–49.
4. TJ to John Page, December 25, 1762, in *Writings of Thomas Jefferson*, ed. Lipscomb and Bergh, IV: 1.
5. Jefferson, *Autobiography*, in *Thomas Jefferson: Writings*, 4.
6. Jefferson, cited in Gaustad, *Sworn on the Altar of God*, 8.
7. Enclosure in TJ to Robert Skipwith, August 3, 1771, in *Thomas Jefferson: Writings*, 744.
8. TJ to Peter Carr, August 19, 1785, in *Thomas Jefferson: Writings*, 814–18.
9. TJ to Peter Carr, August 10, 1787, in *Thomas Jefferson: Writings*, 902.
10. TJ to Benjamin Rush, April 21, 1803, in *Thomas Jefferson: Writings*, 1125. Jefferson often associated his political enemies with Jews. He also complained that "an Anglican, monarchical and aristocratical party, had sprung up" in America; TJ to Philip Mazzei, April 24, 1796, in *Thomas Jefferson: Writings*, 1036. On the Quakers, see TJ to Lafayette, May 14, 1817, in *Thomas Jefferson: Writings*, 1408 ("Delaware ... is essentially a Quaker State, the fragment of a religious sect, ... Dispersed, as the Jews"). On the New England Federalists, see TJ to John Taylor, June 1, 1798: "they are marked, like the Jews, with such a

perversity of character, as to constitute, from that circumstance the natural division of our parties." *Thomas Jefferson: Writings*, 1050.

11. TJ to William Short, August 4, 1820, in *Thomas Jefferson: Writings*, 1437.
12. TJ to Benjamin Waterhouse, June 26, 1822, in *Thomas Jefferson: Writings*, 1458.
13. "Now, which of these is the true and charitable Christian? He who believes and acts on the simple doctrines of Jesus? Or the impious dogmatists, as Athanasius and Calvin? Verily I say these are the false shepherds." Ibid., 1458–9. Jefferson also spoke of "the half reformation of Luther and Calvin." TJ to Salma Hale, July 16, 1818, in *Extracts from the Gospels*, 385.
14. TJ to Samuel Kercheval, January 19, 1810, in *Thomas Jefferson: Writings*, 1213–14.
15. Ibid., 1214.
16. The text of both may be found in *Extracts from the Gospels*.
17. TJ to John Adams, January 24, 1814, in *The Adams–Jefferson Letters*, ed. Lester J. Cappon (Chapel Hill: University of North Carolina Press, 1959), 421.
18. TJ to John Trumbull, February 15, 1789, in *Thomas Jefferson: Writings*, 939–40.
19. Jefferson Bible, first page, *Extracts from the Gospels*, 60.
20. TJ to Benjamin Waterhouse, June 26, 1822, in *Thomas Jefferson: Writings*, 1458; TJ to F. A. Vanderkemp, July 30, 1816, in *Extracts from the Gospels*, 375.
21. TJ to William Short, October 31, 1819, in *Thomas Jefferson: Writings*, 1431. See also TJ to Joseph Priestley, April 9, 1803, in *Extracts from the Gospels*, 328ff.
22. TJ to Benjamin Waterhouse, June 26, 1822, in *Thomas Jefferson: Writings*, 1458.
23. TJ to William Short, April 13, 1820, in *Jefferson's Extracts from the Gospels*, 391–2. See also TJ to William Short, August 4, 1820, in *Extracts from the Gospels*, 394–9. Elsewhere, Jefferson suggested that Jesus was a materialist: "He told us indeed that 'God is a spirit,' but he has not defined what a spirit is, nor said that it is not *matter*." TJ to John Adams, August 15, 1820, in *Adams–Jefferson Letters*, 569. See also TJ to John Adams, January 8, 1825, in *Adams–Jefferson Letters*, 605–6.
24. TJ to Benjamin Rush, April 21, 1803. At the end of this letter, Jefferson reflects that Jesus "taught, emphatically, the doctrines of a future state … and wielded it with efficacy, as an important incentive, supplementary to the other motives to moral conduct." *Thomas Jefferson: Writings*, 1124–6.
25. TJ to Margaret Bayard Smith, August 6, 1816, in *Jefferson's Extracts from the Gospels*, 376. Jefferson tended to say "our God" or "his God" and not simply God, suggesting he may have had questions about the deity in general.
26. TJ to Madame d'Enville, April 2, 1790, in *Thomas Jefferson: Writings*, 966.
27. TJ to Thomas Law, June 13, 1813, in *Writings of Thomas Jefferson*, ed. Lipscomb and Bergh, XIV: 140.
28. TJ to John Adams, October 28, 1813, in *Thomas Jefferson: Writings*, 1306.
29. TJ to John Adams, April 8, 1816, in *Adams–Jefferson Letters*, 467–8. Conkin says that Jefferson never questioned what he calls a "Semitic cosmology," but that's probably not entirely fair. "Religious Pilgrimage," 21.
30. Ernst Cassirer, *The Philosophy of the Enlightenment*, trans. Fritz Koelln and James Pettigrove (Princeton: Princeton University Press, 1951), notes that theodicy was a political problem for men of the Enlightenment.
31. TJ to John Adams, October 12, 1813, in *Adams–Jefferson Letters*, 385. Elsewhere he added that, "knowing nothing more moral, more sublime, more worthy of your preservation than David's description of the good man, in his 15th Psalm,"

he would transcribe it for his correspondent, and he did so from the same translation. Jefferson to Isaac Englebrecht, February 25, 1824, in *Writings of Thomas Jefferson*, ed. Lipscomb and Bergh, XVI: 16.

32. Both these are quoted from Brady and Tate, *A New Version of the Psalms of David*, available on the web, courtesy of *Music for the Church of God*, 2001. www.cgmusic.com/workshop/newver_frame.htm.

33. TJ to John Adams, August 15, 1820, in *Adams–Jefferson Letters*, 567.

34. TJ to John Adams, October 14, 1816, in *Adams–Jefferson Letters*, 491.

35. TJ to John Adams, April 8, 1816, in *Thomas Jefferson: Writings*, 1384.

36. TJ to John Adams, August 22, 1813, in *Adams–Jefferson Letters*, 368.

37. Jefferson, *Notes on the State of Virginia*, in *Thomas Jefferson: Writings*, 285.

38. Ibid., 289.

39. Jefferson's draft of the Virginia Statute may be found in *Thomas Jefferson: Writings*, 346–8. All citations in this paragraph and the next two are from this source, unless otherwise noted.

40. TJ to Benjamin Rush, September 23, 1800, in *Thomas Jefferson: Writings*, 1082.

41. This belief might explain why Jefferson tended to label his political opponents "heretics" or to speak of their "heresies." When the *Rights of Man* was to be published in America, Jefferson wrote that he was "extremely pleased to find it [Paine's book] will be reprinted here, and that something is at length to be publicly said against the political heresies which have sprung up among us." TJ to Jonathan B. Smith, April 26, 1791, in *Papers of Thomas Jefferson*, ed. Julian P. Boyd *et al.* (Princeton: Princeton University Press, 1950–), XX: 290. See also TJ to Mr. Cutting, October 2, 1788, to James Madison, August 11, 1793, and to James Sullivan, June 19, 1807, in *Writings of Thomas Jefferson*, ed. Lipscomb and Bergh, VII: 155, IX: 180, XI: 238, respectively.

42. TJ to Benjamin Waterhouse, June 26, 1822, in *Thomas Jefferson: Writings*, 1459. On this idea, see Johann Neem, "Beyond the Wall: Jefferson's Danbury Address," *Journal of the Early Republic*, 17:1 (Spring, 2007): 139–54, and Richard A. Samuelson, "What Adams Saw Over Jefferson's Wall," *Commentary*, 104:2 (August, 1997): 52–4. On the political calculations involved specifically in Jefferson's letter to the Danbury Baptists, see James H. Hutson, "Thomas Jefferson's Letter to the Danbury Baptists: A Controversy Rejoined," *William and Mary Quarterly*, 3rd ser., 56:4 (October, 1999): 775–90. This issue of the *William and Mary Quarterly* features responses to Hutson's article immediately after it.

43. On Jefferson's revision of the laws and the Virginia Statute, see Daniel Dreisbach, "A New Perspective on Jefferson's Views on Church–State Relations: the Virginia Statute for Establishing Religious Freedom in its Legislative Context," *American Journal of Legal History*, 35:2 (April, 1991): 172–204. The bill titles may be found on 187, 189, 191, 196. See also Dreisbach, *Thomas Jefferson and the Wall of Separation Between Church and State* (New York: New York University Press, 2002).

44. TJ to Dr. Thomas Cooper, November 2, 1822, in *Thomas Jefferson: Writings*, 1564.

45. TJ to John Adams, April 8, 1816, in *Adams–Jefferson Letters*, 467.

11

ANDREW BURSTEIN

Jefferson and the language of friendship

What we know about Jefferson's friendships, we know primarily through his familiar letter writing. While there is anecdotal information in the published accounts of some who interacted with him personally, and family stories that have been passed down, by far the best source for the historian is the large body of correspondence (some 16,000 letters, it has been reliably estimated) in the Library of Congress, University of Virginia, and Massachusetts Historical Society collections. Many, although not all, of these letters have been published.[1]

Though Jefferson, in general, adheres to eighteenth-century conventions, and thereby disguises his emotions, we can be fairly certain that the picture we obtain from his ample correspondence is not always constructed so that we, his posterity, are only able to perceive him as strong, consistent, and well intentioned. That is, there were times when he wrote in a less self-censored way than he ordinarily did; there were times when he felt impassioned and unconstrained, and took a chance in committing his feelings to paper. When he wrote, he wrote to have an impact on the person or persons to whom he addressed his letter – the plural is mentioned here because, in his century, one's correspondence was less private and often shared, unless the letter writer insisted on utter confidence or directed that the letter was meant for incineration. (We know this, because letters that instructed the recipient, "Burn this," were in fact preserved.) Jefferson is public property now, and the meaning we derive from his writing is contingent on our ability to shed twenty-first-century skin and recover the foreign inner world of an eighteenth-century being.

Friendship in literature

In what is perhaps his most famous letter on friendship, the twelve-page dialogue between Head and Heart, written in October, 1786, to the Anglo-Italian portrait painter Maria Cosway, Jefferson purported to open himself up.

At the time, he was the widowed US minister to France, and living in Paris; Mrs. Cosway was in a loveless marriage. In this letter, Jefferson revealed a conflict that he imagined was eternal: whether to commit oneself to another, risking the pain of separation that emotional commitment entails; or to make the deliberate choice of avoiding commitment, so as to pursue more cerebral pleasures. The fact that Jefferson had not long before dislocated his right wrist (he was right-handed) during an outing with Cosway, and wrote this letter painstakingly with his left over the course of at least one day, suggests how committed he was to dispatching this letter. Its mood alternates between melancholy and exhilaration, and its clear intent is that it will be read as a work of art as well as a testament of sentimental attachment. Maria Cosway was an accomplished artist, and they had attended museums together during the months when they kept company in Paris. Jefferson could not communicate with paint, instead producing his art with a quill pen.

To appreciate this letter, and Jefferson's other letters of friendship, we must first understand how Jefferson became familiar with the art of friendship. The study of Greek and Latin was unquestionably the top priority in a young man's education in the mid eighteenth century. Models of thought and behavior derived first from classical antiquity. In his literary commonplace book, a selection of meaningful, extended quotations compiled from approximately 1762 to the early 1770s, Jefferson in his twenties gave attention to the Greek tragedian Euripides, and copied in Greek several passages relating to trustworthiness, fairness, and justice; for instance, "There is nothing better than a trusty friend, neither wealth nor princely power; mere number is a senseless thing to set off against a trusty friend," and, "May he perish and find no favour, whoso hath not in him honour for his friends, freely unlocking his heart to them. Never shall he be a friend of mine." Greek was, for Jefferson, the original language of friendship.[2]

Greek literature had a powerful impact on Jefferson's mind throughout his life. Indeed, he returned to reading Greek texts in his retirement years, and corresponded with a number of people, including John Adams and the Harvard-trained Greek expert Edward Everett, about the beauties of the language. Other Greek influences on Jefferson include Homer's epic *The Iliad*, in which friendship, of course, figures prominently; and Xenophon's *Memorabilia*, with its attention to Socrates, a text Jefferson considered the only "genuine" history of that noble philosopher. Jefferson adored Epicurus, and described himself as an Epicurean, by which he meant that he embraced a style of living that emphasized plainness (lack of artificiality or adornment) and the cultivation of friendship – a friendship viewed almost therapeutically. Jefferson composed his wife's epitaph in Greek, pronouncing that their flame of friendship would "burn on through death."[3]

Of the Romans, Jefferson was quite familiar with the discourses of Cicero, whose style of address was considered masterful and whose friendship with Atticus was legend: "All I beg of you," wrote Cicero to his friend while under political attack, "is, that as you have ever loved me personally, you will continue in the same affections. I am still the same man." In the *Epistolae ad Atticum*, as among the Greeks, friendship was that which was so true and dependable that it could be preserved amid social dysfunction or political ups and downs, something Jefferson, as a public man, well understood.[4]

We should bear in mind, too, that death was never far from any of these classical writings, just as dreaded diseases were a constant part of the lives of Jefferson and his contemporaries, in an age when the best that medical intervention could be expected to do was to ease pain temporarily while nature took its course. It is necessarily difficult for us to encounter friendship on the same level as Jefferson: relationships risked more because of frequent early or sudden death, and because of the logistical distance that separated friends, and their consequent reliance on letters to sustain their friendships.

Closer to Jefferson's time, the French essayist Michel de Montaigne (1533–92), whom Jefferson admired and from time to time quoted, further elaborated on the meaning of friendship, as he wrote with unprecedented introspection and self-revelation. "Free will has no product more properly its own than affection and friendship," he wrote in "Of Friendship." Closeness was built upon the Ciceronian model – a "harmony of wills" – and made spiritual through continual practice. Friendship between men was different from love for a woman. Likening the feeling to a fire, Montaigne described the first as "a general and universal warmth, moderate and even," and the second as a "more active, more scorching, and more intense" fire, an "impetuous and fickle flame," but in the end a "frantic desire." There are misogynistic strains running through Montaigne's writing, and they are quite noticeable here: "To tell the truth," he adds to his assessment, "the ordinary capacity of women is inadequate for that communion and fellowship which is the nurse of the sacred bond; nor does their soul seem firm enough to endure the strain of so tight and durable a knot." These sentiments, unnerving today, were quite readable in Jefferson's time, when it was widely judged that male–male communication was formed more easily than male–female. There are, in fact, examples of conventional misogyny in Jefferson's commonplace book, though it would be wrong to exaggerate their importance.[5]

Jefferson's outlook on human relationships was significantly influenced by the work of a near contemporary, Laurence Sterne (1713–68). Sterne was a maverick writer, the author of a risqué novel, *The Life and Opinions of Tristram Shandy*, and a semi-autobiographical travelogue, *A Sentimental Journey*. Both of these were digressive, and *Tristram Shandy* was downright anarchic. The author, who adored Montaigne, not only defied the literary conventions of his time, but offered an energizing sympathy along with satirical humor and sexual innuendos, the combination of which led overtly moralizing religious conservatives to label Sterne, an Anglican minister, as an embarrassment to polite society. Sterne may have been naughty, but he wrote to move his readers. He highlighted episodes in life in which the highest value lay not in ascetic withdrawal but in sentimental attachment. He wrote confessionally as well as imaginatively, teaching readers how to "mingle tears"; he adhered to what Jefferson knew as "rational Christianity," rejecting the miraculous while at the same time recognizing the limits of pure reason. He wrote to extend self-knowledge.[6]

Jefferson discovered Sterne at an impressionable moment, when he was a college student in Williamsburg. He read *Tristram Shandy* as each new volume emerged between 1759 and 1767. Sterne's meaning to him continued to enlarge over the years, and he carried a pocket-sized edition of *A Sentimental Journey* with him when he became a sentimental traveler himself, in France, in the late 1780s. He was at his most Sternean when he wrote to the Marquis de Lafayette from the French countryside in 1787, aping Sterne's insinuating attitude towards strangers, and striving to make impressions and connections wherever he went: "You must ferret the people out of their hovels as I have done," wrote Jefferson, "look into their kettles, eat their bread, loll on their beds under the pretense of resting yourself, but in fact to find out if they are soft." For Sterne, supping with a country family, it was: "I sat down at once like a son of the family; and to invest myself in the character as speedily as I could, I instantly borrowed the old man's knife, and taking up the loaf cut myself a hearty luncheon." The idea was that it never paid to be too proper, genteel, or stand-offish.[7]

Yet, as we return to the letter to Maria Cosway, it is important to note that *A Sentimental Journey* was filled with flirtation and sexual tease; the author adored women and doted on them, but received pleasure in voyeuristically fantasizing, too. Sterne was unusual in allowing his fantasies to spill onto the printed page. Jefferson did not miss this facet of Sterne's authorial personality, and, indeed, capitalized on it, as if the Anglican cleric was giving him permission to express himself more directly with women than he might otherwise have done.

"My Head and My Heart"

"My dear Madam," Jefferson begins, "Having performed the sad office of handing you into your carriage ..., I turned on my heel and walked, more dead than alive, to the opposite door, where my own was awaiting me." He is about to amplify what he calls a "confession of distress" into a treatise on friendship. We are to understand that he returned to his quarters, thinking of nothing and no one but her: "Seated by my fire side, solitary and sad, the following dialogue took place between my Head and my Heart."

The Head notices that the Heart is in "a pretty trim"; "*Heart*: 'I am indeed the most wretched of all earthly beings. Overwhelmed by grief, every fibre of my frame distended beyond it's [*sic*] natural powers to bear, I would willingly meet whatever catastrophe should leave me no more to feel or fear.'" The departure of this friend has caused the Heart to suffer to the point where it would rather not feel – for to feel was to suffer. The Head, promoting the value of intellectual occupation over spontaneous pleasure, is full of prudent advice. It accuses the Heart of leading the body into "follies," through its "warmth and precipitation" (blind haste, or acting on sympathetic impulse), for which later confession is of little avail. The cost of affection, plain and simple, is pain, especially when the object is a woman who possesses such accomplishments as "music, modesty, beauty, and that softness of disposition which is the ornament of her sex and the charm of ours." Listening impatiently to the swelling Heart, the ever-practical Head figuratively shakes its head: "I never ceased whispering to you that we had no occasion for new acquaintance; that the greater their merit and talents, the more dangerous the friendship to our tranquility, because the regret at parting would be greater." Better not to get involved.

But the Heart is not done praising this Maria, and the time they had together: "Every moment was filled with something agreeable. The wheels of time moved on with such rapidity of which those of our carriage gave but a faint idea, and yet in the evening, when one took a retrospect of the day, what a mass of happiness had we travelled over!" To be imprudent, by the Head's accounting, was to come alive by the Heart's record of events. The Head retorts: "Everything in this world is a matter of calculation. Advance then with caution ... The art of life is the art of avoiding pain." And, more aggressively, "Friendship is but another name for an alliance with the follies and the misfortunes of others."

But the Heart will have none of it, building its case as the letter proceeds. It recognizes that the pain it feels defines its humanity:

> And what more sublime delight than to mingle tears with one whom the hand of heaven hath smitten! To watch over the bed of sickness, and to beguile it's tedious and it's painful moments! To share our bread with one to whom misfortune has left none! The world abounds in misery: to lighten it's burthen we must divide it with one another.

And now, the Heart reaches the high point in its argument:

> Let the gloomy Monk, sequestered from the world, seek unsocial pleasures in the bottom of his cell! Let the sublimated philosopher grasp visionary happiness while pursuing phantoms dressed in the garb of truth! Their supreme wisdom is supreme folly: and they mistake for happiness the mere absence of pain. Had they ever felt the solid pleasure of one generous spasm of the heart, they would exchange for it all the frigid speculations of their lives.

The Heart receives the longest soliloquy of the letter, invoking "the feelings of sympathy, of benevolence, of gratitude, of justice, of love, of friendship." And then the Heart finally gets to rationalize a bit itself, while calling the Head "my friend": "We are not immortal ourselves, my friend; how can we expect our enjoiments to be so? We have no rose without it's thorn; no pleasure without alloy. It is the law of our existence; and we must acquiesce."

Thus Jefferson proves himself a philosopher of friendship, somewhat Socratic, and even more Epicurean. He assigns the fields of science and mathematics to the Head and the field of morals to the Heart. He argues for temptation as he would for the value of art. The Head is impotent in deciding how to live; it is turned so as to avert literal self-destruction, but not emotional hurt. To "live in random," then, is by far preferable to operating so as to avoid dangers that are merely theoretical. What also comes through in Jefferson's dialogue is his use of language to invoke stark differences. The Head's speculations are "frigid," its pleasures "unsocial"; the Heart's delight is "sublime," its pleasure "solid." The Head's words drone on, while the Heart's seem to glide, often alliteratively: when friends offer solace, "How we are penetrated with their assiduities and attentions!"; or: "Friendship is precious not only in the shade but in the sunshine of life." He can be almost breathless: "what a mass of happiness had we travelled over!" These are subtle tools.

As for Sternean suggestions in the letter, Jefferson's Heart relates a story about a missed opportunity to give a carriage ride to a "poor wearied souldier" on a Virginia road during the Revolution. In *A Sentimental Journey*, Sterne's character shows disrespect to a Franciscan mendicant; in both cases, the momentarily insensitive narrators return in an effort to make amends – in essence, to show unselfish concern and befriend a stranger. Jefferson had turned the carriage around, but could not find the soldier; so he vowed never to let such an opportunity pass him by again. Later, in Philadelphia, he spotted a poor woman asking for charity. His Head told him she was "a drunkard", but his Heart convinced him to give. "When I sought her out afterwards," he writes, "she employed the money immediately towards placing her child at school." Opening himself up to his natural emotions, the Sternean loves life. Sterne wrote that the reason for his writing *A Sentimental Journey* was "to teach us to love the world and our fellow creatures better than we do now."[8]

Finally, with regard to the sexual element, Jefferson reserves all such playfulness for another letter – not one, as he explains at one point, which he sends through the notoriously insecure mail system, but one carried by a trusted individual. Here he tells her that he has nothing in particular to say and would be inclined only to give her "a continuation of Sterne upon noses." This was a *double entendre* focusing attention on the length of a man's nose, which every reader of Sterne understood as a phallic reference. After this, Jefferson requested of his fair correspondent a letter in return, "teeming with affection."

He would write even more flirtatiously, not long after, to a friend he had in common with Maria Cosway. In recommending that the two of them travel back to America on the same vessel, he prodded Angelica Schuyler Church: "Think of it then, my friend, and let us begin a negociation on the subject. You shall find in me all the spirit of accommodation with which Yoric[k] began with the fair Piedmontese." In *A Sentimental Journey*, Sterne's Yorick was obliged to bed down in a crowded inn, on a "wet and tempestuous night," sharing a small room with two women. The parties had to engage in considerable "negociation" before bed; and Yorick, unable to sleep, uttered "no more than an ejaculation," which then led to a moment's confusion, an outstretched hand that caught hold of – and the story ends abruptly. So Jefferson knew what he was up to when he merged words of friendship with images of temptation.[9]

Just as Montaigne would have it, friendship with a woman in Jefferson's world could not be developed in the same way as friendship with another man. Leaving aside matters of courtship (and there are no extant letters between Jefferson and his wife), or matters of open flirtation, which the Cosway and Church letters appear to represent, Jefferson maintained warm but very proper epistolary relationships with other women of his class.

Friendship and politics

Friendships between men of the intellectual elite in the eighteenth century generally developed in one of two ways. Either one grew up with a schoolmate, sharing adolescent concerns and recognizing an essential equality; or one had a teacher, a mentor, who facilitated entry into the world of commerce or politics. In Jefferson's case, we have records of both of these kinds of friendships.

John Page was a member of the Virginia gentry, and the same age as Jefferson. They met in Williamsburg, at the College of William and Mary, by the time they were 18, and remained close until Page's death during Jefferson's presidency, nearly a half-century later. In their letters, Jefferson set aside all pretense, and wrote vulnerably: "I can never bear to remain in suspense"; and trustingly: "If this letter was to fall into the hands of some of our gay acquaintance, your correspondent and his solemn notions would probably be the subjects of a great deal of mirth and raillery, but to you I can venture to send it." He could chide Page: "Why the devil don't you write? But I suppose you are always in the moon, or some of the planetary regions. I mean you are there in idea, and unless you mend, you shall have my consent to be there de facto." We can see from these excerpts that Jefferson had a keen sense of wit and wordplay and that friendship was enlarged through teasing and banter.[10]

At William and Mary, Jefferson found a mentor in his law tutor, George Wythe, an exceptionally patient and generous man, an ethical thinker, and in some ways a surrogate father to Jefferson, whose own father died when he was 14. After he had achieved national stature, Jefferson reminded Wythe of "my debt to you for whatever I am myself." After Wythe's death, Jefferson eulogized: "No man ever left behind him a character more venerated." It was Wythe who guided Jefferson to read Homer in the original Greek, and who was probably responsible for Jefferson's "democratic" style of writing, insofar as both men refused to capitalize nouns or person's names. The law student collaborated with his former tutor in 1776, in rewriting Virginia's laws; the two men were entirely compatible, and free of egoistic competition. Jefferson internalized the lessons he learned under Wythe, who joined him in signing the Declaration of Independence, and later imparted those same lessons to the younger men who turned to him for advice.[11]

Republican statesmen James Madison and James Monroe were, of course, close political allies – allies of Jefferson, who introduced them, and of each other. But what is less widely known is that Jefferson was tested, more than once, when Madison and Monroe vied for power and prestige. The way he managed their competition, and assuaged their feelings, is a further testament to the value Jefferson placed on harmonious friendship.

In 1784, just prior to Jefferson's departure for France, Madison was retiring from the Confederation Congress just as Monroe was entering. Jefferson urged Madison, who was a bit older and better known than Monroe, to be responsive to the younger man. Monroe "wishes a correspondence with you," he nudged, "and I suppose his situation will render him an useful one to you. The scrupulousness of his honor will make you safe in the most confidential communications. A better man cannot be." This was quite a recommendation. It is hardly surprising that the two Virginians found common cause.[12]

Recognizing Madison's greater intellectual rigor and self-confidence, Jefferson wrote to this friend – unquestionably his closest confidant – with deliberate concern and consideration, but without flourish and without emotionally based appeals. But neither Jefferson nor Madison was a saint; they were political actors. And so their close alliance allowed them to confide critical views to one another, expanding their vocabularies to get something off their chests. In 1784, Madison wrote to Jefferson of a treaty ceremony in New York State, at which the Marquis de Lafayette arranged to give a speech, so as to advance his personal reputation. Madison suggested that the Frenchman, though a friend to America and a friend of Jefferson's, was also extremely vain. "With great natural frankness of temper," wrote Madison, "he unites ... a strong thirst of praise and popularity." Jefferson concurred at this time: "I take him to be of unmeasured ambition, but that the means he uses are virtuous." Two years later, when Lafayette was back in France, and assisting Jefferson in the promotion of American interests, knowing Madison's opinion, the US minister drew on the earlier opinion, adding: "His foible is a canine appetite for popularity and fame."[13]

Writing about King Louis XVI of France, Jefferson disparages easily: "He is irascible, rude, and very limited in his understanding, religious bordering only on bigotry ... Unhappily the king shews a propensity for the pleasures of the table. That for drink has increased lately." This is more than news; it is opinion of a kind that one only expressed so bluntly to a trusted friend. Not long after, Jefferson gave Madison friendly guidance on how to approach a French visitor: "She is goodness herself. You must be well acquainted with her ... The way to please her is to receive her as an acquaintance of a thousand years standing." Directness always paid off.[14]

With Monroe, however, Jefferson tended to be either paternal or carefully solicitous, in a way that he found unnecessary with Madison. He had tutored Monroe in the law in 1780, while he was serving as Virginia's governor, which suggests that their relationship formed less as equals than in the case of Madison. Nevertheless, that tone of watchfulness does not disappear, even as the years pass, because Jefferson recognized in Monroe a sentimental quality made sometimes unattractive because of a thin skin. In many of the letters Monroe wrote to Jefferson, and Jefferson wrote to Monroe, the word "feelings" or "sentiments" was generally invoked; Monroe's First Inaugural Address, in 1817, opened: "I should be destitute of feeling, if I were not deeply affected." Jefferson understood this, because he himself took public contentions personally.

Monroe frequently felt supplanted by Madison. As early as 1787, Monroe expected to be brought to Philadelphia with the Virginia delegation to the Constitutional Convention, at which Madison, of course, was a dynamic

force. Madison, he wrote to Jefferson, "upon whose friendship I have calculated, whose views I have favored, and with whom I have held the most
confidential correspondence since you left the continent, is in strict league
with [those disposed to "thwart" him] & hath I have reason to believe
concurrd in arrangements unfavorable to me." In 1789, Madison was elected
to the first US Congress by defeating Monroe. Even more critically, when
Jefferson prepared to retire from the presidency in 1808, Monroe thought he,
and not Madison, should succeed.

Eager to restore the harmony that subsisted between the two men during
the greater part of their public careers, Jefferson knew he needed to ease
Monroe's resentment. "I have ever viewed Mr. Madison and yourself as two
principal pillars of my happiness," he wrote; "Were either to be withdrawn,
I should consider it as among the greatest calamities which could assail my
future peace of mind." It was, naturally, on highly emotional grounds that the
retiring president made his appeal to Monroe. He asserted his neutrality,
almost as a catechism: "I feel no passion, I take no part, I express no sentiment." This was the way he knew he could get through to Monroe. And
Monroe, for his part, accepted Jefferson's avowal of neutrality: "I have
expressed myself with too much zeal … It has satisfied me that I had mis-
construed your feelings & dispositions toward me." Eventually, Monroe
overcame his jealousy towards Madison, and served as his secretary of
state, before assuming the presidency himself.[15]

One more example should suffice to give a picture of Jefferson's manner of
juggling the personal and the political. In the case of his relationship with
fellow Republican Edward Livingston, a New Yorker, Jefferson was able to
acknowledge his own impropriety and immoderation. After years of political
accord, Livingston lost favor with Jefferson and subsequently tangled with
the president in court over ownership of a valuable plot of land outside New
Orleans, known as the Batture. Between 1807 and 1814, the two argued over
whether the land was to be considered public or private property. Livingston
ultimately won the court fight, though Jefferson went so far as to prepare a
91-page pamphlet to defend his position. He came to view Livingston as a
selfish speculator, noting his "assiduities and intrigues."[16]

Finally, in 1824, Jefferson agreed to reconcile with Livingston, after the
latter, via President Monroe, made the first effort to restore their severed
communication. First, to smooth the way for a letter to Livingston, Jefferson
wrote to Monroe, honoring the New Yorker in terms of equality – this was
how friendship made the most sense to him: "He may be assured I have not
a spark of unfriendly feeling towards him. In all the earlier scenes of life we
thought and acted together. We differed in opinion afterwards on a single
point. Each maintained his opinion, as he had a right, and acted on it as he

ought." Up to this point, assuming Monroe would share his words with Livingston, Jefferson set up the rationale for their respective past actions. Now he moved on to the emotional: "But why brood over a single difference, and forget all our previous harmonies? Difference of opinion was never, with me, a motive of separation from a friend ... Mr. Livingston would now be recieved [sic] at Monticello with as hearty a welcome as he would have been in 1800."[17]

Livingston was elected to Congress from Louisiana, in 1824, and Jefferson wrote to congratulate him. In this letter, he reiterated what he had said to Monroe: "I have learnt to be less confident in the conclusions of human reason, and give more credit to the honesty of contrary opinion." Perhaps he no longer believed that Livingston had had selfish motives in the Batture case. In any event, Jefferson added a generous sentiment in his letter to the incoming congressman: "You have many years yet to come of vigorous activity, and I confidently trust they will be employed in cherishing every measure which may foster our brotherly union."[18]

The next year, Livingston demonstrated his continuing regard for Jefferson, now 82, by asking him to read and evaluate a code of laws he had drafted. Jefferson declined to venture any opinion owing to his advanced age ("five and twenty chilling winters" having "rolled over my head and whitened every hair" since they had last seen one another), but he repeated the sentiment of his previous letter of reconciliation: "Your work ... will certainly arrange your name with the sages of antiquity." The sage of Monticello signed off his last letter to Edward Livingston with "unabated friendship and respect," the same expression he often used in writing to his oldest allies, James Madison and James Monroe.[19]

In Thomas Jefferson's lifetime, the threads of friendship were interwoven with politics. His closest friends were men who helped to shape the future of America, just as he did. The fact that he wrote of political occurrences to his daughters almost exclusively in terms of how it affected his mood suggests strongly that personal history, as much as personal chemistry, helped him to maintain a sense of order and a sense of peace. "Here," he wrote to Martha Jefferson Randolph from Washington, "there is such a mixture of the bad passions of the heart that one feels themselves in an enemy's country."[20]

Politics tested and often undermined friendship, as the Madison–Monroe and Livingston examples indicate. Politics, of course, exacerbated people's passions. But for Jefferson, who had read deeply in texts, ancient and modern, which dramatized the engagement of the heart, cultivating self-control was never a good enough rationale for withdrawal. Through the medium of letter writing, he continued to reach out. Those who knew him best, who knew him at Monticello, insisted that he never ceased putting forward his gentlest side.

This was one way of pursuing happiness, or what he once called "tranquil permanent felicity."

NOTES

1. John Catanzariti, "Thomas Jefferson, Correspondent," *Proceedings of the Massachusetts Historical Society*, 102 (1990): 1–20.

2. Douglas L. Wilson (ed.), *Jefferson's Literary Commonplace Book* (Princeton: Princeton University Press, 1989), 64–78, quotes at 70, 73.

3. Andrew Burstein, *Jefferson's Secrets* (New York: Basic Books, 2005), 161–5; Henry S. Randall, *The Life of Thomas Jefferson*, 3 vols. (New York: Derby and Jackson, 1858), 1: 383.

4. Andrew Burstein, *The Inner Jefferson* (Charlottesville: University Press of Virginia, 1995), 117–18.

5. *The Complete Essays of Montaigne*, trans. Donald M. Frame (Stanford, CA: Stanford University Press, 1943), 136–9.

6. For insights into the life of Sterne, see Arthur H. Cash, *Laurence Sterne: The Later Years* (London: Methuen & Co., 1986); Wilbur L. Cross, *The Life and Times of Laurence Sterne* (New York: Russell & Russell, 1967); for critical commentary, see Valerie Grosvenor Meyer (ed.), *Laurence Sterne: Riddles and Mysteries* (London: Vision Press, 1984); and Frank Brady, "*Tristram Shandy*: Sexuality, Morality, and Sensibility," *Eighteenth-Century Studies*, 4 (1970): 41–56.

7. Burstein, *The Inner Jefferson*, 100–1.

8. TJ to Cosway, October 12, 1786, in *Papers of Thomas Jefferson*, ed. Julian P. Boyd *et al.* (Princeton: Princeton University Press, 1950–), X: 443–53; Burstein, *The Inner Jefferson*, 75–99.

9. TJ to Cosway, April 24, 1788, and to Church, August 17, 1788, in *Papers*, XIII: 104, 521; "The Case of Delicacy," in Sterne's *A Sentimental Journey*, cited in Burstein, *The Inner Jefferson*, 109.

10. TJ to Page, July 15, 1763, and February 21, 1770, in *Papers*, I: 10–11, 34–6.

11. TJ to Wythe, September 16, 1787, in *Papers*, XII: 129; William Clarkin, *Serene Patriot: A Life of George Wythe* (Albany, NY: Alan Publications, 1970).

12. TJ to Madison, May 8, 1784, in *The Republic of Letters*, ed. James Morton Smith, 3 vols. (New York: W. W. Norton, 1995), 316.

13. Madison to TJ, October 17, 1784, and TJ to Madison, March 18, 1785, and January 30, 1787, in *Republic of Letters*, 348–9, 365, 463.

14. TJ to Madison, June 20, and October 8, 1787, in *Republic of Letters*, 481–2, 494.

15. TJ to Madison, May 8, 1784, in *Republic of Letters*, 316; TJ to Monroe, February 18, 1808, in *The Writings of Thomas Jefferson*, ed. Paul Leicester Ford, 10 vols. (New York: Putnam, 1892–9), IX: 177–8; Monroe to TJ, February 27, and March 22, 1808, in *The Writings of James Monroe*, ed. Stanislav Murray Hamilton, 7 vols. (New York: Putnam, 1898–1903), V: 29, 32–5; Andrew Burstein, "Jefferson's Madison vs. Jefferson's Monroe," *Presidential Studies Quarterly*, 28 (Spring, 1998): 394–408.

16. See Dumas Malone, *Jefferson and His Time: The Sage of Monticello* (Boston: Little Brown, 1981), 55–73; quote from a letter to William B. Giles, at p. 63.

17. TJ to Monroe, March 27, 1824, in Thomas Jefferson Papers, Library of Congress. This episode is also detailed in Burstein, *Jefferson's Secrets*, 232–4.

18. TJ to Livingston, April 4, 1824, in Thomas Jefferson Papers, Library of Congress.
19. TJ to Livingston, March 25, 1825, in Thomas Jefferson Papers, Library of Congress.
20. TJ to Martha Jefferson Randolph, January 16, 1801, in *The Family Letters of Thomas Jefferson*, ed. Edwin Morris Betts and James Adam Bear, Jr. (Charlottesville: University Press of Virginia, 1986), 191.

12

JOANNE B. FREEMAN

Jefferson and Adams: friendship and the power of the letter

On July 4, 1826, Americans witnessed a seemingly providential coincidence: as the nation commemorated the fiftieth anniversary of the Declaration of Independence, both John Adams and Thomas Jefferson died. Thus ended a fifty-year friendship between a cantankerous New Englander with a realist's skepticism and a conflict-averse Virginian with an optimist's selective vision. The two men first encountered each other in the summer of 1775 as the American Revolution took shape and form. Forged amidst the hardships and risks of war, their friendship was strong, though at times it faced challenges; the bitter partisanship of the 1790s strained it to the breaking point. But in the end, it survived, grounded on each man's fundamental appreciation of the other man's character, and, once the turmoil of public life was behind them, it flourished again. They lived long enough to rekindle their friendship through a rich correspondence, two elder statesmen musing on their lives, their experiences, and the heady events of their times in a written conversation that continued for over a decade.[1]

Between 1812 and 1826 Adams and Jefferson exchanged over 150 letters bearing remarkable testimony to their hearts and minds as they reflected on the past, present, and future. Not surprisingly, they often touched on political topics, debating their political differences and ideals, and thinking back on shared allies and enemies and the legacies of their victories and defeats. But their range reached much wider, encompassing topics as diverse as political philosophy, religion, linguistics, and the natural sciences. Their letters have the tone and feel of an ongoing dialogue, the loquacious Adams writing almost twice as many letters as the more reticent Jefferson, but both men clearly reveling in the exchange.

These letters of their retirement years are an incredibly rich archive, bursting with insights into the two men and their times. But this was not their first such exchange. More than thirty years earlier they were close correspondents during their travels as diplomats in France and England. For a brief period they were close neighbors, Jefferson becoming intimate with the Adams family during their stay in France. When the Confederation Congress sent the Adamses to England, they maintained their bond with Jefferson through correspondence. Their letters reveal the difficulties of diplomacy in a new nation struggling to prove itself on the world stage: the slights, indignities, and misunderstandings that greeted them in European courts; the desperate need to secure commercial treaties or risk economic collapse. They also testify to the intellectual benefits of their European travels: the joys of full access to worlds of books in European capitals of culture; the national self-knowledge born of their first exposure to the heights and depths of European society, culture, and politics.

Informal, amusing, personal, and often profound, the Adams–Jefferson letters capture a friendship that – after 1812 – existed only on paper; after Jefferson's election to the presidency in 1801, the two men never again met face-to-face. Indeed, in many ways, the letters themselves form the actual pith and core of their relationship, allowing them to reveal their innermost thoughts and feelings in ways they would not have attempted in person. Their correspondence preserved their friendship, and preserved history as well, capturing the thoughts and experiences of two national "founders." Their lives remain part of America's national narrative; their letters give voice to the turmoil of its origins.

European relations: 1777–1788

For roughly a decade after their partnership in the Continental Congress, Adams and Jefferson remained close friends, though for most of that time they were miles apart. They were together for only ten months in 1784 and 1785, when their diplomatic missions overlapped in France. This brief period added a personal dimension to their previously political friendship; it also forged strong bonds between Jefferson and the entire Adams family, particularly with Abigail Adams and Adams's oldest son, John Quincy.

Prior to their time in France there had been only a handful of letters between them, filled with wartime news and shared concerns for the new nation's political progress. Adams reported to Jefferson on events in Congress; Jefferson reported on news in Virginia and offered political strategies from afar. When both men worried about the difficulties in uniting the states in a confederation, Jefferson reminded Adams of a past conversation that might advance their cause. Adams promised to raise the idea in Congress.[2] Jefferson made a similar suggestion several months later, proposing measures that might calm Virginia's fears about joining the confederation.[3] In a sense, these exchanges prolonged the benefits of their productive congressional partnership during the quest for independence.

Their next sprinkling of letters was in 1784 as Jefferson first made his way overseas. Appointed minister plenipotentiary to France, he was to join Adams and Benjamin Franklin, both his seniors in experience. By this point, Adams had been in a series of diplomatic posts for eight years, accompanied by his son John Quincy through much of it, negotiating first with France, then with Britain, and then with the Dutch, who granted America a much needed loan. In 1782, he returned to France to participate in the negotiations that would end America's war with Great Britain. Two years later, in 1784, his family joined him, as did Jefferson, newly arrived in France.

For the next ten months, Jefferson and the Adamses were in constant company, deepening the bonds between the two statesmen and forging new friendships between Jefferson and the rest of the family. Adams's appointment as ambassador to Great Britain in 1785 brought this period to a close, much to the dismay of all. "The departure of your family has left me in the dumps," Jefferson wrote to Adams five days after the family's departure.[4]

Their separation marked the beginning of an active correspondence. Between 1785 and 1788, the two men exchanged roughly 136 letters blending business and friendship as they informed one another about diplomatic proceedings and political news. Far more personal are Jefferson's and Abigail's exchanges during this period. Frequent correspondents, they inquired about mutual friends and shared their experiences as Americans in foreign climes. Their letters echoed conversations of times past, as Jefferson himself acknowledged. "[W]hen writing to you, I fancy myself at Auteuil, and chatter on till the last page of my paper awakes me from my reverie," he explained at the close of one letter.[5] He had no qualms about asking Abigail to select and send tablecloths and napkins from England, where cloth was much cheaper. Jefferson, in turn, sent fine wine to the Adamses.

The bond between Jefferson and Abigail grew even stronger in 1787 when Jefferson's daughter Polly stayed with the Adamses on her way to her father in France. Over the course of several weeks, the family grew to love Polly. "I am really loath to part with her," Abigail wrote to Jefferson; "She is the favorite of every creature in the House." By Abigail's account, when Polly learned that she was to leave for France, she burst into tears and declared that "it would be as hard to leave me as it was her Aunt Epps" back in Virginia. In preparation for Polly's departure, Abigail bought and made clothing for "Miss Jefferson and the maid ... as I should have done had they been my own."[6] Jefferson had forged a similar bond with John Quincy during their time together in France. In a letter to Jefferson years later, John referred to John Quincy as "our John," explaining, "I call him our John, because when you was at Cul de sac at Paris, he appeared to me to be almost as much your boy as mine."[7]

The Adams's departure for America in 1788 marked the end of such exchanges; separated by such a distance, it would be too difficult to regularly correspond. Adams mourned the loss of their correspondence at the close of a letter to Jefferson discussing Adams's recently published *Defence of the Constitutions of the United States*. "There are but two Circumstances, which will be regretted by me, when I leave Europe," he confessed; "One is the oppertunity of Searching any questions of this kind, in any books that may be wanted, and the other will be the Interruption of that intimate Correspondence with you, which is one of the most agreable Events in my Life."[8]

Partisanship ... and silence: 1789–1812

One year later, in 1789, Jefferson likewise returned to America, only to discover that newly elected President George Washington had appointed him secretary of state in the new national government. The Constitution had taken effect in March of that year, and Adams had been elected vice president. With both Adams and Jefferson living in America's capital city – first New York and then Philadelphia – they had little reason to correspond; between 1790 and 1796, they exchanged only nineteen letters. But there were more complex reasons for their shared silence. Partisan passions came to the fore in the 1790s, and Jefferson and Adams were on opposing sides. By 1792, Jefferson was the leader of the Republican party and Adams was a leading Federalist, advancing to the presidency in 1797.[9]

Only a handful of letters broke their mutual silence, most of them spurred by outside events. In 1791, Jefferson returned a draft copy of Thomas Paine's *Rights of Man* to a printer accompanied by a note praising its effectiveness in combating "the political heresies which have sprung up among us" – an indirect reference to the seemingly pro-British *Discourses on Davila* recently written by Adams and printed in Philadelphia newspapers.[10] Without asking Jefferson's permission, the printer published his note in the pamphlet's opening pages. Jefferson's comments created a public controversy that included a series of letters published in a Boston newspaper, under the pseudonym of Publicola, that vehemently criticized Paine and, by extension, Jefferson. "I was thunderstruck," Jefferson explained to Adams in a letter of apology for his comments. Adams responded with a lengthy explanation of his political views, thanking Jefferson for providing the opportunity. "It was high time that you and I should come to an explanation with each other," he explained, adding that his fifteen-year friendship with Jefferson remained "very dear to my heart."[11] Adams had denied that he was the author of the Publicola letters, but he did not tell Jefferson that Publicola was in fact his son, John

Quincy Adams. An additional letter of explanation from Jefferson closed this exchange, but clearly strains had entered their relationship.

Silence prevailed for more than a decade, broken only by Jefferson's brief retirement from public life when he resigned as secretary of state in 1793. With the "Din of Politicks"[12] somewhat quieted, the two men exchanged an occasional letter until the close of 1796, when Adams was elected president and Jefferson vice president, reawakening their political differences. Shortly after their election, Jefferson tried to salvage their friendship – and gain influence with Adams – with a conciliatory letter, but he never sent it. Worried about its political liabilities, he first showed it to his friend James Madison. Ever the prudent advisor, Madison recommended withholding it, arguing that Jefferson's kind words to Adams would be invaluable political fodder for the Federalists in future campaigns. Jefferson shouldn't give Adams "written possession" of his feelings, Madison warned.[13] Adams's loss to Jefferson in the presidential election of 1800 only deepened the rift, as did Adams's last desperate act in his final hours as president; in an attempt to keep the judiciary under Federalist control, he appointed a large number of Federalists to life-tenure positions as federal judges. Dejected and defeated, Adams left Washington before Jefferson's inauguration.

The next twelve years saw only two brief exchanges, both of them prompted by a death. In 1801, Adams's son Charles died. When a letter describing Charles's funeral was accidentally delivered to Jefferson in Washington, he forwarded it to Adams without reading it, enclosing a brief note of explanation. In his reply, Adams mourned the loss of his son and wished Jefferson "a quiet and prosperous Administration."[14] They had no further correspondence for eleven years.

Polly Jefferson's death in 1804 prompted a letter from Abigail, but not from John. At the close of her letter of condolence, Abigail signed herself: "her, who once took pleasure in subscribing Herself your Friend." Jefferson took this glancing reference to their past friendship as an opportunity to make amends. He and John still shared "mutual esteem" despite their political differences, he insisted, but Adams's appointment of the "midnight judges" was "personally unkind" and had hurt their friendship: it was the "one act of Mr. Adams's life" that gave Jefferson "a moment's personal displeasure."[15] Outraged, Abigail defended her husband's actions and went one step farther, insisting that Jefferson – not Adams – had destroyed their friendship by patronizing James Thomson Callender, a rabid Republican pamphleteer who had turned his vitriol against Adams during the election of 1800. Although they exchanged a few more letters, neither one appeased the other, leading Abigail to close their correspondence. At the bottom of the letter-book copy of Abigail's closing letter, John added a final word: "The whole of this Correspondence was begun and conducted without my Knowledge or Suspicion. Last Evening and this Morning at the desire of Mrs. Adams I read the whole. I have no remarks to make upon it at this time and in this place."[16]

Retirement and rapprochement: 1812–1826

Throughout their political trials, Jefferson and Adams continued to profess their mutual respect in their letters, a thin connecting thread with their intimate friendship of years past. Ultimately, it was just such a profession that rekindled their relationship, thanks to the efforts of a mutual friend. Benjamin Rush, a nationally renowned physician and signer of the Declaration of Independence, was a frequent correspondent of both Adams and Jefferson. Eager to reconcile them, in 1809 he began to prod first one and then the other to re-establish contact.[17] In 1811, his efforts paid off. On December 16, he wrote to Adams describing a letter he had just received from Jefferson, who had recently been assured of Adams's continued affection by a mutual friend. "This is enough for me," Jefferson wrote to Rush; "I only needed this knowledge to revive towards him all the affections of the most cordial moments of our lives."[18] Adams poked fun at Rush's solemn pleas for a rapprochement between the "fellow laborers in erecting the great fabric of American independence."[19] But several days later, he sent Jefferson a copy of John Quincy Adams's *Lectures on Rhetoric and Oratory*, noting that it was written "by One who was honoured in his youth with some of your Attention and much of your kindness."[20] Clearly, the family intimacy of their years in France remained a strong bond.

"A letter from you calls up recollections very dear to my mind," Jefferson responded; "It carries me back to the times when, beset with difficulties and dangers, we were fellow laborers in the same cause." He concluded by assuring Adams that "No circumstances ... have suspended for one moment my sincere esteem for you; and I now salute you with unchanged affections and respect."[21] Adams was quick to reply, noting with pleasure that their correspondence could be frequent and fast due to improved roads.[22] His letter hints at the range of topics in their letters to follow, touching on the state of the union, political enemies of times past, and a sampling of writers and philosophers, both classical and contemporary. A week later Adams wrote again, asking for information on Indian resistance in the western territories; Jefferson was happy to respond.[23]

Thus began a fourteen-year correspondence of over 150 letters touching on an astonishing range of topics; religion, politics, world history, moral philosophy, linguistics, and natural science were all within the reach of their letters, scattered with sprinklings of French, Latin, and ancient Greek. The two men mused on current events, reminisced over past accomplishments, mourned lost friends, and hashed out political differences. Each man clearly gloried in the chance to give his mind free range in letters to a friend fully up to the challenge. As Jefferson explained after writing at length about the "whimsies, the puerilities, and unintelligible jargon" of Plato's *Republic*: "But why am I dosing you with these Ante-diluvian topics? Because I am glad to have some one to whom they are familiar, and who will not receive them as if dropped from the moon."[24] Adams agreed. "Whenever I sett down to write to you, I am precisely in the Situation of the Wood Cutter on Mount Ida: I can not see Wood for Trees," he wrote in 1813; "So many Subjects crowd upon me that I know not, with which to begin."[25]

As suggested by Adams's comment, his letters overflowed with questions and observations, jumping from one topic to the next in his eagerness to explore Jefferson's thoughts and express his own. "[T]hese Letters of yours require Volumes from me," he marveled.[26] Paragraphs seemingly begin at the close of one letter and continue at the opening of the next one. Sometimes, he seems to have been barely able to wait for a response, as in 1813 when he wrote letters almost every other day between June 28 and August 14, when he finally received a response from Jefferson.[27] The cumulative effect is of a mind bubbling over with ideas and enthusiasm, at once wry, humorous, provocative, and profound. Ultimately, Adams wrote twice as many letters as Jefferson, though he dismissed this diplomatically: "[I]f I write four letters to your one; your one is worth more than my four."[28] Because of the range of interests each man held, perhaps none of their contemporaries could have so successfully brought out the best in each correspondent; two well-stocked and lively minds spurred each other on in speculations about language, history, and the nature of virtue and talent.

Although more restrained than Adams on paper, Jefferson matched him in his interests and enthusiasms, as well as in his ability to view their past trials and tribulations philosophically, with a healthy sense of detachment. He ultimately achieved the same tone with Abigail, with whom he re-established contact in August of 1813 with a letter of condolence at the death of Adams's daughter. Abigail was happy to return the favor, though not without glancing at what she considered to be Jefferson's most grievous sin. Although "time has changed the outward form," she wrote, "and political 'Back wounding calumny' for a period interrupted the Friendly intercourse and harmony which subsisted, it is again renewed, purified from the dross." She signed her letter "your Friend."[29] For Jefferson, and for Adams as well, these letters at the close of their lives affirmed in powerful ways deeply held commitment to the power of friendship to overcome political difference. Abigail's close would have been deeply meaningful to Jefferson, considering her parting words in their correspondence of 1804.

Both John and Abigail were unafraid to touch on sensitive topics, though they did so with a light hand. John was particularly eager to explore the political differences between him and Jefferson, a project made easier by the gradual publication of some of Jefferson's letters within the published papers of his contemporaries. Such letters often led Adams to quote Jefferson to himself and then playfully demand an explanation. If Jefferson refused to take the bait, Adams would persist in letter after letter until Jefferson responded. "You and I ought not to die before We have explained ourselves to each other," Adams wrote towards the beginning of their exchange.[30] Jefferson agreed. As he explained after a lengthy discussion of their political differences, "I have thus stated my opinion on a point on which we differ, not with a view to controversy, for we are both too old to change opinions which are the result of a long life of inquiry and reflection; but on the suggestion of a former letter of yours, that we ought not to die before we have explained ourselves to each other."[31] Always, they discussed their differences with care, tempering their comments with humor, wry self-deprecation, and assertions of mutual esteem and affection. Typical of this well-meaning balance is a letter by Adams discussing the publication of some of his letters attacking Jefferson; Adams signed the letter "J.A. In the 89 year of his age still too fat to last much longer."[32]

Adams's comment points to yet another reason for their ability to philosophically dismiss political differences of the past: their full awareness of their mortality. As their correspondence continued and the two men aged, their health began to suffer. By 1812, Adams had a severe palsy in his hands that made it difficult to write.[33] Over time, Jefferson also had difficulty writing; in his final years, his wrists and fingers made it "slow and laborious."[34] In the distance of time, with eternity looming before them, there was no pressing need to prove one of them right; only time would tell. As Adams put it, towards the start of their correspondence, "Whether you or I were right Posterity must judge."[35]

Posterity figures largely in their letters. Both men were certainly aware of their status as "founders." Throughout their retirement, they spent an inordinate amount of time answering letters – often from complete strangers – full of questions about the "truth" behind one or another historical event. Jefferson seems to have been particularly overwhelmed with such requests. Jealous of the amount of time that Adams dedicated to reading, he complained that much of his time was devoted to correspondence. "From sun-rise to one or two aclock, and often from dinner to dark, I am drudging at the writing table," he grumbled; "And all this to answer letters into which neither interest nor inclination on my part enters; and often for persons whose names I have never before heard." Jefferson called this "the burthen of my life, a very grievous one indeed."[36] In 1822, he estimated that in 1820, he had received 1,267 letters. "Is this life?" he asked in utter exasperation.[37]

Adams's response reveals their full awareness of the historical significance of the entirety of their life's correspondence. "I hope one day your letters will be all published in volumes," Adams wrote; "[T]hey will not always appear Orthodox, or liberal in politicks; but they will exhibit a Mass of Taste, Sense, Literature and Science, presented in a sweet simplicity and a neat elegance of Stile, which will be read with delight in future ages."[38] Already, their letters to each other were attracting notice. "I presume that our correspondence has been observed at the post offices, and thus has attracted notice," Jefferson observed in 1815; "Would you believe that a printer has had the effrontery to propose to me the letting him publish it?"[39]

Yet, even as they marveled at such a request, they understood its logic. Jefferson expressed it best in one of his last letters to Adams, asking for permission for his grandson Thomas Jefferson Randolph to pay Adams a call. As Jefferson explained it:

> Like other young people, he [Randolph] wishes to be able, in the winter nights of old age, to recount to those around him what he has heard and learnt of the Heroic age preceding his birth, and which of the Argonauts particularly he was in time to have seen. It was the lot of our early years to witness nothing but the dull monotony of colonial subservience, and of our riper ones to breast the labors and perils of working out of it. Theirs are the Halcyon calms succeeding the storm which our Argosy had so stoutly weathered.

Adams and Jefferson were Argonauts of the "Heroic age" who had weathered storms through the worst of times. Now, in their old age, it was their responsibility to impart their understanding of America's past to younger generations. Adams declared Jefferson's letter "one of the most beautiful and delightful I have ever received."[40]

This exchange, like the hundreds that preceded it, is testimony to a remarkable relationship that did indeed weather difficult storms. Sparked by a shared commitment to American independence, nourished by shared years abroad representing a new nation on the world stage, threatened by the fierce political conflicts of the 1790s, and rekindled through the passage of time and the careful ministrations of a mutual friend, the relationship between Adams and Jefferson followed the rhythms of the evolving American nation. In the end, it was their letters that preserved their emotional bonds over decades of challenges – words on paper, a fitting legacy from two men who contributed so much to America's founding documents, as well as its historical narrative.

NOTES

1. For an excellent brief biography of Jefferson, see R. B. Bernstein, *Thomas Jefferson* (New York: Oxford University Press, 2003). On Adams, see John Ferling, *John Adams: A Life* (Knoxville: University of Tennessee Press, 1992), and Peter Shaw, *The Character of John Adams* (New York: Norton, 1976).
2. TJ to Adams, May 16, 1777, in *The Adams–Jefferson Letters*, ed. Lester Cappon (Chapel Hill: University of North Carolina Press, 1959), 3–4; Adams to TJ, May 26, 1777, in *Adams–Jefferson Letters*, 5–6.
3. TJ to Adams, December 17, 1777, in *Adams–Jefferson Letters*, 8–9.
4. TJ to Adams, May 25, 1785, in *Adams–Jefferson Letters*, 23. For a good account of Jefferson's and Adams's diplomatic dealings during this period, see William Howard Adams, *The Paris Years of Thomas Jefferson* (New Haven: Yale University Press, 1997), esp. ch. 6.
5. TJ to Abigail Adams, September 25, 1785, in *Adams–Jefferson Letters*, 71.
6. Abigail Adams to TJ, July 6, 1787, in *Adams–Jefferson Letters*, 183.
7. Adams to TJ, January 22, 1825, in *Adams–Jefferson Letters*, 606–7.
8. Adams to TJ, March 1, 1787, in *Adams–Jefferson Letters*, 177.
9. On the partisan passions of the 1790s, see Joanne B. Freeman, *Affairs of Honor: National Politics in the New Republic* (New Haven: Yale University Press, 2001). For a good narrative of the political events of the 1790s, see Stanley Elkins and Eric McKitrick, *The Age of Federalism: The Early American Republic, 1788–1800* (New York: Oxford University Press, 1993).
10. TJ to Adams, July 17, 1791, in *Adams–Jefferson Letters*, 246.
11. Adams to TJ, July 29, 1791, in *Adams–Jefferson Letters*, 250.
12. Adams to TJ, April 4, 1794, in *Adams–Jefferson Letters*, 253.
13. See TJ to Adams, December 28, 1796, in *Adams–Jefferson Letters*, 262–3. See also Madison to TJ, January 15, 1797, in *The Papers of James Madison*, ed. Robert Rutland and J. C. A. Stagg, 17 vols. (Charlottesville: University Press of Virginia, 1962–), XVI: 455–7.
14. TJ to Adams, March 8, 1801, and Adams to TJ, March 24, 1801, in *Adams–Jefferson Letters*, 264.
15. Abigail Adams to TJ, May 20, 1804, and TJ to Abigail Adams, June 13, 1804, in *Adams–Jefferson Letters*, 269, 270–1.
16. Abigail Adams to TJ, October 25, 1804, in *Adams–Jefferson Letters*, 282. John's comment does not appear on Jefferson's copy of the letter.
17. See *Adams–Jefferson Letters*, 283–6.
18. Quoted in Rush to Adams, December 16, 1811, in *The Spur of Fame: Dialogues of John Adams and Benjamin Rush, 1805–1813*, ed. John A. Schutz and Douglass Adair (San Marino, CA: Huntington Library, 1980), 199.
19. Adams to Rush, December 25, 1811, in *The Spur of Fame*, 200.
20. Adams to TJ, January 1, 1812, in *Adams–Jefferson Letters*, 290. On the retirement years of Jefferson and Adams, see Andrew Burstein, *Jefferson's Secrets* (New York: Basic Books, 2005); Joseph Ellis, *Passionate Sage: The Character and Legacy of John Adams* (New York: Norton, 1994).
21. TJ to Adams, January 23, 1812, in *Adams–Jefferson Letters*, 292.
22. *Adams–Jefferson Letters*, 294.

23. Adams to TJ, February 10, 1812, and TJ to Adams, April 20, 1812, in *Adams–Jefferson Letters*, 293–6, 298–300.
24. TJ to Adams, July 5, 1814, in *Adams–Jefferson Letters*, 432–4.
25. Adams to TJ, July 9, 1813, in *Adams–Jefferson Letters*, 350.
26. Adams to TJ, June 14, 1813, in *Adams–Jefferson Letters*, 330.
27. Adams wrote letters on June 28, 30, July 3, 9, 12, 13, 15, 16, 18, 22, August 9, and August 14.
28. Adams to TJ, July 15, 1813, in *Adams–Jefferson Letters*, 357.
29. Abigail Adams to TJ, September 20, 1813, in *Adams–Jefferson Letters*, 377. She was responding to Jefferson's letter of August 22, 1813.
30. Adams to TJ, July 15, 1813, in *Adams–Jefferson Letters*, 357.
31. TJ to Adams, October 28, 1813, in *Adams–Jefferson Letters*, 392.
32. Adams to TJ, November 10, 1823, in *Adams–Jefferson Letters*, 602. Adams and Jefferson had been discussing the publication of William Cunningham's "Correspondence between the Hon. John Adams, Late president of the United States, and the Late Wm. Cunningham, Esq., beginning in 1803, and ending in 1813" (Boston, 1823). For more on this pamphlet, see Freeman, *Affairs of Honor*, 155–6.
33. Adams to TJ, February 3, 1812, in *Adams–Jefferson Letters*, 296.
34. TJ to Adams, October 12, 1823, in *Adams–Jefferson Letters*, 599.
35. Adams to TJ, May 1, 1812, in *Adams–Jefferson Letters*, 301.
36. TJ to Adams, January 11, 1817, in *Adams–Jefferson Letters*, 505. See also TJ to Adams, May 17, 1818, and TJ to Adams, June 27, 1822, in *Adams–Jefferson Letters*, 524, 580.
37. TJ to Adams, June 27, 1822, in *Adams–Jefferson Letters*, 580–1.
38. Adams to TJ, July 12, 1822, in *Adams–Jefferson Letters*, 582.
39. TJ to Adams, August 10–11, 1815, in *Adams–Jefferson Letters*, 453.
40. TJ to Adams, March 25, 1826, and Adams to TJ, April 17, 1826, in *Adams–Jefferson Letters*, 613–14.

13

ANNETTE GORDON-REED

The resonance of minds: Thomas Jefferson and James Madison in the republic of letters

It has been called "the Great Collaboration"; the long-term political partnership, professional relationship, and deep friendship of Thomas Jefferson and James Madison, two American statesmen who, together and apart, played pivotal roles in the formation of the American nation. The connection of these two Virginians calls to mind the description of two other famous collaborators in an entirely different field, and from another era: James Watson and Francis Crick, who first described the structure and workings of DNA. A person who knew and observed this celebrated pair said that their partnership was driven by a "resonance between two minds – that high state in which 1 plus 1 does not equal 2 but more like ten." Like Jefferson and Madison, Watson and Crick were men of different temperaments who were, nevertheless, united by their single-minded devotion to their respective goals. However one weighs the relative merits of the contributions of these partnerships – two scientists discovering the building blocks of life versus two politicians/philosophers laying down the groundwork for a new nation – there is no question that a special alchemy was created by both combinations of minds, a catalyst that spurred each individual to greater intellectual strivings than they would have had without the other member of their pair.[1]

The conditions, however, had to be right. One cannot discount the importance of being the right people in the right place at the right time. Watson and Crick were perfectly situated and suited to take advantage of the scientific advances and theories that laid the groundwork for their eventual triumph, having come of age during the post-Second World War era of scientific inquiry and technological innovation. Being the right people in the right place at the right time was, in some ways, even more important for Jefferson and Madison. The details of their personal lives, their vital statistics, played an enormous role in setting the stage for what each man was able to accomplish, individually and in concert with one another.

Contemporary Americans tend to view the pair, and some of the other architects of the American Revolution and the early American republic, as demigods from a world infinitely better than the one we currently inhabit. *There were giants then! And look at us now.* This invidious comparison fails to take into account the entire picture of their time relative to ours. Their unquestioned natural abilities aside, it must always be kept in mind that the world Jefferson and Madison inhabited had been expressly made for a tiny group of individuals who shared their characteristics and profiles. They were born free, white, males in a society built upon African slavery and male dominance. In a world of sharp class distinctions and hierarchy, they were members of the tightly knit, small world of upper-class Virginians with all the privileges attendant to being in that cohort – superior living conditions, access to fine educations, leisure time, and a ready-made supply of possible mentors to help them along; all the advantages that build confidence, create a sense of entitlement, and can smooth an individual's path through life. Both Jefferson and Madison were eldest sons, and though primogeniture was not the official legal rule, eldest males were favored, and considered the de facto heads of their group of younger siblings, female and male. By all measures, these two men came into the world born to lead, and, thus protected from any competition from the overwhelming majority of Virginia's population – enslaved Afro-Virginians, lower-class whites, and all women – who undoubtedly had natural, but uncultivated, geniuses among them, Jefferson's and Madison's innate talents flourished. They were giants, but giants in a place and time where the growth of everyone not like them was deliberately and forcibly stunted.

The two men also flourished at a singular moment in world history. They were in the extremely rare position of being present at the birth of a country during the eighteenth century: a heyday of programmatic thinking about the formation and constitution of governments. Being around for the start of any venture confers an enormous advantage on those first participants who are able, in Bernard Bailyn's phrase about the American Revolution, "to begin the world anew." The just-created United States of America, pledged to the idea of a new style and system of government, needed both determined thinkers and energetic doers to put things in motion. Fresh ideas, concrete plans for the system's operation, battles with opponents about which roads to take; there was much for men like Madison and Jefferson to do, and they set about doing it together when they first met in the pivotal year of 1776 as fellows in the Virginia House of Delegates.[2]

Making and sustaining the collaboration

Jefferson and Madison did not immediately become friends when they met in 1776, as both men conceded. Jefferson, eight years older than Madison, was already something of an elder statesman, a figure much respected for his authorship of the Declaration of Independence. They knew each other in those days mainly from their associations on legislative committees. It was not until 1779, when Madison served on the Executive Council during Jefferson's problematic turn as the governor of Virginia, that the two men really got to know one another and began the correspondence that would cover the next five decades: well over 1,000 letters discussing policy, idle gossip, political maneuvering, family matters, agriculture, and philosophy. Though the sheer volume and steady nature of the correspondence cannot fail to impress, there are different opinions about its overall quality. To Julian Boyd, the renowned editor of the *Papers of Thomas Jefferson*, the Jefferson–Madison letters were "the most elevated, the most significant exchange of letters between any two men in the whole sweep of American History." We can credit Adrienne Koch, who wrote a book about the two men, for the description "the Great Collaboration," a phrase that takes in not only their friendship but the correspondence that was the engine that helped drive their relationship. Other historians have not been so enthusiastic. James Oakes, in a review of James Morton Smith's indispensable compilation of the Jefferson–Madison correspondence, *The Republic of Letters: The Correspondence between Thomas Jefferson and James Madison*, had the following to say: "The truth is that the Jefferson–Madison letters can be awfully dull. Most of them are concerned with minute details of public policy. They are undoubtedly of great value to students of, say, factional intrigue during the Washington administration, diplomatic maneuvers during the Jefferson and Madison presidencies, or the founding of the University of Virginia." Oakes went on to offer that any one who approaches the entirety of the correspondence looking for "a compelling exchange of ideas between two of the finest minds ever to grace American public life" will likely be greatly disappointed. Jack Rakove, who has thought deeply about and written extensively on Madison, offers a good reason for this. It is very likely, and not at all surprising, that the pair's most compelling exchanges took place in their face-to-face casual conversations. These were true friends who had access to one another for most of their time together, personally and professionally. There was no need to hash out, revisit, or explicate matters that were discussed on these more intimate occasions over wine and dinner at their homes or on the long trips they took together traveling between the various seats of government and their homes in Virginia.[3]

One would love, for example, to have some in-depth account of the men's conversations traveling from Philadelphia through upstate New York and New England in 1791, a journey of nearly 900 miles, ostensibly for the purpose of researching the hessian fly, but also for testing the strength of their arch political opponents led by Alexander Hamilton, with whom they were in a pitched (though partly surreptitious) battle. Although it is inconceivable that the pair did not discuss politics and a plethora of other subjects during those weeks, as they rode along isolated roads in a phaeton driven by James Hemings, Jefferson's chef/manservant, neither man chose to write about such matters in the journals they kept of their trip. Instead, both largely confined themselves to talking about the terrain, flora and fauna they encountered, the quality of the inns they used, and the Native American languages they encountered – those last two things from Jefferson. When they returned from their journey, Jefferson to Philadelphia, Madison lingering in New York for a time, they went back to the business at hand in their letters. It is probably no coincidence that the letters they wrote to one another while Jefferson was in France are the sharpest and most compelling, the ocean between them not allowing either man to put off too much of what they wanted to say to one another to another time when they could be together.[4]

Although Jefferson and Madison were not in the habit of revealing details of their inner lives in their letters, there is enough in them to make it clear how important the two men were to one another at every level. Madison was, perhaps, the first to cement his position as a trusted and deep friend when he saw how deeply wounded Jefferson was by the legislative inquiry brought against him for his actions while governor of Virginia, and supported his new friend throughout the ordeal, although they did not write of the matter to one another. Even though the legislature found he had done nothing wrong, Jefferson remained until the end of his life deeply wounded by the criticism of his official conduct. While Madison supported and commiserated with Jefferson, he grew impatient when it seemed that his friend had ventured far beyond the territory of normal sadness about the event into the terrain of paralyzing self-pity. He devoted much energy to getting his friend back into the public arena where he belonged. Jefferson played a similar role in 1783 when the then 32-year-old Madison's engagement to 15-year old Catherine Floyd fell through. Jefferson had actively encouraged the match, speaking with Floyd in favor of Madison. After their relationship imploded when Floyd met and fell in love with a 19-year-old, Jefferson consoled his friend, but then encouraged him to quickly get back to work – that, and time, were the only effective balms to heal wounds.[5]

Partnerships like the one that Madison and Jefferson shared are seldom ever really fifty–fifty in terms of the amount of investment and energy brought to the union; and the balance can shift over time. One gets the overall impression that Jefferson was the more emotionally needy of the two, and seemed not to understand how his personal enthusiasm might, at times, appear almost overbearing to Madison, if not even detrimental to their shared political goals. For example, March of 1791 found both men in Philadelphia – Jefferson serving as secretary of state in Washington's cabinet; Madison, a member of Congress, representing Virginia. By this time the nature of the association was clear to their political friends and foes alike, and there was a perception, unfair or not, that Madison was under Jefferson's sway. Approaching the height of their contest with Alexander Hamilton and his faction, Jefferson proposed that Madison move into his sumptuous home on High Street. "Let me intreat [*sic*] you my dear Sir, to do it, [move in] if it be not disagreeable to you. To me it will be a relief from solitude of which I have too much," Jefferson wrote. Madison politely declined the invitation, assuring Jefferson that it was a "sacrifice" for him to do so. He declared to his friend his affection and esteem, and gave reasons for not making the move somewhat reminiscent of, "I *would* go out with you, but I have to wash my hair tonight."[6]

Jefferson, fresh from his time in France, was used to having friends reside with him, for periods of time, at his even more sumptuous Paris residence, the Hotel de Langeac. He apparently did not think it at all a problem that two public servants, from different branches of government, seen by some as trying to undermine the government of a beloved icon (a government of which one of the public servants was a part), should begin to share a private residence together. Aside from fueling the suspicion that they were always working in concert, what might this mean to Madison – who was already portrayed if not as Jefferson's tool then as his right hand – to actually move in with him? Most instructive of all is that Jefferson conveyed this invitation by letter instead of simply asking Madison when they were together, in casual conversation. They were in close enough proximity to one another for the letter to be sent and responded to on the same day. This might be a case where the very importance of the question made a face-to-face communication too potentially painful. Broaching the subject in writing, the thin-skinned Jefferson could risk rejection – and the thoughtful Madison could reject – from a safe distance.

These most self-conscious of correspondents – they were very clear and open about building their legacies through their letters – constructed their missives with great care to craft how they would be perceived by later generations. A warm and friendly, but, at base, very businesslike, tone pervades the whole enterprise. They very often wrote as if they were posing for the later generations whom they hoped would one day be looking metaphorically over their shoulders. That there may have been people who *during their times* were, for all intents and purposes, looking over their shoulders by opening their mail undoubtedly influenced what and how they wrote. Ever mindful of their positions, and that letters might fall into the wrong hands, the two men often resorted to using code to convey the most sensitive information in their letters. There is little doubt that this particular vulnerability heightened their strict control over the parameters of their conversation.

Madison and Jefferson wanted to put only their best, most discreet and serious, faces forward in their letters to one another. It is instructive, and somewhat puzzling given their extreme intelligence and natural way with words, that both men apparently believed that displays of wit and humor might somehow compromise that particular effort. Jefferson, who has never had the reputation for being particularly funny, really could be funny and charming when he wanted to be. He seldom, however, displayed humor in his letters to Madison; and Madison, who *was* known to have had a sly sense of humor that could border on bawdiness, rarely displayed this in his letters to Jefferson. One wonders if he was taking a cue from his partner about the demeanor to affect in their correspondence. *This is just not what we do in our letters. We save if for when we get together and talk.* There were times, however, when Madison could not help himself. One notable, small, but very welcome bit of respite from the near total drought of wit occurred in 1806 when, at the request of the visiting ambassador to Tunis, then Secretary of State Madison arranged to supply the ambassador and his entourage with the services of local prostitutes to serve as concubines during their stay. Madison said that the payments for the women were to be listed in State Department accounts as "appropriations to foreign intercourse." Months after this episode, in a letter to Jefferson about another matter, Madison made a joking reference to the adventures with the Tunisian ambassador and the prostitutes, stating: "It is not amiss to avoid narrowing too much the scope of *appropriations to foreign intercourse*, which are terms of great latitude, and may be drawn on by any urgent and unforeseen occurrences" (emphasis in the original). He obviously knew that Jefferson would get, and appreciate, the joke, and there had probably been much mirthful conversation between them about what had happened. But, except for this artfully mischievous reference, details about their involvement in this situation were not to be preserved for the ages. It was left to a slightly stunned and disapproving William Plumer of New Hampshire to record in his diary the basic details of what had happened. If one thinks it meaningful to consult and live by "what the founders intended for Americans," and believe that their writings give evidence of their intentions, the absence of humor in the Jefferson–Madison correspondence suggests that, at least as far as these founders were concerned, wit was not to be considered a foundational American trait.[7]

It has also been suggested that, if the correspondence fails to crackle with much energy, it is because Madison and Jefferson did not sharply disagree on many things or engage in estranging arguments that required them to make up on paper. Interested readers lose out when long-term correspondents have few opportunities to explain themselves to one another for any reason, or to try to persuade the other of a position; the words and manner chosen for a debate, or the way one party makes an appeal for compromise or, if needed, reconciliation, can reveal much about the inner workings of a friendship and the friends involved. Jefferson himself noted this late in his life when he offered to Madison that part of the great joy of their association was that they had been essentially as one about the political principles that really mattered to him, an interesting and very telling construction of the contours of friendship. It is not clear that Madison, who appears to have been more open-minded than his Monticello friend, really needed this convergence as much as Jefferson, who did not like to have disagreements with anyone, particularly not with those for whom he had affection. Harmony, the Jeffersonian Holy Grail, was the glue that held friends and other intimate partners together. It was not that people could *never* disagree, but the manner in which they disagreed, and the forum, were extremely important to him.[8]

Writing to one of his daughters, Jefferson, probably recalling his own experiences as a husband, noted that one of the worst things that couples could ever do was to contradict one another in public. Disagreements would come, but they should be discussed out of earshot and eye-view of those who were outside of the couple – that is to say, the entire world. The Jeffersonian will to harmony had its downsides. Some observers have suggested that Jeffersonian harmony could only be achieved when the people around him agreed with his position: like Blackstone's description of marriage, the two would become one and the one would be the husband. If one considers the Jefferson and Madison association as a marriage of sorts, thinking of the two as having formed a committed union, one understands why airing their disagreements in letters destined for the public at large, after their deaths, was not a thing to be done. One suspects that there may have been many more times than we can know when Madison, understanding Jefferson's personality and emotional needs, simply refrained from pressing points (at least in print) in deference to his friend's feelings, as true friends often do.[9]

At the same time, it is clear that Madison was not Jefferson's doormat. He clearly influenced his more volatile friend, tempering his exuberance on occasion, persuading him not to send letters that he wanted to send. When warranted, he went his own way on matters of great importance to him. Both men, concerned about the abuses of the Adams administration under the Alien and Sedition Acts, came up with their own solutions to the problem that reflected their differences: Jefferson's more extreme Kentucky Resolutions and Madison's more moderate Virginia Resolutions, although they intended for their authorship of these documents to remain secret, and had no reason to think there would be any public knowledge of their slightly divergent views on the matter.[10] Their differences occasionally made it into print. Indeed, the most justly famous letter that ever passed between them was one that found them in profound disagreement: Jefferson's letter of September 6, 1789, written while he was still in France, proclaiming that "the earth belongs in usufruct to the living," and, therefore, future generations should not be saddled with the debts of previous ones. He went on to say, even more provocatively:

> On similar grounds it may be proved that no society can make a perpetual constitution or even a perpetual law. The earth belongs always to the living generation. They may manage it then, and what proceeds from it, as they please during their usufruct. They are masters too of their own persons, and consequently may govern them as they please. But persons and property make the sum of the objects of government. The constitution and the laws of their predecessors extinguished then in their natural course with those who gave them being. This could preserve that being till it ceased to be itself and no longer. Every constitution then, and every law, naturally expires at the end of 19 years. If it be enforced longer, it is an act of force, and not of right.[11]

As Herbert Sloan has noted, by defining a "generation" as nineteen years, and welcoming the likely repeated upheavals that would attend societies set to be remade according to that time frame, Jefferson's explication of this idea supports the view that "the standard doctrines of the Enlightenment had a radical potential that made them far more incendiary than their authors intended."[12] As with the Declaration of Independence, Jefferson's ideals would have set the stage for a series of events that he, perhaps, could never have contemplated. The very astute Madison recognized this immediately, and responded with a letter that detailed what he saw as the very practical difficulties of having constitutions and laws that expired roughly every two decades. The threat to property, to the settled expectations of citizens, and to the societal order would be enormous if Jefferson's plan were actually followed. Madison, the newly minted Constitution maker, asked, among other things:

> Would not a Government so often revised become too mutable to retain those prejudices in its favor which antiquity inspires, and which are perhaps a salutary aid to the most rational Government in the most enlightened age? Would not such a periodical revision engender pernicious factions that might not otherwise come into existence. Would not, in fine, a Government depending for its existence on some positive and authentic intervention of Society itself, be too subject to the casualty and consequences of an actual interregnum.[13]

This head-to-head exchange outlines the basic contours of the differences between the two men, and can be seen as Madison's first important turn in the role that he would play during the rest of Jefferson's life: the pragmatic counter to his friend's idealism. James Oakes has identified (and criticized) what he terms as a "'progressive' orthodoxy" that paints Jefferson as the radical egalitarian and Madison as the arch defender of bourgeois stability.[14] Certainly the men's exchange over whether the earth truly belongs to the living displays a radical Jefferson ("radical" defined as one willing to put that most sacred of American rights – the right to private property – in jeopardy, which his proposal definitely would have done) and a conservative Madison (more vigilant in protecting the inviolability of property rights).

In the end, it may well be that the differences between the two men were more about their differing personalities than any really great differences in political views. There are, in fact, radical personalities who, when all is said and done, do not really rigidly adhere to the substantive tenets of what one might call radical politics. They are merely extreme and passionate people. That is why it should be no surprise that some extreme liberals are able to turn with complete ease into extreme conservatives, and, though less often, vice versa. It is not the substance of the ideas that really moves these people; it is more the strong personal need for passionate engagement. For all of his outward appearance of control and mild amiability, Jefferson was a deeply passionate man who found an outlet for his roiling passions by seeing and expressing things in the extreme – this particular dish, wine, plow, or person was the best thing known to mankind – or the worst. Rather than see the French Revolution fail, he "would have seen half the earth desolated. Were there but an Adam and Eve left in every country, and left free, it would be better than it is now." Half the earth desolated? Only an Adam and Eve left in every country ... no Patsy, no Polly, no Sally ... no Jemmy Madison? It was not enough that Unitarianism was a good and worthy religious philosophy that people should consider, one day *every* young man was going to become a Unitarian. Of a piece with all of this was his habit of delving into books and finding (and believing) the sometimes outlandish stories told in them about things like the sexual preferences of orangutans in tropical jungles – an animal he knew nothing about, from a place he never visited.[15]

There was clearly something more going on with Jefferson than reasoned political judgment. In the end, however, it is the Jeffersonian exuberance (often naïve exuberance) that is the chief source of his enduring attraction – one seeks to know him to berate him for it or to revel in it. He appears perpetually young (touching even) in his idealism and faith that he could learn and know it all; while Madison in his more measured and considered statements – his very judiciousness – appears prematurely old. That too great exuberance for espoused ideals can sometimes bleed into unattractive, some-times dangerous, didacticism is merely one of the hazards of passionate idealism – and, again, one of the traits associated with youthfulness. While the young and the old each have their strengths and attractions, for most people fair or not, pitting even the callow enthusiasm of the young against the sober presentation of old age is not much of a contest. By temperament, Jefferson appears as man in a balloon perpetually excited about taking off into uncharted territory, while Madison on the ground holding a rope attached to the balloon tries to pull him back down to earth, or, at least, to some more suitable place in the stratosphere. John Quincy Adams, who it must be said hated Jefferson, was nevertheless astute when he explained that Madison's friendship with Jefferson was "the friendship of a mind not inferior in capacity and tempered with a calmer sensibility and a cooler judgment."[16] Their writings bear this out.

One sees this in what the two men had to say about slavery and race, even though they did not say it to one another on paper. The lack of any serious discussions about slavery – an institution that both men were intimately involved with as a personal and policy matter – is, perhaps, one of the more lamentable omissions in the Jefferson–Madison epistolary record. Slavery was certainly on the table, either directly or indirectly, during the entirety of the years both men were on the public scene, and afterwards. It is not as though they never talked about it with anyone else. They discussed the matter with other correspondents – at times, in great depth. Here Rakove's observation about the primacy of face-to-face communications, along with their well-known concurrence on major issues, provides a likely reason. We will never know for certain, but it is almost inconceivable that Jefferson and Madison did not talk about slavery, what it meant to the new republic they were trying to make, and the nature of black people, over the course of their fifty-year association. What they actually said about slavery and black people to others suggests that they had virtually identical views, or views that were not so different that they required writing or debating in print about them.

While Madison, and every other white person who lived at the time, gets credit (is absolved from racism) for not having written Query XIV in *Notes on the State of Virginia*, he adhered to almost every sentiment about blacks that Jefferson put forth – except the part about the orangutans liking black women, or at least he never wrote that he accepted that idea. Madison believed that "existing and probably unalterable prejudices in the United States" mandated blacks' removal from the country after their emancipation, a thing that both he and Jefferson championed, and that "reciprocal antipathies" would prevent blacks and whites from living together in harmony.[17] He also stated that "if the blacks strongly marked by physical and lasting peculiarities be retained amid the whites, under the degrading privation of equal rights, political and social, they must always be dissatisfied with their position, as a change from one to another species of oppression."[18] Note that he did not say the "peculiarity" of having black skin would be lasting, but referred to the *peculiarities* of black people, as if more than skin color was at issue. What those other lasting peculiarities were he did not say, but the clear import was that black people were different in ways that would not allow their fellow citizens to accept them and live with them under terms of equality. Hence, his assumption that the "privation of equal rights, political and social" would be an inevitable and immutable fixture of any society comprised of blacks and whites. That tracks Jefferson's beliefs as expressed in the *Notes*, entirely. Neither man gave any indication that he would be willing to speak out against the prejudice they saw in others, but which so obviously resided in themselves: not for their generation, not even from the more politically safe position of speaking to the posterity whom they addressed in their correspondence. There are simply no firm grounds to make real distinctions between their views about black people.

Madison, as he was on other occasions, was simply more circumspect in his language than Jefferson, but there should be little doubt that his views on race cast blacks as a perpetual "other" who could never be incorporated into the American experiment. That he seemed to put the blame for this on whites, the same whites he expected to be able to rise to the challenges of the never before known to the world republican experiment, and seems to have tried to separate himself from *all those whites out there who are prejudiced, unlike me*, simply will not do. When criticizing abolitionist Frances Wright's plan for an interracial community of whites and emancipated blacks, he characterized "her views of amalgamating the white & black population" as "universally obnoxious" without explicitly stating whether he was part of that universe.[19]

Jefferson tried similar tacks on a number of occasions. After all, even in the *Notes*, he refers to "deep rooted prejudices entertained by the whites" – the equivalent of Madison's population (presumably white) who "universally" considered race mixture "obnoxious." Both men treated these racial views as if they were something in the air, like the moon, that neither man, who sought to remake the world in other ways, had any chance at all of affecting. Jefferson could not even bring himself to just say outright, "Black people are mentally inferior to whites," and instead ventured it "as a suspicion only," and talked about hesitating "to degrade a whole race of men from the rank in the scale of beings which their Creator perhaps may have given them." In the 1820s, he told a visitor to Monticello that he personally believed that it was time for the United States to recognize Haiti, but white people (*those white people over there*) were simply too prejudiced against black people to tolerate such a thing, as if he, of course, was above all that.[20]

There were then, as there are now, preferred conventions of communication and presentation. Just as the trope of the disinterested statesmen who had no ambition required politicians of Jefferson's and Madison's day to proclaim in letters, and to all who would listen to them, that they did not want, or were hesitant, to take offices they silently and desperately craved, one must view the protestations that *I'm not prejudiced against blacks. It's all those other whites, and in deference to those white people (whom, of course, I fundamentally believe are more important than blacks), black people have to leave the country they helped to build* as a similar form of cover. But, cover from what? Perhaps the fear of being thought "prejudiced," of being one who made decisions on the basis of emotions rather than the reason that was supposed to reign for Enlightenment thinkers, shaped how both men presented their thoughts about black people. It is almost certain that Madison and Jefferson, both intelligent men, knew that at least some of their discomfort about blacks came from a realm that was beyond all reason. They knew their statements about black people's utter hopelessness and helplessness were not necessarily true, for they were well acquainted with black people who were free and functioning in society. Madison's personal valet, William Gardner, whom he freed, and his wife Henrietta, also a free woman, were able to make their way in the world. Henrietta Gardner was Jefferson's laundress for all the time he lived in Philadelphia as secretary of state and vice president. And, of course, Jefferson knew the Hemings family who had many talented artisans in their number, and had the experience of treating some of them as paid employees. Jefferson's grappling with race has been the subject of numerous studies, and a detailed look at them is beyond the scope of this chapter. Of Madison, we can say that he well knew that the "physical distinctions," between blacks and whites that he saw as a stumbling block to black citizenship could be virtually eradicated in two or three generations. He had seen the Hemings family. Indeed, one of the "whitest" among them, one who was actually "white" by Virginia law, Jefferson's third son with Sally Hemings, was named James Madison Hemings.[21] That was a subject, along with the true nature of black and white relations in Virginia overall, that could never be discussed in their letters.

Brothers in arms

If "marriage" or "union" are metaphors that come to mind when thinking about Jefferson and Madison's relationship over the years, there is one more that, in the final analysis, may most accurately describe what their correspondence and actions suggest they really were to one another: brothers in arms. That might appear a strange characterization, because neither man was ever an actual soldier, and there is no evidence that either had a burning desire to play that role. It was, in part, their lack of military service that contributed to the dismissive attitude that men like Alexander Hamilton and John Marshall, both Revolutionary War veterans, had towards both of them. They did not have the experiences of forging deep bonds with their fellows during combat, or making decisions in the heat of to-the-death battles, but if politics is war by other means, Jefferson and Madison were soldiers, and extremely effective ones at that.

Those contending to be the leaders in the new American nation of Jefferson and Madison were at war by other means. It was left to Jefferson to state most explicitly what he always hoped would be the ultimate outcome of this war. He, along with his political generals and soldiers, would, he said, "sink federalism into an abyss from which there [could] be no resurrection for it."[22] He and Madison forged their friendship in this joint effort just as surely as if they had fought together on a real battlefield, sharing defeats and embarrassments – the debacle with Philip Freneau and the *National Gazette* which destroyed Jefferson's currency with George Washington – and their victories – Jefferson's and the Republicans' triumph in 1800 and Madison's succession to the presidency. By the end, Jefferson could ask his long-term friend and political comrade in arms to "take care" of him after he was dead, confident that Madison would readily accept the charge and that, of everyone he knew, he would be the one person best suited to do that.[23] Even after his death, his brother would not desert him.

NOTES

1. Adrienne Koch, *Jefferson and Madison: The Great Collaboration* (Connecticut, 2004); *Papers of Thomas Jefferson*, ed. Julian P. Boyd et al. (Princeton: Princeton University Press, 1974), XIV: 544–51; Robert Wright, "Francis Crick and James Watson," *Time Magazine*, March 29, 1999.
2. Bernard Bailyn, *To Begin the World Anew: The Genius and Ambiguities of the American Founders* (New York: Alfred Knopf, 2004); Ralph Ketchum, *James Madison: A Biography* (Charlottesville: University of Virginia Press, 1990), 75.
3. James Morton Smith (ed.), *The Republic of Letters*, 3 vols. (New York: W. W. Norton, 1995), 36–8, 3; James Oakes, "Was Madison More Radical Than Jefferson?" *Journal of the Early Republic*, 15 (Winter, 1995): 649; Jack N. Rakove, review of *Republic of Letters: The Correspondence between Thomas Jefferson and James Madison, 1776–1826* by James Morton Smith, *William and Mary Quarterly*, 3rd ser., 53:3 (1996): 672–4.
4. "Notes on the Lake Country Tour," in *Papers*, XIV: 25; "The Northern Journey of Jefferson and Madison," in *Papers*, XX: 438.
5. Madison was upset at Jefferson's talk of retiring from public life and championed the idea of Jefferson going to France to represent the United States in peace negotiations with Great Britain. Dumas Malone, *Jefferson and His Time: Jefferson*

the Virginian (Boston: Little Brown, 1948), 398; Annette Gordon-Reed, *Thomas Jefferson and Sally Hemings* (Charlottesville: University Press of Virginia, 1997), 112.

6. TJ to James Madison, March 13, 1791, and James Madison to TJ, March 13, 1791, in *Papers*, XVI: 551, 552.

7. See Gordon-Reed, *Thomas Jefferson and Sally Hemings*, 231–2.

8. TJ to James Madison, February 17, 1826, in *Republic of Letters*, 1966.

9. TJ to Martha Jefferson, in *Papers*. See Drew McCoy, *The Last of the Fathers: James Madison and the Republican Legacy* (Cambridge: Cambridge University Press, 1989), 25–33, recounting various contemporaries' assessments of Jefferson and Madison.

10. R. B. Bernstein, *Thomas Jefferson* (New York: Oxford University Press, 2003), 125–6.

11. TJ to James Madison, September 9, 1789, in *Papers*, XV: 392.

12. "'The Earth Belongs in Usufruct to the Living'", in *Jeffersonian Legacies*, ed. Peter S. Onuf (Charlottesville: University Press of Virginia, 1993), 299.

13. James Madison to TJ, February 4, 1790, in *Republic of Letters*, 651.

14. Oakes, "Was Madison More Radical?" 650.

15. TJ to William Short, January 3, 1793, in *Thomas Jefferson: Writings*, ed. Merrill Peterson (New York: Library of America, 1984), 1004; TJ to Benjamin Waterhouse, June 26, 1822, in Papers of Thomas Jefferson, in Library of Congress, 39680; Thomas Jefferson, *Notes on the State of Virginia*, in *Thomas Jefferson: Writings*, 265.

16. Adams quoted in McCoy, *The Last of the Fathers*, 32.

17. James Madison to Robert J. Evans, June 15, 1819 in *Letters and Other Writings*, III: 134.

18. Ibid.

19. James Madison to Marquis de Lafayette, February 20, 1828, in *Writings of James Madison*, IX: 311.

20. *Thomas Jefferson: Writings*, 270; William Peden, "A Bookseller Invades Monticello," WMQ, 3rd ser., 6 (October, 1949): 631–6, 633.

21. See *Jefferson's Memorandum Books, Accounts With Legal Records and Miscellany, 1767–1826*, ed. James A. Bear, Jr., and Lucia Stanton (Princeton: Princeton University Press, 1997), for numerous references to payments to "Mrs. Gardner" at pp. 808, 814, 1014, 1019, and many others. Jefferson's relationship with the entire Hemings family will be discussed in Annette Gordon-Reed's, *The Hemings Family of Monticello: A Story of American Slavery*, forthcoming from W. W. Norton in 2008. Gordon-Reed, *Thomas Jefferson and Sally Hemings*, 197, 247.

22. TJ to Levi Lincoln, October 25, 1801, in Papers of Thomas Jefferson, Library of Congress, 21869.

23. TJ to James Madison, February 17, 1826, in *Republic of Letters*, 1967, 1965.

14

DOUGLAS ANDERSON

Jefferson and the democratic future

When Thomas Jefferson summarized his legacy to the democratic future in the instructions that he left for his gravestone inscription, he omitted most of the historical and biographical landmarks of his long public career. His presidency goes unmentioned in Jefferson's austere self-assessment. The only book that he wrote, *Notes on the State of Virginia*, continued to occupy him with corrections and appendices long after its original 1787 publication, but Jefferson's epitaph ignores it. His diplomatic service, his terms as governor of Virginia, as secretary of state and as vice president, his revision of the Virginia legal code, the Louisiana Purchase, his instigation of the Lewis and Clark expedition – all disappear from view as Jefferson drafts the words that he believes will best commemorate his life:

could the dead feel any interest in Monuments or other remembrances of them, when, as Anacreon says

Ολιγη δε κειςομεςθα
Κονις, οςτεων λνθεντων

the following would be to my Manes the most gratifying:
On the grave a plain die or cube of 3.f without any mouldings, surmounted by an Obelisk of 6.f height, each of a single stone: on the faces of the Obelisk the following inscription, & not a word more

"Here was buried
Thomas Jefferson
Author of the Declaration of American Independence
of the Statute of Virginia for religious freedom
& Father of the University of Virginia."

because by these, as testimonials that I have lived, I wish most to be remembered. to be of the coarse stone of which my columns are made, that no one might be tempted hereafter to destroy it for the value of the materials. my bust by Ciracchi, with the pedestal and truncated column on which it stands, might be given to the University if they would place it in the Dome room of the Rotunda. on the Die of the Obelisk might be engraved

> 'Born Apr. 2. 1743. O.S.
> Died____ [1]

Though unsigned and undated, this scrap of manuscript reads like a codicil to the formal will that Jefferson drew up in March, 1826, a few months before his death. His heirs clearly viewed the page in that light and arranged to carry out Jefferson's wishes. But by design his words suggest a kind of anti-will as well: a testament from Jefferson's otherworldly "Manes" rather than from Jefferson himself. The Greek homily that he drew from his literary common-place book to introduce this gravestone description establishes the ultimate futility of monuments: "A scanty dust to feed the wind, / Is all the trace 'twill leave behind."[2]

These instructions, like so much of Jefferson's life, paint a portrait of deep-seated ambivalence, a posture curiously similar to the profound ambivalence that many contemporary students feel about Jefferson himself. His doubts, in this case, center on the importance of history. The "true Jeffersonian legacy," as Joyce Appleby aptly notes, "is to be hostile to legacies."[3] His well-known opposition to the cumulative burden of a national debt, or his life-long insistence that no single human generation has the right to bind the actions of its successors, are celebrated instances of this aversion. Jefferson never relinquished either conviction. Both are integral features of what Joseph Ellis terms the "antigovernment ethos" of Jefferson's temperament: a cast of mind that (according to Ellis) renders most of his thinking simply irrelevant to 21st-century life. "On the most disturbing and controversial problems in contemporary American society," Ellis concludes, Jefferson "has little to say."[4] Perhaps so. But this carefully orchestrated presentation of a few grave-stone "testimonials" suggests that Jefferson fully appreciated both the limita-tions and the potency of his example. He was far from indifferent to the impact of his words on the future of American independence and acutely aware that dramatic simplicity was the most effective vehicle at his disposal to secure the attention of posterity.

A meticulous custodian of his papers, Jefferson clearly intended for the plain sheet describing his monument to come to light just as it did: carefully folded among the keepsakes of his wife's death but unpolished and unsigned, a coarse preamble of its own to a complicated exercise in remembrance. The material value of the stones themselves will be negligible, Jefferson insists, though in describing them he cannot resist a multilayered pun on the com-pleted "course" of individual life, as well as the discarded bodily "corse" that is slowly decaying beneath a cubic yard of unadorned rock, selected to match "my columns." Surely Jefferson refers to Monticello's columns, but the stipulation is oddly fastidious. Why should the house of the dead and the house of the living match, except perhaps to invoke another pun? In a variety of senses, Jefferson's life was hedged in by columns: the tabular data that he loved to arrange in his scientific notebooks and that continue to bedevil readers of *Notes on the State of Virginia*; the ledgers that recorded his struggle to fend off the debts that stalked his existence; the newspaper columns to which he vowed never to contribute himself but which have continued to march back and forth over his private and public affairs for the last 200 years, stirring up the scanty dust of his reputation.

To these tentative, reflexive echoes of Jefferson's mind, the Greek lines add a further dimension. In Thomas Moore's translation, they comprise a complete epitaph in themselves, but Jefferson casually brushes aside this conventional expression of Epicurean melancholy as easily as the Anacreontic poets brushed aside thoughts of death in favor of celebrating wine and love. By 1826, his sensual appetites must certainly have cooled – Jefferson would turn 83 that April – but he is not about to accept the reduction of life's significance to a scattering of dust. The cool, geometric "faces" of his obelisk capture this essential ambivalence too. His gravestone might or might not survive. The University of Virginia might or might not choose to display his fine marble bust, just as the stone cutters might choose to include or to neglect the traditional numerical record of his birth and his death on the cubic base. Much certainly depends on chance, on how the "Die" falls. But chance is not the ultimate arbiter of Thomas Jefferson's universe.

Perhaps it is foolish to scrutinize this note so closely, but its haunting, ruminative tone is difficult to dismiss. As Andrew Burstein points out, Jefferson lodged it in a particularly sacred place among his personal mementoes.[5] The monument that it describes was built and then rebuilt, after years of souvenir chips had damaged the stone, each time replicating the sketch that Jefferson drew in the upper left-hand corner of the page: a carefully beveled obelisk complete with scribbled lines to simulate the placement of the inscriptions. For the moment, at least, let's consider the paper itself as the genuine monument: a more intimate and more substantive message to its readers than Monticello's physical shrine provides, pointing to the dialogue between permanence and impermanence, reason and feeling, optimism and resignation that marks so much of Jefferson's thought. As his life drew to a close, he struggled to finish an elaborate house and a simple tomb employing the same materials: adjusting and readjusting the scope of his ambitions and achievements as he measured the vanity and futility of life. The resonant claims of the Declaration of Independence diminish from a broadly human to an "American" event. Religious freedom is a Virginia statute, not a national or a universal principle. The University of Virginia is a fledgling dream at the foot of Jefferson's little mountain.

But the epitaph also rises as it descends: from a contingent state of political independence to mental liberty, from the crazy sectarian marketplace of religious freedom to the unifying, rational faith that Jefferson hoped to enshrine at his new university, purged of the "daemonism," the atheism, the contemporary storms of "ideology" that he and his old colleague John Adams jointly lamented and ridiculed in their remarkable correspondence between the war of 1812 and the uncanny coincidence of their deaths. There would be no professor of divinity at the University of Virginia, no professional expositor of "the mystical generation of Jesus" to delude the students with fables. With "the dawn of reason and freedom of thought in these United States," Jefferson assured Adams, two days before his eightieth birthday, "the primitive and genuine doctrines of this the most venerated reformer of human errors" would shed their "artificial scaffolding." The ramshackle inheritance of revelation, along with its philosophical supporters and opponents, would collapse of its own weight, leaving the universe itself to impress "a conviction of design, consummate skill, and indefinite power" on the human observer. Adams gleefully concurred: "Allegiance to the Creator and Governor of the Milky Way and the Nebulae, and Benevolence to all his Creatures, is my Religion."[6] For both of these former revolutionaries and career politicians, the Argument from Design was a means of escaping the brutal entanglements of history, a cultural trajectory that is implicit in the enigmatic display of Jefferson's grave.

***

"I have sometimes asked myself whether my country is the better for my having lived at all?" Jefferson posed this sober question in another undated and unsigned manuscript that he drafted early in the nineteenth century, prompted perhaps by a period of self-doubt during the contentious years of his presidency. Titled simply "A Memorandum (Services to my Country)," it too names the Declaration of Independence and the Virginia Bill for Establishing Religious Freedom as important achievements, but they do not have the same prominence that they assume in the comparatively spare gravestone inscription. "I have been the instrument of doing the following things," Jefferson tentatively begins, "but they would have been done by others; some of them perhaps, a little better."[7] Very early in his career, he recalls initiating steps aimed at improving navigation on the Rivanna River. This public service project is the first item that he mentions as he reviews the difference that his life might have made to the well-being of the nation: an "Act of Assembly" for removing obstructions and permitting the river "to be used completely and fully for carrying down all our produce."

Other legislative acts which the memorandum itemizes, however, have less tangible, less complete, or less immediate results. They were, in fact, done by others more effectually than Jefferson himself was able to do them. His revision of the Virginia criminal code, for instance, only passed into law eleven years after Jefferson and his committee of revisal had first prepared it, and only then under different legislative sponsorship and in different language from the version that Jefferson had written. The "act for religious freedom" waited eight years before being shepherded into Virginia law by James Madison. In the process of presenting his résumé of achievements, Jefferson, a bit ruefully, concedes that these central contributions to civic life required the help of deft intermediaries – as well as some laundering to remove the taint of the Virginia Voltaire – before his fellow citizens could be brought to endorse them.

An elaborate plan that Jefferson had drafted for a state-wide system of public education, culminating in three-year scholarships to William and Mary College for the poorest but most able students, aroused "great enthusiasm at first," he recalls, but the courts ultimately thwarted its intent: "Whether the act for the more general diffusion of knowledge will ever be carried into complete effect, I know not." Similar uncertainty plagued the opening of the University of Virginia, the institutional offspring that Jefferson was still nursing into being in the last months of his life. Early in 1826, the Virginia House cut off funds for the school less than a year after it had admitted its first students, prompting Jefferson to freeze all unnecessary construction so that "the circular room for books and the anatomical theatre" at least could be finished. Otherwise (as he reported to James Madison), the newly ordered library couldn't be unpacked. His epitaph designation as "Father" of the University of Virginia may reflect a measure of concern that the term "Founder" might yet prove darkly prophetic – an unwitting pun on the wreckage of his educational hopes.

Informal though the Memorandum as a whole may appear to be, like the epitaph it has an implicit dramatic vitality. Jefferson might have summarized this dimension to its significance very simply, if doing so did not dilute much of the impact of a hard-won realization: removing inconvenient obstructions from rivers is child's play; removing them from the human mind is a much more formidable challenge. The same lesson takes slightly different form as Jefferson recalls two horticultural experiments still underway at the time he recorded these notes. During his diplomatic service in France, he had arranged for the export of some olive trees from Marseilles to Charleston, where he hoped they might eventually be established in South Carolina and Georgia. "They were planted," Jefferson recalls, "and are flourishing; and, though not yet multiplied, they will be the germ of that cultivation in those

States."[8] In 1790, shortly after returning to America and joining George Washington's cabinet, he repeated this effort, importing "a cask of heavy upland rice" from Africa for use in the same two states, where in time he hoped it would replace the wet rice fields that made parts of the south "so pestilential through the summer."

"The greatest service which can be rendered any country," Jefferson concludes, rather oddly for a sitting chief executive, "is, to add an useful plant to its culture; especially, a bread grain; next in value to bread is oil." The words themselves are particularly remarkable in the context of Jefferson's unique contribution to the process of cultural germination that had produced the government he served: the seeds of liberty and of religious tolerance for which he bore at least some responsibility and was entitled to take at least some credit, the bread and oil of democratic life. But, like Mediterranean olives and African rice, these crops too were imperfectly established importations – promising but dormant germs, like "the act prohibiting the importation of slaves" that the Memorandum enumerates among Jefferson's accomplishments. Do not dispute about the origins of evil, the fate of nations, or the destiny of man, Candide and Pangloss ultimately conclude in Voltaire's celebrated fable. The surest route to happiness is to cultivate your garden. To some degree, at least, Jefferson embraced this famous admonition.

But only to some degree. The urge to dispute was strong, though Jefferson managed more frequently than not to contain it. He was so angered by John Marshall's biography of George Washington that, in 1818, a decade after leaving the presidency, he collected the scraps of paper that he had saved from twenty-five years of public service – "ragged, rubbed, & scribbled as they were" – and had them bound into three volumes in preparation for "a calm revisal." Here is yet another effort, late in life, to fix his legacy. History at its worst was a "Congeries" of "suspicions & certainties, rumors & realities, facts & falsehoods" that "may be made to wear any hue, with which the passions of the compiler, royalist or republican, may chuse to tinge it."[9] Jefferson meant to have his say in this competition for posterity's ear, but only when "the passions of the time" had dissipated and only in a private, annotated scrap book, not for publication. Ambivalent even in his resentments, Jefferson preferred to enter the fray through his executors, perhaps because a posthumous defense might seem less defensive.

Marshall's icy partisanship, Jefferson insisted, made it impossible for him to capture the emotional heart of Washington's story and of the times through which he had lived:

> No act of heroism ever kindles in the mind of this writer a single aspiration in
> favor of the holy cause which inspired the bosom, & nerved the arm of the patriot

warrior. No gloom of events, no lowering of prospects ever excites a fear for the issue of a contest which was to change the condition of man over the civilized globe. The sufferings inflicted on endeavors to vindicate the rights of humanity are related with all the frigid insensibility with which a monk would have contemplated the victims of an auto da fé. Let no man believe that Genl. Washington ever intended that his papers should be used for the suicide of the cause, for which he had lived, and for which there never was a moment in which he would not have died ... Were a reader of this period to form his idea of it from this history alone, he would suppose the republican party (who were in truth endeavoring to keep the government within the line of the Constitution, and prevent it's being monarchised in practice) were a mere set of grumblers, and disorganisers, satisfied with no government, without fixed principles of any, and, like a British parliamentary opposition, gaping after loaves and fishes, and ready to change principles, as well as position, at any time, with their adversaries.[10]

Liberty was a boisterous sea, as Jefferson famously proclaimed to Philip Mazzei in a 1796 letter; despotism, an icy calm. The same two antagonists come to grips in Jefferson's vivid attack on the "cold indifference" of Marshall's biography. Indeed, they inhabit Jefferson himself, the calm despot of Monticello who never ceased to urge the appeal of boisterous liberty on his neighbors. The extraordinary dialogue between the Head and the Heart that Jefferson wrote for Maria Cosway in 1786, a year before the publication of *Notes on the State of Virginia*, depicts this interior blend of conflict and cooperation.

Beginning as "a mutual confession of distress" between Jefferson and a companion who shares his regret at the Cosways' departure from Paris, the letter abruptly turns its confession inward as Jefferson sits by his fire, listening to Head chastise Heart for exposing their collective peace of mind to danger: "This is one of the scrapes into which you are ever leading us," Head begins, exposing us to fresh emotional attachments, with the inevitable burden of sorrow that departure entails. The calm despot and the boisterous sea reappear in this exchange, wearing another set of metaphorical costumes and staging what at first glance seems to be a gentle farce rather than a grand historical tragedy. Heart dismisses Head's mind-numbing "diagrams & crochets."[11] Head defends the utility of its studies: the construction of a handsome public market in Richmond, the improvement of navigation on the Schuylkill (as the young Jefferson had improved the channel of the Rivanna) the better to "warm and feed" Philadelphia's poor.

Their exclamations and complaints deftly expose the Head's susceptibility to beauty and to feeling, as well as the Heart's generous response to architectural and engineering wonders. The two form a partnership more intimate and far-reaching than the brief infatuation that Jefferson felt for the young artist-wife of a gifted English miniaturist in pre-revolutionary Paris. As the misunderstanding unfolds, Head and Heart seem both petty and sublime, carrying on a minor squabble that subtly echoes the foretaste of death and divine abandonment in Genesis. "Paint to me the day we went to St. Germains," Heart joyfully asks his companion, in the midst of their disagreement, placing implicit faith in Head's memory and aesthetic gifts: "Oh! My dear friend, how you have revived me by recalling to my mind the transactions of that day!" The Cosway letter underscores Jefferson's pleasure in dramatic forms – in the volatility and vigor displayed by both of his speakers, each of whom contains the same psychological and intellectual duality that the outer dialogue embodies. A poor orator Jefferson may have been, but he responded deeply and appreciatively to theatrical energy. In his early twenties, he stood at the lobby door of the House of Burgesses during the Stamp Act debates to hear Patrick Henry deploy his celebrated verbal powers. "They were great indeed," Jefferson remembered half a century later, "He appeared to me to speak as Homer wrote."[12]

Head and Heart begin by conducting a domestic disagreement in the household of Thomas Jefferson's consciousness, but their discussion too, like that of Virginia's colonial legislators, gradually ascends to loftier heights. Heart suggests that the artistic Cosways, should they agree to visit Virginia, could not help but be drawn to the American landscape in general and to Monticello in particular. "With what majesty do we there ride above the storms!" Heart exclaims, "How sublime to look down into the workhouse of nature, to see her clouds, hail, snow, rain, thunder, all fabricated at our feet!" Head adopts precisely the same figurative language in defense of the power of intellectual pleasures to "ride serene & sublime above the concerns of this mortal world, contemplating truth & nature, matter & motion, the laws which bind up their existence, & that eternal being who made and bound them up by those laws."[13]

Despite the superficial opposition between them, each inner speaker is drawn by different paths to the same destination. Each appreciates the relentlessly destructive impact of the wheels of time, the speed with which they hurry us past the pleasurable (or grief-stricken) present towards the kind of evening "retrospect" that Heart embraces in its celebration of the day's "mass of happiness," or that Jefferson's late memorandum undertakes as he assesses his services to his country, or that he and John Adams jointly construct in their retirement letters. When, in his first inaugural address, Jefferson announces to a deeply divided Congress that they are, in fact, "brethren of the same principle," he is not simply temporizing. The celebrated assertion that "We are all Republicans, we are all Federalists" points to the compound of Heart and Head, of hope and fear, of boisterous energy and cool reason, that shapes Jefferson's vision of communal as well as individual psychology.

Implicit in Jefferson's epistolary fable is the recognition that, at best, men are notoriously changeable beings. "I do not know that I ever did a good thing on your suggestion, or a dirty one without it," Heart reminds Head in the sweeping speech that concludes the Cosway letter, words that comprise both an accusation and a confession, dramatizing the ethical complexity of their partnership.[14] Jefferson recasts the darker implications of this symbiotic bond in some of the most chilling passages from *Notes on the State of Virginia*, those springing from Jefferson's anguished recollection that, twice amid the intense anxieties of the Revolution, the Virginia House of Delegates had contemplated surrendering their powers to a dictator. "The very thought alone," Jefferson cried, "was treason against the people; was treason against mankind in general; as riveting for ever the chains which bow down their necks, by giving to their oppressors a proof, which they would have trumpeted to the universe, of the imbecility of republican government." These words fall near the end of Query XIII, an extended analysis of the Virginia Constitution which evolves, in Jefferson's hands, into a brief, passionate treatise on human nature.

"Mankind soon learn to make interested uses of every right and power which they possess, or may assume," Jefferson admonishes the members of the Assembly, urging them to anticipate the relentless erosion of principle by the insidious forces of interest:

> They should look forward to a time, and that not a distant one, when corruption in this, as in the country from which we derive our origin, will have seized the heads of government, and be spread by them through the body of the people; when they will purchase the voices of the people, and make them pay the price. Human nature is the same on every side of the Atlantic, and will be alike influenced by the same causes. The time to guard against corruption and tyranny, is before they shall have gotten hold on us. It is better to keep the wolf out of the fold, than to trust to drawing his teeth and talons after he shall have entered.[15]

This recognition of the stubborn proclivity to corruption was almost certainly among those portions of Jefferson's book that pleased John Adams. But Jefferson's peculiar genius taught him to present the outcome of this fateful process as a hybrid monster of his own making: a wolf with "talons" to which only the human imagination might give birth.

Among all the members of the revolutionary generation, Jefferson was himself the most hybrid consciousness: a mind wholly infatuated with the power and potential of reason, at the same time that it possessed an acutely gothic sensibility, rendering him deeply sympathetic with the psychic nightmares that plagued Romantic artists and thinkers in the early nineteenth century. Readers usually remember Jefferson's faith in the curative power of free argument and debate as being far more serene than it is. The Bill for Establishing Religious Freedom and Query XVII of *Notes on the State of Virginia* both insist that "Truth can stand by itself" in its perpetual contest against error, without any coercive reinforcement from the state. Indeed, coercion is capable of producing only tyranny and hypocrisy, not ethical, political, or religious uniformity in a heterogeneous population. But how long can truth reasonably expect to be "left to herself" as "the proper and sufficient antagonist to error"? Not long, Jefferson believed.

History is a litany of bloody inquisitions, not unfettered inquiry. Even his famous bill closes with the extraordinary gesture of envisioning, and protesting against, its ultimate revocation by a future generation of persecutors. Query XVII, "The Different Religions Received into That State?," is still more emphatic in its fears. "I doubt whether the people of this country would suffer an execution for heresy, or a three years imprisonment for not comprehending the mysteries of the Trinity," Jefferson boldly claims in those pages. Almost immediately, however, the shadows descend:

> But is the spirit of the people an infallible, a permanent reliance? Is it government? Is this the kind of protection we receive in return for the rights we give up? Besides, the spirit of the times may alter, will alter. Our rulers will become corrupt, our people careless. A single zealot may commence persecutor, and better men be his victims. It can never be too often repeated, that the time for fixing every essential right on a legal basis is while our rulers are honest, and ourselves united. From the conclusion of this war we shall be going downhill. It will not then be necessary to resort every moment to the people for support. They will be forgotten ... They will forget themselves, but in the sole faculty of making money, and will never think of uniting to effect a due respect for their rights. The shackles, therefore, which shall not be knocked off at the conclusion of this war, will remain on us long, will be made heavier and heavier, till our rights shall revive or expire in a convulsion.[16]

Surely these words speak to the challenges of 21st-century democratic life with painful urgency and force.

The sleep of reason breeds monsters. Francisco Goya – Jefferson's nearly exact contemporary – illustrates this aphorism in a famous plate from "Los Caprichos" (1799) that encapsulates one of the essential insights of the so-called Enlightenment, a perception that Jefferson grasped only too well. By the end of their lives, John Adams would escape far more completely than Jefferson from the grip of the old theology. "Howl, Snarl, bite, Ye Calvinistick! Ye Athanasian Divines," Adams exclaims in a series of letters to his old revolutionary colleague, as he rejects the grim doctrine of predestination and tries out a comparative mish-mash of "heretical Divinity" on Monticello's far more celebrated heretic.[17] Jefferson shared every bit of

Adams's scorn for what he termed the "Cannibal priests" of sectarian religion, but was unable to join his old colleague's exuberant spiritual flights. In the end, Adams soared higher, Jefferson believed, than a "chaste and correct imagination" ought to go.

By contrast, Jefferson's own exuberance was subject to a grim chastening. He spent the last eighteen years of his life in a house that never seemed able to shed its scaffolding and stand alone, surrounded as he worked and wrote by vivid daily reminders of the moral weakness that smothers our finest instincts and principles: the dirty enterprises of the head that seduce the heart. "They will be forgotten," he might have said of the nobler human aptitudes, as he did of the neglected rights of free Virginians; "They will forget themselves."[18] His beautiful house in its breathtaking mountain setting was a Palladian temple of reason brooding over subterranean secrets, a Goya etching in a Virginia landscape.

In *American Scripture: The Making of the Declaration of Independence*, Pauline Maier offers a finely detailed, appreciative analysis of the changes imposed on Jefferson's draft of the Declaration by the Continental Congress acting as a committee of the whole on July 2 and July 3, 1776. "This was no hack editing job," she insists, noting repeatedly the stylistic improvements that resulted from these two excruciating and fruitful days. Jefferson's vanity suffered, but the Declaration became, on the whole, a more streamlined and more forceful document.[19] One change, however, substitutes rhetorical for psychological acuity in a revealing and disturbing way. Where Jefferson had called his American compatriots a "people who mean to be free," Congress substituted the concise and confident designation "a free people." It is easy to see the tactical reasons for the change. But it is just as easy to recognize the basis for Jefferson's own, wary approach to such a resonant claim. What works for slogans and for songs is seldom true to the dark complexities of human experience. If Joseph Ellis is right that Jefferson has little to say about the specific problems of our society, his belief in the continuing necessity to strive towards a yet unattained freedom for all continues to matter. We are not yet what we mean to be. This is the anti-monumental message latent in the inscriptions on Jefferson's tomb: a reminder that the house of the living, like the house of the dead, is never finished.

NOTES

1. *Thomas Jefferson: Writings*, ed. Merrill D. Peterson (New York: Library of America, 1984), 706.
2. Douglas L. Wilson (ed.), *Jefferson's Literary Commonplace Book* (Princeton: Princeton University Press, 1989), 129–30.

3. Joyce Appleby, "Jefferson and His Complex Legacy," in *Jeffersonian Legacies*, ed. Peter S. Onuf (Charlottesville: University Press of Virginia, 1993), 1–16.
4. Joseph J. Ellis, *American Sphinx: The Character of Thomas Jefferson* (New York: Alfred A. Knopf, 1997), 355.
5. Andrew Burstein, *Jefferson's Secrets* (New York: Basic Books, 2005).
6. Lester J. Cappon (ed.), *The Adams–Jefferson Letters* (Chapel Hill: University of North Carolina Press, 1959), 594, 406.
7. *Thomas Jefferson: Writings*, 702.
8. Ibid., 703.
9. Ibid., 662.
10. Ibid., 662–3.
11. TJ to Maria Cosway, October 12, 1786, in *Thomas Jefferson: Writings*, 866–77.
12. *Thomas Jefferson: Writings*, 6.
13. Ibid., 870.
14. Ibid., 875.
15. Jefferson, *Notes on the State of Virginia* (New York: Penguin, 1999), 127.
16. Ibid., 167.
17. *Adams–Jefferson Letters*, 374–83.
18. Jefferson, *Notes*, 167.
19. Pauline Maier, *American Scripture* (New York: Alfred A. Knopf, 1997).

GUIDE TO FURTHER READING

Editions

Adams, Dickinson W., ed. *Jefferson's Extracts from the Gospels*. Princeton: Princeton University Press, 1983.
Boyd, Julian P. *The Declaration of Independence: The Evolution of the Text*, ed. Gerard W. Gawalt. Washington, DC, and Charlottesville: Library of Congress and Thomas Jefferson Memorial Foundation, 1999.
Cappon, Lester J., ed. *The Adams–Jefferson Letters: The Complete Correspondence Between Thomas Jefferson and Abigail and John Adams*. Chapel Hill: University of North Carolina Press, 1959.
Notes on the State of Virginia, ed. Frank Shuffelton. New York: Penguin Putnam, 1999.
Papers of Thomas Jefferson, ed. Julian P. Boyd *et al.* 35 vols. to date, plus 5 vols. in the *Retirement Series*, Princeton: Princeton University Press, 1950–.
Smith, James Morton, ed. *The Republic of Letters: The Correspondence Between Thomas Jefferson and James Madison*. 3 vols. New York: W. W. Norton, 1995.
Thomas Jefferson: Writings, ed. Merrill D. Peterson. New York: Library of America, 1984.
The Writings of Thomas Jefferson, ed. Paul Leicester Ford. 10 vols. New York: G. P. Putnam, 1892–9.
The Writings of Thomas Jefferson, ed. Andrew A. Lipscomb and Albert Ellery Bergh. 20 vols. Washington, DC: Thomas Jefferson Memorial Association, 1903.
Wilson, Douglas L., ed. *Jefferson's Literary Commonplace Book*. Princeton: Princeton University Press, 1989.

Biographical studies

Bernstein, R. B. *Thomas Jefferson*. New York: Oxford University Press, 2003.
Burstein, Andrew. *The Inner Jefferson: Portrait of a Grieving Optimist*. Charlottesville: University Press of Virginia, 1995.
Malone, Dumas. *Jefferson and His Time*. 6 vols. Boston: Little Brown, 1948–81.
McLaughlin, Jack. *Jefferson and Monticello: The Biography of a Builder*. New York: Henry Holt, 1988.
Peterson, Merrill D. *Thomas Jefferson and the New Nation: A Biography*. New York: Oxford University Press, 1970.

Critical and historical studies

Adams, William Howard. *The Paris Years of Thomas Jefferson.* New Haven: Yale University Press, 1997.
  Thomas Jefferson Architect: The Built Legacy of Our Third President. New York: Rizzoli, 2003.

Ambrose, Stephen. *Undaunted Courage: Meriwether Lewis, Thomas Jefferson, and the Opening of the American West.* New York: Simon and Schuster, 1996.

Banning, Lance. *Jefferson and Madison: Three Conversations from the Founding.* Madison, WI: Madison House, 1995.

Becker, Carl. *The Declaration of Independence: A Study in the History of Political Ideas.* New York: Harcourt Brace, 1922. Rev. edn. New York: Alfred Knopf, 1942.

Bedini, Silvio. *Thomas Jefferson, Statesman of Science.* New York: Macmillan, 1990.

Boorstin, Daniel. *The Lost World of Thomas Jefferson.* New York: Holt, 1948.

Burstein, Andrew. *Jefferson's Secrets: Death and Desire at Monticello.* New York: Basic Books, 2005.

Cogliano, Francis D. *Thomas Jefferson: Reputation and Legacy.* Charlottesville: University Press of Virginia, 2006.

Cunningham, Noble E., Jr. *The Process of Government Under Jefferson.* Princeton: Princeton University Press, 1978.

Dunn, Susan. *Jefferson's Second Revolution: The Election Crisis of 1800 and the Triumph of Republicanism.* Boston: Houghton Mifflin, 2004.

Engeman, Thomas, ed. *Thomas Jefferson and the Politics of Nature.* Notre Dame, IN: University of Notre Dame Press, 2000.

Finkleman, Paul. *Slavery and the Founders: Race and Liberty in the Age of Jefferson.* Armonk, NY: M. E. Sharpe, 1996.

Fliegelman, Jay. *Declaring Independence: Jefferson, Natural Language, and the Culture of Performance.* Stanford: Stanford University Press, 1993.

Gaustad, Edwin S. *Sworn on the Altar of God: A Religious Biography of Thomas Jefferson.* Grand Rapids, MI: William B. Eerdmans Publishing, 1996.

Gilreath, James A., ed. *Thomas Jefferson and the Education of a Citizen.* Washington, DC: Library of Congress, 1999.

Gordon-Reed, Annette. *Thomas Jefferson and Sally Hemings: An American Controversy.* Charlottesville: University Press of Virginia, 1997.

Hellenbrand, Harold. *The Unfinished Revolution: Education and Politics in the Thought of Thomas Jefferson.* Newark: University of Delaware Press, 1990.

Horn, James, Jan Ellen Lewis, and Peter S. Onuf, eds. *The Revolution of 1800: Democracy, Race, and the New Republic.* Charlottesville: University of Virginia Press, 2002.

Jackson, Donald. *Thomas Jefferson & the Stony Mountains: Exploring the West from Monticello.* Urbana: University of Illinois Press, 1981.

Jayne, Allen. *Jefferson's Declaration of Independence: Origins, Philosophy, Theology.* Lexington: University of Kentucky Press, 1998.

Kelsall, Malcolm. *Jefferson and the Iconography of Romanticism: Folk, Land, Culture, and the Romantic Nation.* New York: St. Martin's Press, 1999.

Lehmann, Karl. *Thomas Jefferson, American Humanist.* New York: Macmillan, 1947.

Levy, Leonard W. *Jefferson and Civil Liberties, The Darker Side.* Cambridge, MA: Harvard University Press, 1963.

Lewis, Jan Ellen, and Peter S. Onuf, eds. *Sally Hemings and Thomas Jefferson: History, Memory, and Civic Culture*. Charlottesville: University Press of Virginia, 1999.

Maier, Pauline. *American Scripture: Making the Declaration of Independence*. New York: Alfred A. Knopf, 1997.

Matthews, Richard K. *The Radical Politics of Thomas Jefferson: A Revisionist View*. Lawrence: University of Kansas Press, 1984.

Mayer, David N. *The Constitutional Thought of Thomas Jefferson*. Charlottesville: University Press of Virginia, 1994.

McDowell, Gary L., and Sharon Noble, eds. *Reason and Republicanism: Thomas Jefferson's Legacy of Liberty*. Lanham, MD: Rowman and Littlefield, 1997.

Miller, Charles A. *Jefferson and Nature: An Interpretation*. Baltimore: Johns Hopkins University Press, 1988.

Onuf, Peter S., *Jefferson's Empire: The Language of American Nationhood*. Charlottesville: University Press of Virginia, 2000.

The Mind of Thomas Jefferson. Charlottesville: University of Virginia Press, 2007.

Onuf, Peter S., ed. *Jeffersonian Legacies*. Charlottesville: University Press of Virginia, 1993.

Peterson, Merrill D. *The Jefferson Image in the American Mind*. New York: Oxford University Press, 1960.

Peterson, Merrill D., and Robert C. Vaughan, eds. *The Virginia Statute for Religious Freedom: Its Evolution and Consequences in American History*. New York: Cambridge University Press, 1988.

Seefeldt, Douglas, *et al.*, eds. *Across the Continent: Jefferson, Lewis and Clark, and the Making of America*. Charlottesville: University of Virginia Press, 2005.

Sheehan, Bernard W. *Seeds of Extinction: Jeffersonian Philanthropy and the American Indian*. Chapel Hill: University of North Carolina Press, 1973.

Sheldon, Garrett Ward. *The Political Philosophy of Thomas Jefferson*. Baltimore: Johns Hopkins University Press, 1991.

Simon, James F. *What Kind of Nation: Thomas Jefferson, John Marshall, and the Epic Struggle to Create a United States*. New York: Simon and Schuster, 2002.

Sloan, Herbert E. *Principle and Interest: Thomas Jefferson and the Problem of Debt*. New York: Oxford University Press, 1995.

Staloff, Darren. *Hamilton, Adams, Jefferson: The Politics of Enlightenment and the American Founding*. New York: Hill and Wang, 2005.

Stanton, Lucia. *Slavery at Monticello*. Charlottesville: Thomas Jefferson Memorial Foundation, 1996.

Tucker, Robert W., and David C. Hendrickson. *Empire of Liberty: The Statecraft of Thomas Jefferson*. New York: Oxford University Press, 1990.

Wallace, Anthony F. C. *Jefferson and the Indians: The Tragic Fate of the First Americans*. Cambridge, MA: Harvard University Press, 1999.

Wills, Garry. *Inventing America: Jefferson's Declaration of Independence*. New York: Doubleday, 1978.

Wilson, Richard Guy. *Thomas Jefferson's Academical Village: The Creation of an Architectural Masterpiece*. Charlottesville: Bayly Art Museum of the University of Virginia, 1993.

Yarbrough, Jean M. *American Virtues: Thomas Jefferson on the Character of a Free People*. Lawrence: University of Kansas Press, 1998.

INDEX